THE

Ancient Coptic Churches

of Egypt

𝕷𝕠𝕟𝕕𝕠𝕟

HENRY FROWDE

OXFORD UNIVERSITY PRESS WAREHOUSE

AMEN CORNER

Dair Abu's-Sifain, Old Cairo, from the South.

THE

Ancient Coptic Churches

of Egypt

BY

ALFRED J. BUTLER, M.A. F.S.A.

Fellow of Brasenose College, Oxford

IN TWO VOLUMES

Vol. I.

𝔒𝔵𝔣𝔬𝔯𝔡

AT THE CLARENDON PRESS

1884

PREFACE.

THE aim of this book is to make a systematic beginning upon a great subject – the Christian antiquities of Egypt. Few subjects of equal importance have been so singularly neglected. One writer admits that the Coptic Church is still 'the most remarkable monument of primitive Christianity'; another that it is 'the only living representative of the most venerable nation of all antiquity'; yet even the strength of this double claim has been powerless to create any working interest in the matter. No doubt the attention of mere travellers has been bewitched and fascinated by the colossal remains of pagan times, by the temples and pyramids which still glow in eternal sunshine, while the Christian churches lie buried in the gloom of fortress walls, or encircled and masked by almost impassable deserts. Yet the Copts of to-day, whose very name is an echo of the word Egypt, trace back their lineage to the ancient Egyptians who built the pyramids, and the ancient tongue is spoken at every Coptic mass: the Copts were among the first to welcome the tidings of the gospel, to make a rule of life and worship, and to erect

*religious buildings: they have upheld the cross un-
waveringly through ages of desperate persecution:
and their ritual now is less changed than that of
any other community in Christendom. All this
surely is reason enough to recommend the subject to
churchman, historian, or antiquarian.*

*But although I need offer no apology for the essay
contained in the volumes, I am fully aware of its
many shortcomings. It is the result of seven months'
research in Egypt; and that brief period was inter-
rupted and shortened by a fever. The work was
begun, too, it must be confessed, at a time when the
writer's mind was a mere blank as regards architecture, ritual, and ecclesiology—a fact of which the
traces cannot have been quite obliterated by subsequent
study. Nor indeed was study possible in Egypt,
where it would have been most valuable in guiding
and correcting observation; for there is scarcely a
more bookless country now than that which once
boasted the best library in the world. The lack of
special training, and the sense of unfitness thence
arising, would certainly have deterred me from un-
dertaking a task beyond my powers, had there appeared
any likelihood of a more competent person devoting
himself to it. But that was not the case; and it
seemed better to make a beginning, however inadequate.
It was, of course, a great advantage to be living as a
resident in Egypt, to have even a smattering knowledge of the native Arabic, to be on friendly terms*

with many of the Copts, and, above all, to have plenty of leisure. For no one who has not tried can imagine what time and trouble it has often cost to obtain access even to some of the churches at Old Cairo; no one would believe how many fruitless journeys under a scorching sun can go to a scanty handful of Coptic notes. And if one searches for oral information, trouble multiplies a hundredfold. Very few indeed of the Copts know anything about their own history or their own ritual, or can assign a reason for the things which they witness in their daily services. A question on a point of ceremonial is usually met either by a shake of the head or by a palpably wrong answer veiling ignorance. Moreover the oracle, when discovered, generally prefers speaking to-morrow.

The difficulties, then, both physical and moral, which face the enquirer are rather exceptional; but they are such as tact and patience will mitigate, if not conquer. I have briefly indicated in the text how much remains to be done in Upper Egypt in the way of exploring and describing the early Christian churches there; and the very incompleteness of this work proves how much is still lacking to an adequate treatise on Coptic rites and ceremonies. Nor is there less scope for the historian than for the antiquarian and the ecclesiologist; for the history of Christian Egypt is still unwritten, or at least that part of it about which the most romantic interest gathers, the

*period which witnessed the passing away of the
ancient cults and the change of the pagan world. We
have yet to learn how the cold worship, the tranquil
life, and the mummified customs of that immemorial
people dissolved in the fervour of the new faith;
how faces like those sculptured on the monuments of
the Pharaohs became the faces of anchorites, saints,
and martyrs.*

*Even of later Coptic history very little is known.
It had been my wish to sketch roughly some portion
of the meagre records; but space has failed me;
and besides I could add nothing fresh to the story.
Renaudot's 'Liturgiarum Orientalium Collectio' and
'Historia Patriarcharum Alexandrinorum,' Al
Makrîzi's 'History of the Copts,' translated by the
Rev. S. C. Malan, Neale's 'Eastern Church' (a work
full of errors)—these are almost the only authorities:
and all that they relate has been ably summarised in
Mr. Fuller's article on the Coptic Church in the
Dictionary of Christian Biography.*

*It has not come within my province to discuss points
of doctrine which separate the Jacobites from the
Melkites, the Copts from the orthodox Alexandrians.
Nor need I enter into the origin of the Monophysite con-
troversy. I may however remark that the great mass
of the Copts to-day are entirely free from any strong
bias or even from any knowledge on the question; and
a few years ago political obstacles alone hindered the
union of the two Churches. The few who can call*

themselves theologians among the Copts cling to their ancient formula of μία φύσις, *not however denying either the humanity or the divinity of our Lord, but alleging that ' out of the two natures arose a single nature,'—*من الطبيعتين قام طبيعة واحدة *in the words of their chief authority.*

And, as I have not felt called upon to treat of the doctrine apart from the practice of the Copts, so I have been anxious to avoid any signs of party prejudice in relation to the questions which divide our Church of England. My purpose throughout has been merely to give a statement of facts, and neither to twist the facts nor to colour the statement in any controversial manner. If anything that I have written has any bearing on the tenets of English churchmen, I leave it to others to point the moral. But while I have candidly striven to write in an unsectarian spirit, it would be foolish and disingenuous to pretend blindness to the nature of the conclusions likely to be drawn from a study of Coptic ritual. No fairminded person who has any regard for the teaching of the early Church can make a careful comparison of our present liturgy and ritual with an unchanged liturgy and ritual, like the Coptic, without regretting the reckless abandonment of much that we have abandoned.

The rendering of Arabic names and words in English characters is a problem which no writer on oriental subjects has yet solved satisfactorily. The '*missionary alphabet*' *devised by Professor Max Müller, and mainly adopted by the translators of the Sacred Books of the East, seems originally designed rather with reference to the Indian languages; and though it finds indeed an equivalent for every Arabic letter, it has recourse to no less than three separate founts of type, and modifies all three by the use of diacritical marks. Thus a simple phrase like* غطيان المذبح *(altar coverings) would have to be rendered* ghuṭlân âl maḍḥba'h—*surely an intolerable combination. It is far better with Spitta Bey to use a single fount of type largely varied by points and dots. But neither Spitta Bey's system nor any other yet devised can be called clear, consistent, and faultless. It is next to impossible to transliterate Arabic so as to render consonants, vowels, and vowel points in any manner at once coherent and readable. I have merely tried to indicate Arabic words in terms intelligible to an Arabic scholar without straining after an unattainable precision. Thus* ك *is rendered by* k*,* ق *by* ḳ*,* ه *by* h*,* ح *by* ḥ*, and so forth:* ا *and* و *are generally distinguished from the corresponding vowel points by* â *and* û *or* ô*, but not when they are either initial or final. I write, for instance,* abu *not* âbû*, and* anba *not* ânbâ*, because in such cases there is no real ambiguity. But I cannot claim any sort of absolute accuracy, for the simple reason that in many cases where a proper name has been learnt by ear, or borrowed from another writer, I have been unable to* *ascertain exactly the Arabic spelling. Some mistakes therefore are inevitable.*

All the plans in the text are carefully drawn to scale with the exception of some of the small plans of Cairo churches. It had not been my intention to publish these, but merely to use them for my own guidance: however on consideration it seemed better to give a slight plan than none at all. These plans, then, rough as they are, will serve to give an idea of the general arrangement of buildings quite unfamiliar to English readers: and in most if not in all cases measurements will be found in the text sufficient to give the scale approximately.

A pleasant task remains—to acknowledge the kindness of those who have aided me in my work. The largest measure of thanks—a measure larger than I can find words fitly to express—is due to my friend Mr. J. Henry Middleton, to whom I owe the best plan and many of the most beautiful drawings in the text, drawings which I am forbidden to particularise. Nor have I profited less by the immense learning than by the rare draughtmanship of Mr. Middleton. Indeed but for his most generous assistance and encouragement I do not know that this book would have been written. My thanks also are gladly rendered to Sir Arthur Gordon, Governor General of Ceylon, for three very interesting plans of churches in Upper Egypt; to the Very Reverend Dean Butcher, of Cairo, for much help and befriending in my task;

to the Coptic Patriarch for his authority and countenance in my journeys and researches; to Abûna Philotheos, Ḳummuṣ of the Cathedral in Cairo, and to 'Abdu 'l Massîḥ Simaikah for much information; and to many others, whose names if unrecorded here are gratefully remembered.

A. J. B.

Oxford,
October, 1884.

GLOSSARY OF ARABIC OR COPTIC TERMS.

Anba, the Coptic term for father : this title is usually but not exclusively given to the patriarch.

Dair, a ring-wall enclosing Coptic churches or monastic buildings.

Galilaeon, one of the holy oils of Coptic ritual : the term is a corruption of ἀγαλλιάσεως ἔλαιον.

Haikal, the central of the three chapels in a Coptic church, or principal sanctuary, containing the high altar : literally the word signifies 'temple.'

Isbodikon, the central part of the Coptic eucharistic wafer : from δεσποτικὸν (σῶμα).

Ḳaṣr, the keep or tower of a dair in the desert.

Ḳorbân, literally the oblation; and so either the wafer or the mass.

Ḳummuṣ, either archpriest, or in a monastery the abbot.

Manḍârah, the guest-room of a church or monastery.

Mâri, the Coptic term for saint.

Mushrabîah, a peculiar kind of finely jointed lattice-work used for windows, etc.

Myron, Arabic *mîrûn*, the μύρον or chrism, the chief of the holy oils.

Paṭrashîl, a kind of stole ; Greek ἐπιτραχήλιον.

Shamlah, a kind of amice.

Ṭarbûsh, the red cap or fez round which the turban is wound.

CONTENTS

OF THE FIRST VOLUME.

CHAPTER I.

CHAPTER II.

CHAPTER III.

CHAPTER IV.

Contents.

LIST OF PLANS AND ILLUSTRATIONS
IN VOL. I.

THE
ANCIENT COPTIC CHURCHES
OF EGYPT.

CHAPTER I.

On the Structure of Coptic Churches in general.

THE seed sown by St. Mark was quick in bearing fruit. Christian doctrines spread and Christian churches sprang up through all the land of Egypt. The Delta was covered with them: singly or in clusters they were dotted along the banks of the Nile for at least a thousand miles south towards the sister churches of Ethiopia: and even the silence of the desert was broken by hymn and chaunt from chapels built upon scenes that were hallowed by the life and death of holy anchorites. For monasticism began in Egypt, as pious or frail believers were driven by the vanities or persecutions of the world into the dreary solitudes where neither the fear of the sword nor the allurements of the flesh could follow them.

To trace the history of these churches, to show how Christianity, at first driven into holes and caves, came forth from the dim catacombs of Alexandria, stood in the light, and in spite of fierce opposition

won its way from the Mediterranean to the tropics
—this would be a work for which time and material
alike fail.   Still more impossible is it to give anything like a complete description of the ancient
church buildings.   With comparatively few exceptions the churches, like the heathen temples before
them, are fallen and gone.   Of the many ancient
churches at Alexandria not one now remains : Tanis
(the Zoan of Scripture), once the site of many
churches, is now a desolate morass, out of which
stand here and there heaps of ruins : of the monasteries at the Natrun Lakes, while a few remain, the
greater part lie buried in the sand : and of the
churches in Upper Egypt perhaps not one tenth is
left.   Fortunately, however, some of the most interesting in point of history and of structure are at
once the best preserved and the most accessible.
With the single exception of St. Mark's church in
Alexandria, which is quite destroyed, there is scarcely
any building of foremost renown in Coptic history
which may not be seen to-day.   But the centre of
interest is Cairo, or rather Old Cairo, not Alexandria.
The earliest churches there date at least from the
third century of our era, and cannot be much later
than the earliest in the northern city.   Even before
the Mohammedan conquest there are signs of a
struggle for supremacy between the two cities ; and
once the Muslim rule was established, the seat of the
patriarchate was removed to Old Cairo, which thus
became practically the religious as well as the political
capital for the Christians, though the spiritual claims
of Alexandria, acknowledged at first by a tribute of
money and the homage of every new patriarch, are to
this day neither abated nor denied.

The predominant type of Christian architecture in Egypt is basilican. It has been the fashion to regard this type as adopted from the secular Roman basilica by the early Christians; but in his recently published 'Essay on the History of English Church Architecture,' Mr. G. Gilbert Scott shows good reason for assigning an earlier and independent origin to this form of building. According to his theory the germ of the Christian basilica was a simple oblong aisleless room divided by a cross arch, beyond which lay an altar detached from the wall. This germ was developed by the addition of side aisles, and sometimes an aisle returned across the entrance end: over these upper aisles were next constructed, and transepts added, together with small oratories or chapels in various parts of the building. On the other hand, the secular basilica is shown to have begun with a colonnade enclosing an open area, to have been roofed in, to have lost the colonnades, and to have passed into a lofty hall covered with a brick vaulting. I have little or no hesitation in accepting this theory, more especially as the churches of Egypt are rich in evidence that favours it. It is of course clear that the two separate developments at one point closely coincided, and that the resemblance, at first accidental, became in later times conscious and designed: but the secular basilicas of the fourth century are very different from the Christian churches of that epoch, which resemble rather the pagan basilicas of three centuries earlier. The question may perhaps be narrowed down to a smaller issue. Since it is quite certain that the earliest places of worship in the East were plain aisleless rooms, and that aisles were a later addition, can it reasonably be maintained that aisles were in no case thrown out before the suggestion had been caught from a Roman basilica? This seems in the last degree improbable: for the logic of thought and logic of fact are alike against it. The rock-cut church at Ephesus, called the Church of the Seven Sleepers, which is not later than the third century, already shows a triple division lengthwise, corresponding to nave and aisles, though there are no actual columns. One of the simple and very early rock-cut churches at Surp Garabed in Cappadocia [1] shows side pilasters which have only to be detached to make an aisled basilica. The crypt at Abu Sargah in Old Cairo, which may, in spite of its Saracenic capitals, date from the second or third century, is tripartite. If I remember rightly, a similar division might be traced in a church among the catacombs of Alexandria near the so-called Baths of Cleopatra—though the fire of the English fleet is likely enough now to have laid that very spot in ruins. Further, the uniformity in the arrangement of the three eastern chapels in the oldest monuments of church building in Egypt, gives a strong presumption that the tradition dates from the remotest Christian antiquity. Al Makrîzi mentions a wholesale destruction of churches in Alexandria by order of Severianus about 200 A. D.; and of churches at Jerusalem nearly a century earlier under Hadrian. These can scarcely all have been devoid of aisles and columns.

But though the Christian basilica had thus probably a non-Roman origin in Egypt and elsewhere, no doubt certain determinations of detail and finish

---

[1] Texier and Pullan's Byzantine Architecture, p. 39.

were received either directly from Roman basilican models in Alexandria and Babylon, or indirectly from the type of Roman architecture which was brought into the East by Constantine.   In example may be cited the classic entablature over the nave columns, in churches like Abu Sargah and Anba Shanûdah; perhaps the upper aisles or large triforia found in most churches; and the outer or second aisles (as in Al Mu'allakah and Al 'Adra in the Hârat-az-Zuailah), which are of frequent occurrence in the period of Constantine, occurring for instance in the church of the Holy Sepulchre at Jerusalem and the basilica at Tyre, both built by that emperor.

Setting aside however the question of origin, and granting merely that most of the Egyptian churches may be roughly termed basilican, it remains to notice a subordinate though powerful influence of another kind, which, for want of a better name, must be called Byzantine.   The leading characteristics of the Byzantine style, exemplified for instance at St. Sophia in Stambûl and the little churches of Athens, are the domed roofing, the absence of many-pillared aisles, and sometimes a cruciform design.   Of these the dome—by far the most important—is distinctively of eastern origin : and I think it far more probable that Byzantium borrowed it from Alexandria than the reverse.   The dome would more easily pass from India to Egypt than to the remoter West; and seeing that Egypt lies nearer the cradle of our religion and her Church was founded by St. Mark, there is every likelihood that Alexandria was before the rest of the world in building churches as in general civilisation, and started the type of architecture which, becoming familiar to Europeans in Byzantium, was called after that city. The use of the dome in Babylonia is certainly of the highest antiquity, and domed buildings were common in the time of the Sassanides: so that without any disparagement to the genius of Anthemius, the architect of St. Sophia, one may imagine that, like the architects of Greece in classic times, he owed much to Egypt. But abandoning any attempt to push the theory, it will be interesting to examine the churches of Cairo with a view to determining the relative importance of the Latin and the Byzantine element in their structure, and to note any peculiarities that may be called distinctively Coptic.

Among all the buildings that I have visited in Egypt proper and the desert, and I believe among all the churches scattered up and down the Nile, there is not a single specimen of purely Byzantine architecture. The Coptic builders seem to have had no liking for or no knowledge of the cruciform groundplan. It would be less difficult, though not easy, to find an instance of a purely basilican church, the best example being the Jewish synagogue at Old Cairo, once the Coptic church of St. Michael. This little building, with its side aisles, aisle returned across the western end, upper aisles, its single broad-curved apse breaking from the straight eastern wall, and its finely ornamented triumphal arch above the sanctuary, presents most of the characteristics of the Latin style. But though the cruciform groundplan is unknown, the dome is almost if not quite universal. Many of the churches are roofed entirely with a cluster of equal domes: wherever a church is figured in a Coptic painting it is always a domed building: and even those churches of the two Cairos that are most markedly basilican (with the single exception of Al Mu'allaḳah, where there are special reasons for the absence of the dome), have at least one dome over the sanctuary, and far more usually one over each of the three altars. The result is that in the majority of cases the architecture of the Coptic churches is of a mixed type, half-basilican and half-Byzantine : while in other cases there is a type entirely non-basilican yet not entirely Byzantine. But there is no case, as far as I know, of an architecture unleavened by either of these two elements, however variously they enter into combination with each other and with other elements.

To take the non-basilican order first. The best examples of this style are perhaps to be found in the monasteries of the desert. There are two twelve-domed churches in Dair Mâri Antonios in the eastern desert by the Red Sea : and though the churches of the Natrun valley in the western desert are not distinguished by any great number of domes, yet the domes there are wider in span, lower in pitch, and finer in structure than anything in Cairo. At the village of Bûsh on the Nile, near Bani Suíf, there occurs the very unusual and, as far as I know, unique arrangement of a central dome with four semi-domes attached and four small domes at the angles of a square about it. As a rule the Coptic architect not merely placed his noblest domes to overshadow the altars, but seldom cared to raise any other domes at all. In Cairo, however, both of the churches in the Ḥârat-ar-Rûm, namely Mâri Girgis and Al 'Aḍra, are covered in with a twelve-domed roofing. The plan of each is a square, divided into twelve minor squares, or, to be more accurate, nine squares and

three apsidal figures.   Each division has its own
dome, and the roof is upheld at Al 'Aḍra by six
piers, at Mâri Girgis by pillars.   The terms aisle and
nave can scarcely be applied in strictness at either
church : and were it not for the absence of a cruciform groundplan, and perhaps the presence of the
triple apse, these little churches might be regarded
as typical Byzantine structures.   With them may be
classed the two churches in Dair Tadrus at Old
Cairo, which are of quite the same style though
less regular in design, and the upper church in
the Ḥârat-az-Zuailah.   These then are the cases in
which the architecture is of decidedly non-basilican
order.   But I must not omit to notice that among
the Cairo churches there is one solitary example of
the central dome, namely Ḳ. Burbârah ; and this is
the only church with anything like a cruciform plan,
though generally its details are basilican.   The
central dome was the most characteristic feature of
the Byzantine style, and after the time of Justinian
' became universal in all towns of the eastern
empire[1].'   Egypt however makes a striking exception to this rule.   The Coptic dome further differs
from the Byzantine in showing externally either plain
brick or a surface of white plaster, and in having no
regular windows, still less anything like the beautiful
arcading of Moné Tes Koras at Constantinople, the
Katholikon in Athens, and the monastery of Daphni
towards Eleusis, or like the extremely rich decoration
of the domes on the church of the Holy Apostles at
Thessalonica.   Further, that which is the rule in the
Coptic churches is at least the exception in all other

---

[1] Texier and Pullan, p. 21.

churches; for I believe there is no case of a Byzantine church out of Egypt in which the apses are covered with full domes: whereas the churches of Maṣr almost always terminate eastward with three fully domed apses, and never in semi-domes.

This peculiarity is found in the basilican as well as the Byzantine edifices. Thus Abu-'s-Sifain, Anba Shanûdah, and most other churches, have three domes, one over each of the three chapels. Abu Sargah has a dome over each of the side chapels, while the haikal curiously enough is roofed with a wagon-vaulting of wood. The wagon-vaulted roof is found also in the church of Sitt Mariam; in the main church and in the chapel of St. Banai at Mâri Mîna; the chapel of Sitt Mariam belonging to Abu-'s-Sifain; the basilica in the Ḥârat-az-Zuailah; and Al Mu'allaḳah. In the last named the aisles and nave are both wagon-vaulted and the vaulting is continued over the eastern chapels in place of the customary domes. If this be the original arrangement, as it very well may be, we have a solitary instance of a domeless church. It is probable that the Copts borrowed this form of roof from the Romans at a very early period, and it is not surprising that the most marked instance of it should occur in the church built upon the gateway of the Roman fortress. But its frequent employment in Coptic churches is very remarkable and deserves to be noted as a Coptic peculiarity—because the wagon-vaulted roof was never used for basilican churches in any part of western Christendom with the solitary exception of Ireland. In Egypt it is more common than the high-pitched timber roof like that at Abu-'s-Sifain and Anba Shanûdah. There is no evidence to show that this skeleton roof of the nave was ever underdrawn with a flat ceiling coffered and gilded, such as was common in churches built by Constantine: but that work of the kind was used for ceiling is proved by the beautiful remnants of coloured woodwork in the south upper aisle at Abu-'s-Sifain as well as by the analogous but far earlier decoration of the entablature in Anba Shanûdah and elsewhere.

The entrance to a Coptic church is almost invariably towards, if not in, the western side, while the sanctuaries lie always on the eastern. The one eastern entrance at the Hârat-az-Zuailah is modern, and even there the altars are at the same end. Whatever may have been the primitive arrangement of the Latin Church—and it would be difficult to refute the evidence by which Mr. G. Gilbert Scott proves that the earliest buildings in south Italy had eastern doorways and a western altar—it is quite certain that there is no trace or tradition of any such arrangement in a Coptic sacred building. There, in every instance, the orientation of the altar is clear and decided, although accidents of site have of course in some cases deflected the axis of a church slightly from the true east. It is quite possible that the orientation of our European churches, which was not the usual practice in the beginning, but which became almost universal in the middle ages, may have been derived from Egypt. The Copts seem to have aimed at securing three western doors: and in their earliest churches this arrangement was doubtless the ordinary one. But almost from the beginning of their Christianity they were harried with incessant persecutions: thus, more especially after the Muslim conquest, when they found their lives and possessions exposed to ceaseless outbursts of fanatical violence and rapacity on the part of their conquerors, it became a necessity of existence to fortify their churches. Hence the absence of windows other than small skylights in all Coptic churches, and the early disuse of the triple western doorway. The latter was retained at Al Mu'allaḳah, which, owing to its peculiar structure 'in the air,' depended for its security on other defences. At Abu Sargah there is one existing door at the west, with clear evidence of one if not two others having been blocked up: while at Ḳadīsah Burbârah, Abu-'s-Sifain, and Anba Shanûdah, there is a single western entrance with no indication of any other having ever existed. The Jewish synagogue (church of St. Michael) differs from all others at the present day in retaining its single original western entrance in the centre: in the other cases quoted the western door opens into one of the side aisles. Many churches have their doorway on the north or south side, the arrangement being determined by the accidents of the situation and the facilities afforded by masses of surrounding buildings. At Mâri Mîna there is a western door opening into the south aisle, and another opening into the north aisle, though the latter has been walled off and excluded from the sacred building. The interesting basilica in the Ḥârat-az-Zuailah seems to have had one or more western doorways, though from the west, as the level of the city rose about the church, the entrance was removed to the south, and finally to the east.

In nearly all cases the western wall of a Coptic church aligns the street, but in the little isolated dairs of Mâri Mîna and Tadrus, which have no

street within them, and in upper churches like those
at Cairo proper, the rule is of course departed from.
It is this western side which is generally exposed to
view, but the wall, instead of ending with the limits
of the church, is nearly always prolonged and lost
in neighbouring houses. For there is no instance
of a sacred edifice standing clear and detached like
an English church in its churchyard. A Coptic
church outside never shows any outline: around it
is huddled a mass of haphazard buildings which
show that the architect's idea was concealment of
the exterior rather than adornment. These buildings serve of course to shelter the church, and though
they have long ago been turned from their original
monastic uses, many of them are still inhabited by
the priests or other satellites employed in the church
services; while in many cases, as at Abu Sargah
for instance, the upper aisles or triforia which opened
into domestic chambers adjoining have been turned
into women's apartments for the priest's family. At
Dair Tadrus the chambers are all silent and deserted,
not a soul residing within the walls, and this was
the case even a hundred and fifty years ago, when
Pococke visited Old Cairo: Dair Bablûn has three
or four inhabitants: Mâri Mîna keeps its rooms
unswept and unfurnished for the pilgrims that come
there once every year: in the Hârat-az-Zuailah nuns
are still living in the old monastic buildings attached
to the church. The houses, then, piled at random
about a Coptic church had two purposes, monastic
and defensive: but it is obvious that they made
anything like exterior ornamentation impossible, and
one may say roughly that an Egyptian church has
neither outline nor exterior architecture. The out-

side is a rude shapeless congeries of brickwork intended rather to escape notice than to attract admiration ; it was meant that there should be nothing to delight the eye of the Muslim enemy prowling without, while architectural and liturgical splendours alike were reserved for the believer within.

This entanglement of the sacred fabric in other buildings, wall against wall, and this absence of out-side adornment, may be set down as distinctly Coptic peculiarities: they are found neither in Syria nor in Byzantium, nor in Latin Christendom : because, while in other countries it was felt that the outside as well as the inside of the church deserved a grand and glorious architecture, to the Copts this outer plainness was a condition of existence. Another external peculiarity is the arrangement or want of arrangement in the accessory chapels, which open from either aisle or from the triforia, which are sometimes grouped three or four together under one roof, which occupy an upper or a lower story indif-ferently, are walled or not walled on to the mother church, and are sometimes piled in almost impossible positions one on top of another. Almost every church furnishes examples ; but I may refer specially to the two upper churches of Mâri Girgis in Cairo proper, to Mâri Mîna, Anba Shanûdah, and above all to Abu-'s-Sifain. Details will be found in the description of those churches.

Many of these chapels possess the full complement of three altars each within its own sanctuary, and therefore deserve rather to be called churches, except in so far as they are grouped about a larger church and are under the direct ministration of its clergy.

Abu-'s-Sifain, for example, though an ecclesiastical and in some sense an architectural unit, is really a group of churches. The neighbouring group at Anba Shanûdah lies within the circuit of Dair Abu-'s-Sifain. Several similar units or groups are enclosed by the ring-wall of the Ḳaṣr-ash-Shamm'ah : so too the churches of Dair Tadrus lie in a walled enclosure not sixty yards in diameter; and the monasteries in the western desert are built on precisely the same model. This whole arrangement corresponds singularly with the earliest monastic buildings of Ireland, where it was customary to erect several small churches close together, instead of large churches, and to enclose each group with all its monastic buildings—cells, chambers, kitchens, &c.—in a 'cashel' or ring-wall[1]. Another curious coincidence between Irish and Coptic practice is the use of the wagon-vault to roof nave and chancel, there being apparently no other parallel for its early employment in western Christendom. Mr. Warren, in his 'Liturgy and Ritual of the Celtic Church[2],' quotes a statement that seven Egyptian monks are buried at Disert Ulidh in Ireland, and are invoked in the Litany of Oengus. So that the coincidence may be not wholly accidental. Moreover, Ledwich[3] relates that a colony of Egyptians settled in the isle of Lerins, off the south coast of France, and adds that in England 'the Egyptian plan was followed at Glastonbury.' The monks of Bangor, St. Columba, Congel, &c., adopted the rule of St. Basil : and the

---

[1] English Church Architecture, by G. Gilbert Scott, pp. 72, 73.
[2] P. 56.
[3] Antiquities of Ireland, 2nd ed., pp. 88, 89.

distinguished antiquaries Sir R. Cotton, Sir H. Spel-
man, W. Camden, and J. Selden, when appealed to on
the subject, 'drew up a certificate wherein they de-
clared that previous to the coming of St. Augustine
in 597 the Egyptian rule (of monastic life) was only
in use.'

Before quitting this part of the subject, I may
remark that no Cairo church has any spire or tower:
neither the Byzantine campanile nor the Muslim
minaret has any counterpart in the ordinary buildings of the Copts.   But this peculiarity arises not
from any dislike on the part of the Christians to
bells, but from the Muslim prohibition of their usage.
Accordingly we find bell-towers still standing and
still in use in the desert monasteries of the Natrun
valley and other remote places, where there is no
chance of Muslim interference.   These towers are
built of brick and covered with plaster: as far as
they have any character they may be called Byzantine.   Each tower is usually two stories high, square
on plan, and each side in the upper story is relieved
by two open arches, highly stilted and round-headed.
The position which the tower occupies with regard
to the church is quite immaterial, but it is always
virtually detached.

We may now turn to the interior structure and
arrangement of the Cairo churches, distinguishing
as before such features as may be called basilican
or Byzantine or Coptic.

Generally speaking the nave is divided from the
aisle on each side by a row of Greek or Roman
columns.   The favourite arrangement was to have
twelve such columns distributed round the three
sides of the nave, as at Abu Sargah, leaving the

eastern side open, but making a narthex or returned aisle at the west end. It is extremely rare to find the rows of columns ending abruptly in a western wall without any cross-row, as for instance was the case in the old basilica of St. Peter's at Rome and perhaps the cathedral at Ravenna : but it is equally rare now to find the cross-row of columns standing clear and making a true returned aisle, such as may be seen in the synagogue at Ḳaṣr-ash-Shamm'ah. For the spaces between the pillars of the returned aisle have in most cases been walled up, so that the western aisle has become rather a true narthex. A comparison of the plan of Abu Sargah or Ḳadîsah Burbârah with the ancient basilica of Thessalonica [1] will show the same transition from the returned aisle to the narthex proper in widely different localities. As far as I know, Al Mu'allaḳah affords a solitary instance of an exo-narthex which contains, like that at Thessalonica, a fountain for ablutions. At the period when Abu-'s-Sifain was built, i.e. the tenth century, the narthex was so far necessary that it is made a distinct feature of the church instead of being an adaptation : while the adjacent but much earlier building of Anba Shanûdah shows no sign of any narthex.   The narthex was of course the place appointed for catechumens during the service of the church, besides being the place of discipline and admonition for penitents, and sometimes the place of baptism.   But the state of decay and disorder into which this part of the sacred edifice has fallen shows a very long discontinuance and oblivion of such primitive usage.   At Abu Sargah, Abu-'s-Sifain, and

---

[1] Figured in Texier and Pullan's Byzantine Architecture, p. 173.

Al 'Adra Hârat-az-Zuailah the large Epiphany tank is sunk in the floor of the narthex : but although the orthodox place would seem to be at the west end, its position in other churches varies so much that it can only have been determined by random choice or hazard.   Still, in these three principal buildings the narthex was used at the feast of Epiphany (when the people plunged into the waters blessed by the priest), long after its original uses were forgotten. At Kadîsah Burbârah the central part of the narthex is walled off and serves as mandârah or guest-room, while the entrance passes through the north part, and the south part is walled off into a separate sacristy.

The narthex is finely marked in some of the ancient churches of Upper Egypt.   Thus the church of the White Monastery near Sûhâg, which dates from at least the third or fourth century, has a central western entrance and a narthex completely walled off from the aisles as well as from the nave : a single central door in the eastern wall of the narthex gives admission to the church.   This narthex once contained a beautiful baptistery, and it remains even now one of the most splendid monuments of early Christian ritual.   Among the monasteries of the desert, the rite of baptism was comparatively rarely exercised, because it very seldom happened that any resorted thither who had not already been signed with the cross of Christ.   Consequently many of the churches there are quite destitute of baptisteries, and even where the font is found, it is seldom or never placed at the western entrance : and such is the modifying influence of ritual upon architecture, that there does not occur one instance of a true narthex in all the churches of the Natrun valley; although the western

returned aisle is not unfrequent. A glance at the
plan of Al 'Adra Dair-as-Sûriâni will show how
easily a narthex might have been built in place of
the returned aisle, had need so required.

The walls of the nave in basilican churches are
generally carried on a continuous wooden architrave
joining the columns, and are lightened by small
relieving arches. But instead of the classic entablature, which was blazoned with colours and gold,
adorned with Coptic texts and carved crosses, we
find the pillars spanned by arches on the north side
of Al Mu'allaḳah: while at Abu-s'-Sifain there are
neither columns nor architrave but heavy solid piers
united by arches. The structure of Mâri Mîna is
somewhat similar: while in the more Byzantine
buildings we often find piers not in line but in
groups, with arches springing from all four sides.
Of these two methods of construction, the arched is
of course later than the trabeated; and many of the
Coptic churches are remarkable for their combination
of both methods, showing in fact with curious felicity
the history of the transition. The Greek architects
set their columns close together, or, in technical
language, employed the pyknostyle arrangement:
but the Romans, choosing to place wider intervals
between the columns, were obliged to find some
way of distributing the heavy bearing which resulted
from this araeostyle construction. Accordingly they
introduced relieving arches, which were at first not
open, but hidden in the wall above the architrave.
The next step was to show the relieving arches
boldly, as they are shown for instance at Abu Sargah
and Anba Shanûdah, and to substitute a wooden for
a stone architrave; and it is easy to see how the

widening of the relieving arches would finally do away with the necessity for the architrave altogether. Such are the changes arising from a change in the method of intercolumniation: and even from this brief review it will be obvious that where we find so decided examples of the trabeated and of the arched style of construction in the same building, as at Al Mu'allaḳah, we must assign them to different epochs. I may add that a continuous marble architrave with small relieving arches visible occurs in the church of Sta. Maria in Trastavere at Rome.

Over the lateral aisles, and over the returned aisle or the narthex, upper aisles are nearly always built, of equal dimensions with those below. These upper aisles, or triforia as they may be called for convenience, were used to accommodate women at times of service at least as early as the days of St. Augustine[1]. They opened into the nave by large bays with an arrangement of columns. Whether the spaces between the columns were screened or not is uncertain, but the parapet of the gallery would be sufficient almost to hide the worshippers from the congregation below. Good examples of these galleries may be seen at Abu Sargah and Ḳadîsah Burbârah, while they are quite unknown in the contemporary churches of the desert monasteries, where of course there were no women. In lapse of time however, as it became customary for women to attend service in the body of the church, a special place westward was railed and screened off for them. Consequently, when the gallery was no longer required, the spaces between the pillars were walled up

---

[1] Civ. Dei, iii. p. 27.

and the galleries were turned to other uses. This change was facilitated by their arrangement, for the entrance to them is in all cases from without the church by a doorway communicating with the adjacent monastic dwellings: so that it was easy to sever this part of the church from the general service of the sacred building. The first step was to convert the women's galleries into chapels; and this was done at an early period at Kadîsah Burbârah, and most likely at Abu Sargah, though there I was forbidden to enter the triforium to examine. The church of Abu-'s-Sifain is remarkably interesting in this connexion as having been built at a time when the transition had already taken place. For the divisions below into men's section and women's section are undoubtedly part of the original arrangement dating from the tenth century. Accordingly we find that, inasmuch as provision was made at the first for women in the body of the church, although the basilican tradition so far determined its structure as to necessitate a continuous gallery over the aisles and narthex, yet this gallery is, with the exception of one small and almost inaccessible opening, entirely shut off from the nave by solid walls, so that no one in it could follow the service below. But the gallery is furnished with chapels of its own, contemporary with the main building, and designed for quite separate services. It may then be taken for granted that the practice of admitting women to the nave of the church, though the two sexes were kept apart, had become general if not universal by the tenth century.

But the chapels erected in the galleries have themselves long fallen into disuse, as the zeal and the number of worshippers diminished: though the

traces of gorgeous colours and gilding, of elaborate
frescoes and beautiful wood-carving, still bear witness
to the olden splendour of these oratories and the
pomp of their vanished ceremonial. To-day the
upper aisles are either entirely disused, or service is
held in each chapel on one solitary day in the whole
year's round, the feast-day of the patron saint ; or the
entire gallery is given up to the women of the
priest's household, who make it their special apartment and deck it with hangings and mirrors. Even
now, however, on the occasion of great festivals, when
the congregation of women is too large for the place
set apart in the nave, they are admitted into the
gallery wherever, as at Abu Sargah, latticed gratings
have been let into the walls which block the ancient
bay openings. It is interesting to notice that the
present restoration of Al Mu'allakah displays a
reversion to primitive practice ; for there the screens
that separated the sexes in the nave have been
entirely abolished, and the women are relegated to
the galleries. In the modern cathedral of Cairo too
the women are not allowed in the body of the church,
but have two stories of latticed galleries over the
aisles, from which they see and hear the service.

Examples of churches with large upper aisles for
women are found at Rome (St. Agnes without the
walls and St. Lawrence): the basilica of the fifth
century at Thessalonica preserves the same arrangement ; though it was not found in the great Roman
basilicas of St. Peter or St. Paul. I may add that
there is no instance of a clerestory in Coptic architecture: nor is there anything resembling the narrow
triforium of our Gothic buildings. The broad
triforium at Westminster Abbey offers perhaps the

closest parallel to the Coptic upper aisles, and the resemblance is the more complete as there is evidence to show that it once contained chapels.

The transept is a very rare feature in the churches of Egypt. Abu Sargah contains a short northern transept, and Kadîsah Burbârah both northern and southern. The latter church (I repeat) is the one example of a cruciform plan, irregular as it is, and over the centre of the cross rises a large and lofty dome; but in other respects the church is decidedly basilican. Besides these two I have seen no other church in Cairo with a transept.

The division of the nave into men's section and women's section by means of screens, which, as I have shown, is at least as ancient as the tenth century, is the normal arrangement at the present day in the main churches, and is carried out even in many of the little chapels and baptisteries. The division is in all cases across the body of the church, so that the women are ranged entirely behind and westward of the men. Thus, as the whole congregation faces eastward, no interchange of glances is possible.

Allusion has already been made to the large Epiphany tank which forms a regular part of a Coptic church. These tanks are eight or ten feet long, six feet broad, and five or six feet deep. They seem to have been boarded over when not actually in use. It is reasonable to suppose, especially from their prevalent position in the narthex, that these tanks were meant in the early ages of the Church for baptism by total immersion, although there is no distinct evidence or tradition to that effect, except perhaps the fact that they generally occupy the place assigned to the font in the churches of the West. It is however certain that any such custom has been abolished for centuries, during which time these tanks have been used exclusively on the feast of Epiphany; and this latter usage was suppressed from the disorder it occasioned within the memory of the present generation. But there is another tank of much smaller size which forms no less characteristic a feature of the Egyptian churches. This is a shallow rectangular basin about two feet long by one foot broad, which is sunk in the floor and edged about generally with costly marbles. Its usual position is in the westward part of the nave, where it may be seen at Abu-'s-Sifain, Anba Shanû-dah, Abu Sargah, Al Mu'allakah, &c.; but in many of the desert churches it lies rather more eastward. In olden times it was undoubtedly used for the mandatum, and possibly also for ablutions.

From the canons of Christodulus, as late as the eleventh century, we know that men were required to come barefoot to church; and the tank was perhaps placed in the floor in order that worshippers might conveniently 'shake off the dust of their feet' before service: and the dust of Cairo is by no means an imaginary evil or pollution. At the present day however, the practice of wearing shoes has rendered this cleansing less necessary, and the use of the tank for ablutions is wholly unknown except on Maundy Thursday, when the ancient ceremony of feet-washing, once common alike to the eastern and western churches, but with us long neglected, is still performed by the priest. While the Epiphany tank seems a peculiarity of the Coptic ritual, the font or tank for ablutions was common to all the oriental

churches, and even the churches of the West retain
in their holy-water stoups the same tradition [1]. But
the Coptic practice differs from that of the Syrian
and Byzantine churches in the position of the tank;
for both in the great basilica of Tyre as restored by
Constantine, and in the church of St. Sophia, the
tank lay in the centre of the atrium external to the
main building, and surrounded by quadrangular
cloisters or colonnades. So too at Thessalonica
the fountain lies outside at the north-east corner
of the church. It is worth remarking that a similar
tank for washing the feet before prayer, or else a
fountain, is invariably attached to the Mohammedan
mosques of Egypt: and moreover the position of
the fountain in the centre of the courtyard at all the
larger mosques, and the surrounding cloisters, almost
exactly reproduce the Christian atrium. The analogy is carried even further in the many cases where
the Muslim fountain is covered with a dome resting
on a circle of pillars; for this was a common Christian
arrangement, and was found at the early church of
St. John at Constantinople as described by Clavijo,
and still exists at the churches of Zographe and St.
Laura at Mount Athos.

In the arrangement of the choir in Coptic churches
there are three distinct methods discernible. In
some of the more Byzantine buildings, as Al 'Adra
Ḥârat-ar-Rûm and Abu Ḳîr wa Yuḥanna, the choir
is neither marked off from the nave by any screen
nor distinguished by a higher level: in other churches,
like Al Amîr Tadrus, a single step divides choir and
nave, while a high lattice screen intervenes: again,

---

[1] History of English Church Architecture, p. 16 n.

in the chief basilican churches the choir is raised
two steps above the nave and screened by lattice-
work. To this latter class however there are two
singular exceptions, Al Mu'allaḳah and Ḳadîsah
Burbârah, in which choir and nave are at one continuous level, and the screens that parted the two
have been removed; so that an unbroken view may
be had from the west to the sanctuary. At Abu-'s-
Sifain, the choir-screen is solid and pierced by a
small square sliding-door or window on either side:
the entrance closes by folding-doors, across which
hung in olden times a curtain. At Abu-'s-Sifain,
Abu Sargah, and Al 'Aḍra Ḥârat-az-Zuailah the
screen recedes about three feet eastward from the
edge of the choir platform, leaving in the nave
a kind of stone bench. This probably corresponds
to the solea of the Greek Church, where candidates
for ordination stood till the Cherubic Hymn was
ended, when they were led into the sanctuary. It
should be remarked that there is a solea before
the *sanctuary*-screen at Al Mu'allaḳah, though
there is no choir now otherwise distinguished than
by the lecterns. It is doubtful whether, in the
very earliest times, the choir was separated from
the nave or had any distinct existence, as the first
clear mention of it seems to be in the seventh
century. Later it was marked off from the nave
by a low railing something like the wall or balustrade common in early Italian basilicas, with this
difference in the Coptic churches, that the choir-
railing always extended across the whole building
instead of returning along the wings or aisles eastward. There was a front railing, in fact, but no
side railings. The reason for this difference of

structure lies in the fact that a Coptic church has three chapels eastward, shut off either by a single continuous screen or by three screens in the same line, and requiring therefore a continuous choir. The choir then in all cases extends the whole breadth of the church, and is even drawn out along the transepts, where such exist, as at Ḳadî-sah Burbârah. There is a very curious arrangement in some of the churches in the Natrun valley, for example at Al 'Aḍra Dair-as-Sûriâni, where the choir is entirely separated from the nave by a wall reaching the whole height of the building, and opening from the nave only by a central doorway fitted with folding-doors. One may remark also that these monastic churches have often low screens of solid stone instead of the lofty lattice screens of the Cairo buildings.

The choir-screen is sometimes, though not always, adorned with a series of pictures ranged along the top: the subjects are either sacred scenes or figures of apostles and saints; but it seems a fixed rule that the central painting over the choir door should represent the crucifixion. The analogy with the western practice is the more obvious when we remember that in later times at all events the rood was generally a crucifix. It was before this door, in the Coptic as in the Roman ritual, that processions made a station while singing antiphons. A rood proper or cross of wood is sometimes, though rarely, found on the choir-screen, as in the chapel of St. Antony at Abu-'s-Sifain. At Al 'Aḍra Ḥârat-ar-Rûm, which has no choir-screen, a large rood with pictures of Mary and John attached rests upon a rood-beam fastened between the two piers, which in the ordinary arrangement would be joined by the choir-screen; while at Al 'Adra Hârat-az-Zuailah, there is a true rood over the door, not of the choir but of the haikal; and the same is the case at Al 'Adra in Dair-as-Sûriâni in the western desert. The Coptic choir, measured from west to east, is seldom more than ten or twelve feet deep; it contains no stalls either for clergy or 'chorus cantorum,' and no seats of any description, but usually two moveable lecterns and a tall standard candlestick. The pulpit is placed in the nave, near the north-east corner: sometimes it resembles closely our western pulpits, in other cases it may more rightly be called an ambon: and sometimes again it has quite disappeared. Fine examples of the ambon occur at Al Mu'allakah, Abu-'s-Sifain, and Mâri Mîna: but its position never varies, and its greater length is invariably east and west, not north and south, as was usual in the early churches, as for example at St. Sophia. It is never mounted by two flights of steps, does not stand in the centre of the church, and has no column to serve as paschal candlestick. The usual pulpit in the monastic churches of the desert is a recess in the nave wall furnished with a rude balustrade.

Every church has three contiguous sanctuaries and three altars, neither more nor less. Many other chapels are attached externally to the main building, or are located in the upper aisles; but in the main body of the church no altars are allowed to be scattered about the building, but all must be ranged in a line at the eastern end. There are only two altars at present at Al Amîr Tadrus and at Abu-'s-Sifain: but it is almost certain that at the former church an altar has been removed, and even if the same is not true

of Abu-'s-Sifain the comparatively late date of that
edifice makes its exceptional structure less noteworthy. Ḳadîsah Burbârah and Al 'Aḍra Ḥârat-az-
Zuailah, though both very ancient buildings, include
part of a still earlier foundation; and I have no
doubt this tradition rightly accounts for the additional altars possessed by those two churches. But
the concurrence of evidence is so overwhelming, and
the exceptions so few and doubtful, that the general
law of three altars is very clearly established. Even
in the tiny chapels adjoining the main churches, as
St. Banai at Mâri Mîna and Sitt Mariam above
Abu-'s-Sifain, it is extremely rare to find a single
altar: three always were built wherever space could
be devised for placing them side by side. Each altar
has its own dedication, but the central is invariably
the high altar: each stands detached in the middle
of its sanctuary. A continuous wooden screen divides
the three sanctuaries from the common choir, and
the central is parted from the side sanctuaries by walls,
with or without open passages of communication.
These chapels, of which the central corresponds to
the Greek bema, or presbytery, are generally, though
not invariably, raised one step above the level of the
choir, never more than two.

The sanctuary screen is always of solid opaque
woodwork, enriched with intricate arabesques or
geometrical patterns, and inlaid with superbly
carved crosses and stars of ivory. Each chapel
has its own low round-arched doorway, fitted with
double doors, and over each door is a Coptic or
Arabic text inlaid in ivory letters. In one or two
of the older churches, as Abu Sargah and Al 'Aḍra
Ḥârat-az-Zuailah, the screen of the haikal, instead

of aligning with that of the side chapels, projects out three or four feet into the choir, and is returned so as to allow of a door on the north and south as well as on the western side of the high altar—an arrangement that clearly points to the ceremonial processions of the greater and the lesser entrance. Besides these doors there is often, but not always, found on each side of the haikal door a small square opening, with a sliding shutter, about five feet from the ground. At Abu-'s-Sifain these windows exist in the choir-screen as well as in the haikal-screen, though in neither case could they ever serve the purpose of allowing the congregation a glimpse of the celebration within, like the hagioscopes of our own churches. Before the sanctuary there hang always a number of lamps, which are sometimes of silver, and the door is veiled by a silk curtain, often of great magnificence, with texts, crosses, and sacred figures wrought in silver embroidery. On entering the church a worshipper always prostrates himself and kisses the hem of this curtain—a reverent custom that ascends to the remotest antiquity. The hanging is drawn aside during the whole period of the celebration, and the doors fold back inwards towards the altar. At the centre of the doorway arch is fastened a ring from which at a certain point in the mass the priest suspends the censer of burning incense in full view of the congregation. Along the top of the screen, which is seven to ten feet high, are ranged several pictures or a continuous tablet divided into panels. The central panel or picture usually represents the Virgin and Child, and those on the sides the figures of apostles or prophets.

Thus the Coptic haikal-screen, with its pictures

or icons, answers very closely to the Greek iconostasis. Originally the sanctuary-screen seems to have
been of trellis, or some kind of light open-work,
whether in wood or metal. At the great church of
Tyre were, as Eusebius relates, wooden gratings
'wrought with so delicate an art as to be a wonder
to behold' — perhaps like the Arab mûshrabîah.
St. Sophia in the sixth century boasted a screen
of silver divided by columns into panels, upon which
were medallions chased with icons of Christ and
other holy figures, the door being surmounted with
a crucifix. At the church of Patras there was a
flabellum ornamented with cherub-heads on each
side of the rood[1]. Clavijo speaks of silver-gilt doors
with silk hangings at the church of St. John,
Constantinople. The mosaics of St. George's at
Thessalonica show a low screen in front of the
altar: and a low stone screen or wall, supporting
slender columns which are joined above by an architrave, forms a type of iconostasis not uncommon in
the early Italian churches. According to Goar, the
opaque form first came into vogue in the eighth
century, and was adopted to gain more space for
pictures in virtue of a sharp reaction against the
iconoclasts. But this canon does not necessarily
apply to the churches of Egypt. There is not
the slightest sign of a low stone screen *before the*
altar in any one of the Coptic buildings, nor of
any altar-screen other than a lofty and opaque
iconostasis. The central haikal-screens at Abu Sargah and Al 'Adra Hârat-az-Zuailah are not later
than the tenth century, and might, I think, reason-

---

[1] Lenoir, Architecture Monastique, vol. i. p. 345.

ably be placed quite a century earlier. But these examples have already the low round-arched doorway with double doors, which is only a development from an earlier arrangement. In proof of this statement I rely on a very curious and interesting discovery which I have made at the monasteries of the Natrun valley. In Dair-as-Sûriâni the grand basilican church of Al 'Adra has for its haikal-screen a pair of very lofty folding-doors—each in three leaves—the jambs of which stand against the side walls of the sanctuary. These doors throw open, or fold back, in such a manner against the walls as to leave the whole interior of the haikal open to view; but when they are closed they form a solid screen entirely concealing the altar and its surroundings. The character of the Syriac inscription on the lintel and jambs fixes the date of the doors as not later than the year 700 A.D. Now it so happens that in the neighbouring monastery of Anba Bishôi the haikal-screen is made after the same model with the exception that each door has only two leaves instead of three. But there the four lofty leaves have been closed permanently to form an immoveable screen: and about five feet six inches from the ground the two inner leaves have been sawn through in a semicircle, the result being to leave a low round-arched doorway with one leaf on each side opening inwards, or in other words an entrance to the haikal identical with that at Abu Sargah. I may add that these very ancient iconostases have of course no pictures on their top, but the icons are inlaid in ivory upon the panels of the doors.

But although it be thus conclusively proved that the arrangement at Abu Sargah is not the earliest

form of the Coptic altar-screen, it is still early enough
to surpass most surviving examples of the iconostasis, eastern and western. For most of the western
churches have lost their ancient screens through
decay, removal, or restoration : while even those
eastern churches which escaped total destruction
at the hands of the Turks and were turned into
mosques—as some of the churches at Constantinople and Thessalonica—even these had all their
fittings broken to pieces when the crescent replaced
the cross.

Each of the side chapels in a Coptic church has
its own set of icons over the screen, but as a rule
the door is not curtained. At Abu-'s-Sifain and Mâri
Mîna the choir, like the sanctuaries, has a separate
iconostasis—a solid screen with central folding-
doors and a row of pictures above instead of the
ordinary light lattice screen that divides choir from
nave. These examples of the double iconostasis
are curious, and I believe unparalleled in any other
churches.

It has already been shown that a Coptic church
has always three eastern chapels, each with its own
altar, its own entrance, and its own iconostasis, and
all standing in a line upon the same platform.
There are also three divisions in a Greek church—
bema, or presbytery, prothesis, and diakonikon.
The prothesis lies on the north of the sanctuary
and contains a table which is set against the wall,
but *no altar*. It is the place where the elements
are made ready and set in order for consecration.
The diakonikon, on the south side of the sanctuary,
contains also a table and serves as a vestry and
sacristy: here are kept the books and vestments,

vessels, incense, and tapers; but here also there is no altar. In fact a Greek church has only one altar, a Coptic church has three; and this is a vital distinction between them. For although in many of the Egyptian churches the southern side-chapel is used, like the diakonikon, as a sacristy, such usage is rather an abuse arising from the neglect into which the minor altars have fallen, than a tradition of primitive custom.

The eastern wall of all three chapels generally, but more especially of the haikal, is apsidal; the apse, however, is invariably internal, so that standing outside one sees a plain rectangular ending to the church, unbroken by any outward curvature. This internal apse is a feature of very great antiquity, and it was characteristic of all the earliest churches of Asia and Europe. The single apse is sometimes said to be earlier than the triple; it is found at Al 'Adra Ḥârat-az-Zuailah, for example, Ḳ. Burbârah, and the satellite church at Al Mu'allaḳah. Yet Al Mu'allaḳah itself has three apses; so had Mâri Mîna and Abu-'s-Sifain, though in each case one has been blocked up. Mr. Freshfield's canon[1] that a Greek triapsal church is later, and a monapsal church earlier, than the time of Justin II, i.e. about 550 A.D., has a tempting precision about it, but cannot be applied to determine the date of the churches of Cairo. For the change from the single to the triple apse was made by the Greeks deliberately to suit the ritualistic requirements of a new processional hymn; but, as I have already explained, the Greek prothesis and dia-

[1] Archæologia, vol. xliv. p. xxiv. ·

konikon have no counterpart in the side-chapels of
a Coptic church, which always contained altars, and
therefore always had their own distinct ritual asso-
ciations. And it must be remembered that the
monastic churches in the Natrun valley, which
yield to none perhaps in point of antiquity, and
which yet represent different epochs, are entirely
destitute of apses, but have all three chapels rectangular. We must therefore be content with the
fact that *out of Egypt* a single apse points to a building of high antiquity. Thus the ancient churches
of Dana on the Euphrates, Kalb Lûzah, and
those of central Syria generally, have only one
apse: three apses, however, are found in the main
church, a single apse in the satellite church at Kalât
Samân 460–560 A.D. The Katholikon and Panagia
at Athens, and the small monastic church at Daphni,
the church of the Virgin at Mistra, of St. Sophia at
Thessalonica, are all triapsal. The early basilicas of
St. Peter and St. Paul, also Sta. Maria Maggiore and
Sta. Agnese at Rome, and S. Apollinare Nuovo at
Ravenna, may be quoted as examples of single-
apsed churches. In England, the church of Wing
in Buckinghamshire has one apse and two square-
ended side-chapels; and the same arrangement was
made in the original plan of the church at Brixworth. The Saxon. church of Deerhurst, near
Tewkesbury, still retains one of its three original
apses. The same number existed at Lindisfarne
priory, while Lanfranc's cathedral at Canterbury
had no less than five apsidal chapels. In all these
churches, and with scarcely an exception in all
churches beyond the limits of Africa, the curve of
the apse wall shows on the exterior.

Whether the Christian apse was suggested by a like feature in the pagan basilica or not, in the Christian churches it had a specific and independent purpose. In its normal structure the curve is followed by a tier of curving steps, at the top of which a bench runs round the wall, divided in the centre by a raised seat or throne; while the altar of course stands detached. The throne was meant for the bishop, the bench for twelve presbyters or elders of the church, who thus sat along the wall facing westward and looking down upon the celebration of the mysteries. This arrangement, styled a tribune, was common in the early churches of the West, and may still be seen in the well-known seventh-century church of Torcello near Venice, and the cathedral of Parenzo in Istria. But nowhere has the idea taken so large and lasting hold upon Christian architecture as in Egypt, and nowhere are finer early specimens of the tribune preserved. The churches of Abu Sargah, Al 'Aḍra in the Ḥârat-az-Zuailah, and Abu-'s-Sifain, furnish beautiful examples of raised marble tribunes with central thrones: while smaller tribunes may be seen at Al Mu'allaḳah, Al 'Aḍra Ḥârat-ar-Rûm, and in most churches. Generally behind the throne a round-headed niche is let into the wall, and in it there often hangs an ever-burning lamp. Even the square-ended churches of the desert retain the niche and have straight instead of curved tribunes.

So strong is the tradition of the tribune with the Copts, that a second and even a third are sometimes found in the side-chapels, as at Al Mu'allaḳah, where the low tiers of steps seem quite too narrow for use and have perhaps only an ideal value. Since

too the tribune is associated with an apse, since all
the early Cairo churches were built with an apse and
with a tribune together, it is curious to note that
even in the very rare cases where a church exists
with square-ended chapels, there is always preserved
some reminiscence of the apse or tribune. Thus in
the church of Sitt Mariam Dair Abu-'s-Sifain all three
chapels are singularly enough square-ended, but in
the eastern wall of the haikal is a large shallow niche
covered with fine Damascus tiles. So at Mâri
Girgis Hârat-ar-Rûm, the only other church where
all the chapels are square, the haikal has a tribune of
two straight steps with five steps leading up to the
throne, which is set under a rectangular recess : and
in the south side-chapel there is another round-
niched throne mounted by a flight of seven steps.
No Coptic chapel is found, I believe, without a niche
in the eastern wall, though these recesses were never
used as in the West for images. Sometimes they are
painted with the figure of our Lord in the attitude
of benediction, and sometimes a hanging lamp burns
before the niche : but more often in the present day
they are uncoloured and lampless. Whether they
had any definite ritual purpose, or whether they are
merely a feature of the full apse and meant to recall
it, must remain undecided.

The walls of the Coptic tribune are generally faced
with slabs and panels of many-coloured marble, which
form a dado six or eight feet high, such as may be
seen at Al 'Adra in the Hârat-az-Zuailah. This use
of variegated marble for wall-facing and paving is
common both in the ancient churches and in the
earlier mosques of Egypt : a very beautiful example
for instance may be seen at the mosques of Al

Ashraf and of Ḳait Bey, among the so-called tombs
of the Khalīfs at Cairo, where both wall and floor are
decorated with the most exquisite designs and colours.
This form of art is however Christian, not Muslim,
in origin, and was borrowed by the Muslim builders :
or rather was lent by the Coptic architects and
builders, whom the Muslims employed for the construction of their mosques.   In the West the art
seems to have decayed comparatively early : though
·at Torcello the marbled walls of the apse still remain
uninjured in curious likeness to those at Al 'Aḍra.
In the East the art was applied to church decoration
at least as early as the fourth century : for Eusebius,
speaking of the church of St. Saviour at Jerusalem
in 333 A.D., tells of walls covered with variegated
marble.   Texier and Pullan give a splendid illustration of a mosaic pavement at St. Sophia in Trebizond,
which they assign to the second or third century.
Long after the Arab conquest, when the beautiful
churches of central Syria had fallen in ruins, this
form of decoration lingered on in Egypt—where
most likely it first arose,—and in the twelfth and
thirteenth centuries, when in greatest danger of
decaying, was adopted by the Muslim conquerors
for the adornment of their mosques, and during that
period, always in the hands of Coptic artists, attained
its most sumptuous perfection.

The same remarks hold good of another like form
of art—Coptic mosaic.   This differs from the sectile
marble-work more in degree than kind ; for it is made
of exceedingly minute pieces of coloured marbles
and porphyries tesselated together, but contains also
a curious admixture of mother-of-pearl.   The whole
constitutes an inlay of almost incredible fineness.

In the churches of Egypt this work is lavished on the places of greatest honour, and may be seen chiefly in the niche of the haikal. Perhaps the best early example is in the tiny baptistery of the little church at Al Muʻallakah : while the southern chapel of the larger church displays both mosaic and sectile work of great splendour. The ambon of Abu-'s-Sifain contains a mosaic design of most extraordinary intricacy, though unmixed with mother-of-pearl. Among the Arab mosques the same style of mosaic in conjunction with sectile work may be seen at the tomb-mosque of Al Ashraf and of Ḳait Bey without the walls of Cairo : within the walls also the mosques of Al Hâkim and Al Ghûri furnish rich and gorgeous examples.

This Coptic mosaic differs entirely from the mosaic that has become familiar to western eyes at St. Sophia in Constantinople or St. Mark in Venice. There the tesserae vary little in shape, being nearly all cubes, and they are composed of coloured enamel, i.e. pastes of glass rendered opaque and coloured by metallic oxides. The gilt tesserae were made by fusing on to a cube of earthenware two thin plates of glass with a film of gold-leaf between them. Mosaic with gold backgrounds made in this manner is anterior to the reign of Justinian. Among the Copts the use of vitreous pastes and metallic oxides is quite unknown : their mosaic is composed only of natural marbles cut into minute pieces of all shapes, —square, round or triangular,—and arranged in ornamental patterns according to their natural colours. There is this further difference, that the Coptic churches show no single instance of a *picture* in mosaic : the artists confined themselves to con-

ventional designs, aware that with the stiffness and
hardness of their material and its colours they could
achieve nothing like the harmonious richness and
softness required for a mosaic picture.   No doubt
the Coptic is earlier than the Byzantine form of
mosaic-work, and it was never disturbed by its later
rival in Egypt.   For although the Saracens in Syria
borrowed the art from Byzantium and used vitreous
enamels for the decoration of their mosque walls, as
well as for inlaying jewellery and steel armour on a
smaller scale, yet the Mohammedans of Egypt never
adopted any but the native or Coptic marble mosaic;
partly because its unpictorial character suited their
taste, and partly because they found ready made both
art and artists,—artists whose names have perished,
but whose skill is still recorded in work of unex-
ampled splendour which adorns the great mosques of
Cairo.   In visiting these mosques one is met by a
striking coincidence : for just as every Coptic church
and chapel has its eastern niche, so every mosque
also has its kiblah or niche in the like position : and
as in the Coptic church, so in the Muslim mosque,
it is the niche that is covered with the most delicate
and beautiful mosaics.   It would however be perhaps
too bold to conjecture that the Coptic architects
introduced the niche as well as the mode of its
decoration from their own sacred edifices.

Marble and mother-of-pearl mosaic is of very rare
occurrence in the West, though examples are found,
as in the church of St. Vitale, Ravenna, and the
cathedral of Parenzo : but it is not so much the
mere admixture of mother-of-pearl, as the extraordinary minuteness of the tesserae and the be-
wildering intricacy of the designs that form the

distinguishing characteristics of the Coptic mosaic, and make it unique in manner and in charm.

But to return from this digression. While the lower part of the apse wall in the haikal is covered with marble slabs, above there should always be ranged in order the figures of the twelve apostles, and in the centre, over or in the niche, our Lord enthroned in the attitude of benediction. These figures of course are painted in fresco or on panel, statues being entirely forbidden. This arrangement may be seen at Abu-'s-Sifain, Dair Bablûn, and in most churches. Sometimes it may be there is no marble, and the wood or fresco painting descends to the floor, but the figures in the conch are as regular a part of church adornment as the icons on the screen. Goar's[1] testimony shows that the same practice holds in the Greek Church, and the remains at Torcello preserve precisely the same method of decoration as an example in western Christendom.

There seems no fixed rule as regards communication between the haikal and side-chapels. In some cases it exists on both sides, sometimes on one side only, and often is entirely wanting. Presumably the earliest arrangement was the simplest and originally the haikal had no communication with either chapel : for however early the three altars became normal, the side-altars must still be later than the central. In the desert churches the party-walls are generally pierced with doorways, as in Dair-as-Sûriâni : but there is not the remotest sign of uniformity in the arrangement of the churches of the two Cairos. While for instance Al Mu'allaḳah

---

[1] Euchologion, p. 14.

has not even party-walls dividing haikal from the side-chapels, but merely piers carrying arches and once closed either by screens or hangings, Anba Shanûdah has a screen on the north of the high altar, and on the south a stone wall divided by an open passage; K. Burbârah has stone party-walls and no passage; Sitt Mariam in Dair Abu-'s-Sifain has a passage through to the north chapel only; while at Mâri Mîna and Dair Bablûn the only thoroughfare is on the south side; in the two churches in the Hârat-ar-Rûm, Al 'Adra and Mâri Girgis, the haikal communicates directly through pierced party-walls with *both* side-chapels; and lastly, in the small satellite churches there is as a rule no communication. In such a strange variety of usage, it is not easy to believe that the piercing of the party-walls had any ritual significance, or was more than a matter of accidental convenience.

The side-chapels in a Coptic church are now generally used but once a year—each upon the festival of the saint to whom it is dedicated. It is however a curious fact, of which the writer can offer no explanation, that the chapel on the south side of the haikal is often much more richly ornamented than that upon the north, as for example at Mâri Girgis satellite of Mâri Mîna, Abu Sargah, and Al Mu'allakah. Moreover if a second chapel is used at all habitually, it is always the south chapel; and if an altar has been demolished, it is always the north altar.

A baptistery is attached to every church, but its position varies greatly. It is found in the north aisle, as at Abu Sargah; in the south, as at Abu-'s-

Sifain; at the western end in the narthex, as at Sitt Mariam near Abu-'s-Sifain; outside the main building in a satellite church, as at Al Mu'allakah; or in an adjoining passage, as at Mâri Mîna and at most other churches. It scarcely admits of question that originally the baptistery was *outside* the church in most countries; but this rule does not apply to Egypt, where the need of secrecy was felt very early, and where the font is always found inside. Doubtless in some cases the baptistery has been removed out of its original place, which was in the narthex. This is true of Abu-'s-Sifain, where the font stands before a blocked aisle-chapel, and of Abu Sargah, for instance. The Coptic churches then hardly bear witness to the very ancient practice of administering the rite without the sacred building, as recorded by Tertullian and Justin Martyr. For there is no instance of an entirely isolated baptistery, such as that built by Constantine near the church of Sta. Agnese without the walls at Rome; or like that at Nocera, which has been converted into a church. In very early times the baptistery was often in the atrium[1] before the church, and the Coptic Epiphany-tanks are perhaps a reminiscence of this usage, and their border, paved with marble, may recall the tradition that the place where Christ was baptized in the Jordan was marked with marble walls and steps, and thronged with crowds of people at the feast of Epiphany. At St. Sophia the baptistery was outside near the western door, and so also at Parenzo in Istria, in the sixth century, and commonly in Roman basilicas. The

---

[1] Lenoir, Architecture Monastique, i. p. 101.

Coptic font is now usually a deep circular basin,
very much resembling those of our own churches,
but set like a copper in a solid bench of masonry
against a wall, not detached or supported on a
pedestal. The very early font near the chapels of
St. James and St. John adjoining Abu-'s-Sifain
differs in being deeper and in having on each side
of the well a short flight of steps; in other words it
is adapted more for immersion than sprinkling. The
other fonts in use at present would serve only for
aspersion, except in the case of very young children;
though the Epiphany-tanks are large and deep
enough for several grown-up people to stand in
together.

There is no altar in the Coptic baptistery, though
the eastern wall, against which the font is set, generally contains a niche, just as early Roman baptisteries—those for instance at Aquileia and Nocera—
had an eastward apse. The niche is decorated either
with a moveable picture, or else with a fresco painting of our Lord's baptism in the Jordan. Belonging
to the font is always a small hand-cross of silver
or other metal, and few baptisteries are without a
gospel-table set with prickets for candles: for tapers
are always kindled at the service. According to
ancient custom a separate apartment is screened
off for women.

There is no trace in any of the churches of Cairo
of any detached *circular* or *hexagonal* baptistery,
such as was common at an early date in western
Christendom and also in central Syria.

Concerning the outbuildings attached to Egyptian
churches there is no need here of lengthy notice.
All over the East the annexation of such buildings

was a common practice. Eusebius speaks of spacious
outhouses belonging to the church at Tyre and also
at Antioch. Augustine too mentions a large room
attached to the church at Cæsarea. This doubtless
corresponds to the Coptic mandârah or reception-
room, where worshippers meet for conversation. At
Abu-'s-Sifain the mandârah is quite distinct from the
church though adjoining it; elsewhere, as at Abu
Sargah, it is a small open courtyard surrounded by
benches; but the finest specimen of an ancient mandârah is that at Mâri Girgis in Ḳaṣr ash-Shamm'ah,
now alas in ruins, but once enriched with stucco-
work and carved woodwork of great magnificence.
Later innovations have sometimes removed the
reception-room within the sacred building, as at
Ḳ. Burbârah, where it now occupies the narthex.

Since every Coptic church was complete in itself
as a miniature monastic establishment, it contained
dwelling-rooms for the priest or priests, a well with
storage for water, and an oven for baking the eucharistic bread. Nowhere, however, is there found
among the Cairene churches the same developed
system of building, with cells, refectory, &c., which
is seen in the kindred monasteries in the Libyan
desert. Moreover now-a-days the domestic chambers are often quite deserted, as at Abu-'s-Sifain,
Al Mu'allaḳah, Dair Tadrus, and elsewhere; or else,
as at Mâri Mîna, they are used only at the time of
the festival to lodge the pilgrims that resort in large
numbers; while in other cases, as at Abu Sargah
and Ḳ. Burbârah, the priest with his family not
only lives in the old rooms, but has usurped the
galleries of the church. Abu Sargah differs from
the other churches in having the well within its

walls—in the choir : no doubt by reason of the special sanctity of the fountain that gave water to the Holy Family.   It is however curious to remark that a sacred well is also mentioned by Paul the Silentiary as lying near the ambon in the church of St. Sophia, and its coping is said to have been brought from Samaria.   In the Jewish synagogue at Old Cairo, the ancient Christian well is situated at the eastern end, almost behind the apse, and from its size resembles rather a tank.

The Copts now usually bury their dead in cemeteries, but some of the ancient churches, such as Mâri Mîna, have separate churchyards not unlike our own, but outside the dair walls and not accessible directly from the church, though they adjoin the sacred enclosure.   The practice of burying within the church is not unknown, but the honour was always reserved for patriarchs or persons of great distinction : thus within Abu-'s-Sifain, Al Mu'allakah, and St. Stephen by the cathedral, spots are pointed out as the tombs of patriarchs.   Yet there is no single instance of any inscription or monument to mark the resting-place of great men buried within the church. So too when a rich man has given a vessel to the altar, it is inscribed as a gift and a short prayer is lettered upon it, but the donor's name is almost invariably unrecorded.   This is the silence that is golden, and full of golden lessons.

To the same right oblivion are consigned the bodies of such as were honoured with burial within the enclosure about the church, as at Anba Shanûdah. In vaults beneath the dark rooms which adjoin the western end of that church many great worthies are buried without a line to perpetuate any remembrance ·

beyond that which is graven in the minds of men.
Still within the precincts of the church, but somewhat
farther removed from the building, are the curious
early sepulchres at Ḳ. Burbârah under the Roman
wall. There also the dead rest nameless and forgotten. It is only in modern graveyards and cemeteries, such as that at Ḳaṣr-ash-Shamm'ah, that the
Copts have begun to cumber the ground with sculptured monuments recording worthless names, forgetting the truth their forefathers well understood,
that none deserve to live or can live after death
save those whose works have made them remembered. But the old tradition lingers still in the
solitude of the Natrun valley, where nothing is
more remarkable than to find that the monks, with
all their multitude of churches, have not one single
graveyard: with them God's acre is the boundless
desert: and though they retain the bones of some
few saints as relics, yet for all the countless dead
who have passed away during the space of full
fifteen centuries, they cannot show one single tomb[1].

---

[1] It is strange that no previous traveller should have remarked
so strange a fact.

CHAPTER II.

Dair Mâri Mîna (مارى مينا).

BETWEEN Cairo and Old Cairo lies a dair, or walled enclosure, which is marked by an Arab domed sibîl or drinking-fountain fronted with bronze grillwork. It contains an ancient church dedicated to St. Menas, who was an early Coptic martyr, born, it seems, at Mareotis, and slain in the persecution under Galerius Maximinus at Alexandria. His name recalls that of the first king of Egypt, the reputed founder of Memphis. This saint must not be confounded with Anba Mîna, patriarch in the eighth century. The ring-wall of the dair is weak and low; the double door large and slender: both obviously are of recent construction, and were renewed at a time when the need for bulwarks and posterns had almost passed away. Inside the wall is first a small garden and a few rude dwelling hovels by which a path leads to the church. On the left one sees a flight of stone steps and a door leading to a new[1] and uninteresting Armenian church; and a short way beyond on the same side in the same wall is a modern-looking doorway. The door, built of huge vertical beams of timber cramped across with iron, stands back on its hinges: one sees within a small courtyard surrounded on three sides by build-

---

[1] The foundation of the Armenian church is very ancient, though the fabric is new.

ings of which the upper stories project and rest on pillars and have open balconies. On the fourth side is the church, so sunken now that one enters by a short flight of downward steps from the door which is at the western end of the south aisle. The west front is as usual a plain high blank wall whose limits

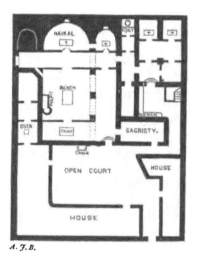

A. J. B.

Fig. 1.—Plan of Mâri Mina and the adjoining church of Mâri Banai.

are lost in the buildings which align with it on either side. There seems no trace of any central western entrance: for the present doorway leads into the south aisle; and although there is a corresponding doorway into what was once the north aisle, the third entrance into the nave is wanting.

The church is small—only about 60 ft. long and 50 ft. wide, the latter measure being taken across the choir. The peculiarities of its structure are that it has no narthex nor any sign of one having existed; that the northern aisle as far as the choir has been entirely shut out of the church and is now occupied by outhouses including a bakehouse for the eucharistic bread: and that there is no regular triforium, although part of one of the upper chapels lies over the south aisle. This aisle is narrow and low, roofed with a groined vaulting and separated from the nave by three heavy piers.

The nave is covered with a wagon-vaulting of brick strengthened by stone ribs. The west end is divided from the rest of the nave and aisle by only a rude lattice-work screen, and serves for the women's section. Here too is the Epiphany tank. Over the eastward door of this screen is a curious picture of the Baptism of our Lord. St. John, who stands to the right on a low Nile-like bank, carries a staff with a Coptic scroll flying from the end: he wears a loose robe, and his feet are bound with sandals and buskins half way up to the knee. Before him is a small lamb with one forefoot raised: Christ on a large round boulder in mid stream is crushing under his left foot a huge dolphin-headed serpent with fiery tongue protruding and tail coiled round under the rock. On the left bank, kneeling and gazing upward at the dove, which is descending in a golden halo set round with rays, is an angel, who is receiving Christ's robe as it parts from his shoulders. Christ stands with his arms crossed on his breast, bending his left shoulder forward towards St. John, whose upraised hand is pouring water on his head. The expression of both and the type of countenance, the long flowing hair, beard and moustache, are almost identical[1].

---

[1] The composition exactly resembles that of the same subject in a French ' Liber Precum,' date 1430.

The body of the nave, or men's section, is about 22 ft. long by 12 ft. wide. Against the north wall is a very interesting ambon or pulpit, the floor of which is about 7 ft. above the nave floor : it rests on wooden beams projecting from the wall, and these again on crossbeams upheld by two slender octagonal pillars. There are as usual two parts, a sort of straight entrance balcony and the pulpit proper which is circular. Both are of marble—the pulpit proper inlaid with various devices in red, black and white marble mosaic; while the side of the balcony is formed by a slab of white marble carved with five beautiful designs in low relief. Of these designs three are large conventional roses : the other two in panels dividing them represent graceful vases overflowing with chrysanthemums and other flowers. At present there is no access to the pulpit, and no trace of a staircase : it was probably mounted by a moveable ladder. Under the pulpit a little corner is railed across, and in the rail are two or three score of T-shaped staves or crutches for worshippers to lean upon during the service.

The pictures in the nave, painted on canvas and so not very early, are as follows :—

On the north wall a large picture in a frame inlaid with ivory shows Mâri Mîna on horseback slaying a dragon.

Then at about 10 ft. from the ground begins a series of pictures which is continued across the screen and on the south wall.

On the north wall are two :—

1. A composition containing two almost identical figures, each wearing a mantle, short tunic, and buskins : each has a glory, each raises his right

forefinger before his breast, and in the left hand each carries a severed head, the symbol of his martyrdom.

The right figure is labelled in Arabic ' James, bishop of Jerusalem :' the left figure ' John the Baptist.'

2. Another composition containing two figures of extraordinary appearance exactly alike in attitude and feature. They stand side by side full face to the spectator with a grave wistful look in their fixed farseeing eyes: they are naked save for a camels' hair girdle round the loins : but their long white narrow beards flow nearly to their feet: and the hair of their upper lip and their head is very long and snowy white. Their arms are bent at the elbow, the left hand carrying a cross and the right uplifted before the chest in benediction. In the background is a single palm-tree laden with yellow fruit. Clearly they are anchorites. The right figure is the familiar Barsûm al 'Ariân: the left is called Abu Nafr as Salah, i. e. Abu Nafr the Wanderer. Both are Coptic saints. Abu Nafr is called now among the Copts the ruler of snakes, scorpions, etc.; and if a Copt sees a scorpion or a viper in his house he exclaims ' Abu Nafr is angry,' and sends in propitiation a candle to the church to be burnt before the picture.

The west screen is of open woodwork coloured: over the door is a picture—Christ being uplifted on the cross. The cross is slanting, in the act of being raised, and a soldier is loosening the cords that bound the hands before they were nailed. High above the screen near the roof is a large picture of the Crucifixion: women are at the foot of the cross and soldiers behind: the two thieves have their arms tied over and behind the branches of the cross, not nailed on in front.

Resuming now the continuous series, on the screen there are seven :—

1. The Resurrection. An empty tomb with people gazing in : above in the clouds is seated the Virgin, and an angel flies on either side : slightly to her left below another angel in clouds is receiving a stole or pall which is falling from her hand.

2. Christ and Mary Magdalen.

3. The Crucifixion.

4. Christ carrying the cross.

5. Christ before Pilate.

6. Judas kissing Christ in the garden ; in the background are soldiers with spears, one with a flaming cresset, and one with a scourge.

7. 'Joseph the carpenter taking the hand of the Messiah.' This is a literal rendering of the Arabic title. Christ is a boy of twelve years, and both are walking on a solitary mountain-top. The imaginative unconventional character of this picture is remarkable.

The series is continued with seven more pictures on the east wall :—

1. The child John the Baptist greeting the child Christ. A very interesting picture. The scene is under a tree in the wilderness ; where, kneeling on one knee at the Virgin's right, St. John upraises folded hands while his crook slopes over his right shoulder. As he looks up with an expression of mingled humility and rapture, the child Christ leans forward from his mother's arms raising his right.

forefinger over John's uplifted face. The expression
on Christ's face of conscious power and authority, yet
gentleness and childlikeness, harmonises admirably
with John's look of deep adoration. The Virgin is
bending slightly to allow of Christ's forward move-
ment, but her face is half averted from John, at
whom she is looking askance with an air of prophetic
anxiety.

2. The Birth of Christ, who is represented laid in
a manger : above is a choir of angels in the clouds.
This painting is remarkable for the sweetness and
beauty of the Virgin's face as she watches with
drooping eyelids over her son. It is very rare in
these pictures to find a really beautiful face; though
it is difficult to define the prevailing type. The
apostles and saints are generally of a fine Jewish
cast, but the women are neither Greek, nor Jew, nor
Egyptian—rather perhaps like the modern Syrian
women, who seem a blended type, recalling at once
Hellenic and Canaanite models, without the marked
beauty of either.

3. The Annunciation. The subject is treated in
the conventional manner as described in Abu-'s-
Sifain pictures, with this difference, that the holy
dove is slanting down towards Mary, as usual in
Italian paintings.

4. Virgin and Child. The Virgin, a half-length
figure, holds the child with both arms: his legs are
crossed and arms outspread, possibly in a manner
meant to foreshadow the cross. The drapery of the
figures is well rendered, and the faces have decided
expressiveness.

5. A curious bearded figure with halo and large
white wings, neither saint nor angel, for no saint or

martyr is represented as winged elsewhere, and no angel has a beard. He is standing in a lonely desert-looking place on a little hill : he bends forward to his right and carries in his left hand an open scroll : over his left shoulder slopes a long staff with a cross-piece and a flag : his right hand is uplifted in benediction or possibly in preaching. In the background is a rude tree with an 'axe laid to the root,' or rather balanced across a division in the trunk near the ground. I tried from every side and every point of vantage—steps and bench and pulpit—to distinguish the dim Arabic title, but I could not make out a letter. The attendants of course knew nothing of this or any other picture, and could only tell me that it was 'Christ.' The probability is that it represents John the Baptist, and was painted by some artist not familiar with all the conventions of such art. Indeed there is an absence of convention in the whole series.

6. Christ bearing the cross.

7. Virgin and Child. The Virgin, a half-length figure, is carrying on her left arm the child, who looks like a girl of twelve : he is fully robed, his right hand is outstretched, and in his left is a golden book with a cross upon the cover. Above are two angels each holding one end of a flying scroll, which forms an arch above the Virgin's head.

Next to these, in the same line but not in the same series, follow three pictures in mushrabìah framework :—

1. St. Irene.

2. Anba Saràbàmûn, who is robed as a patriarch with a gold cross in his right hand, in his left a book and pastoral staff. The crozier, as depicted here

and in other paintings in this church, is rather
unusual, having merely a double curl at the upper
end ᴄᴩ, instead of the more common serpent
heads.

3. Mâri Mîna.

The choir as before mentioned opens out on either
side beyond the width of the nave. It contains two
ordinary lecterns and a pair of tall standard candlesticks. Before the sanctuary-screen hang six silver
lamps of graceful shape, with ostrich eggs over them:
there are two ostrich eggs without lamps but mounted
in metal with a little metal cross above and pendants
below. Six wretched glass chandeliers and some
plain bowl-shaped glass lamps complete the list. The
screen of the north chapel has disappeared if there
ever was one : at present there is a bare wall in its
place, and the chapel itself, which like most north
chapels was used as a store-room, is now blocked up
and disused. The sanctuary-screen, and the eastward side of the choir-screen, are both inlaid with
ivory crosses which are followed round by mouldings
but not carved. The door of the choir-screen is
very curious : above it is a large picture of Aaron
robed as priest, with a by-scene representing the
stoning of Stephen, and on each side is a folding
door, the upper part of which closes over the picture
so as to form a kind of triptych with it. When the
doors are closed their lower and middle part would
of course be seen from the nave ; but oddly enough
even when the doors are shut they do not meet
together, but are parted by a gap of nine inches.
Each door is divided into four panels, one above
another, variously painted. The lowest panel is
merely decked with a pattern of small flowers.

On the northward leaf of the door the three subjects are:—

1. Pentecost. The twelve are sitting in a semi-
circle, while from above spear-headed rays or tongues
are descending upon them.

2. The Ascension.

3. Feast of St. Thomas (حس ثوما).

On the southward leaf the panel pictures are :—

1. The Nativity. An extraordinary mixture of
various scenes in one picture, each scene being
marked off by a wide irregular border of colour. In
the middle is a rough oval slanting sideways, and in
it the Virgin is shown lying down with pillows under
her head. Below is a country scene with sheep and
shepherds, and the child is being washed at a large
vessel of water. Above a star has descended in
a train of light and now is resting over the mouth of
a mountain cave, within which Christ is lying in a
manger and two bodiless heads of oxen are looking
over the side. To the left of the cave outside, but
in the plain at some distance, the Magi are depicted
bringing gifts and kneeling. Exactly the same mixed
composition, common in the Coptic churches, is found
in early western work : it may be seen for example
in a panel in the pulpit at Pisa carved by Niccolo
Pisano in 1260, and in a Carlovingian ivory of the
ninth century now at the South Kensington Museum.

2. The Presentation in the Temple.

3. The Baptism of Christ.

Above this is a tablet of fine small pictures in line.
The Last Supper is in the middle, and the others are
the Entry into Jerusalem, the Appearance after the
Resurrection, the Crucifixion and the Resurrection.
Then above the screen is a series of eleven icons—

large pictures, angels and apostles, very similar in treatment to the series on the southward side of the choir-screen at Abu-'s-Sifain : the resemblance is specially remarkable in the centre figure—our Lord. Underneath these is a broad band of Coptic writing, and other Coptic inscriptions are scattered on available spaces in the screen below. On the piers, into which the screen runs, are two pictures of an angel facing each other.

On the western wall are :—

1. The Virgin : a fine painting. The central figure is surrounded by forty little figures, each painted off in a little oblong space by itself, each wearing a crown and carrying the usual cross and palm.

2–6. Angels and saints.

The northern wall is entirely hidden by a wooden panelling consisting of three elaborate niches, containing each a picture. The three have a more modern and Italian look than usual, and perhaps more delicacy and more freedom, less of Byzantine coldness and stiffness.

1. The Baptism of Christ.

2. Virgin and Child. Her head is hooded as usual, and bent to the left, over the child, whose face is full of life and spirit. Both faces are faintly smiling. On each side of the Virgin's head above is a sleeping cherub-head.

3. St. John the Evangelist. Here too the treatment is unusual. St. John is walking alone, and pondering with eyes fixed before him ; the left hand is holding an open gospel, the right, which is lifted to a level with the shoulder, holds a quill for writing. The body is curved slightly to the left ;

for the left leg is bent at the knee, the foot just lingering as it leaves behindward a boulder on which it has been planted. The large, deep, meditative eyes give admirably the key to the whole attitude, which is that of a man arrested in mid-step by some profound thought or divine remembrance. It is a great man communing with his own spirit in the wilderness, and finding inspiration.

On the eastern wall before what should be the north chapel are five more pictures of saints, including Mâri Mîna and Abu-'s-Sifain. Next comes a little detached painting representing a family of five martyr sons standing in a group, or rather line, with their mother. The drawing is rude, but the scene is pathetic. It is called ' The Five and their Mother,' and bears a date corresponding to about 1790 A. D. A date is also fixed for the next picture, 1780 A. D. It is a representation of Mâri Mîna, the patron saint of the church ; who is honoured by a large niche of woodwork. The shrine contains of course a bolster of relics ; but instead of the ordinary spikes or prickets for candles, before it stands a bronze taper-holder of very singular and original design. Two winged dragons or serpents stretched at full length cross their tails together ; the head is retorted, with the mouth upwards, and the wings are above the body, but there is no twist in the dragon's neck as one would expect. A bar of bronze slightly curved joins the dragons above ; on this bar are thirteen bell-shaped sockets for tapers, and one in each dragon's mouth and on each wing—seventeen in all. The design is either copied from or copied in the adjoining Armenian church ; of the two candelabra the Armenian certainly looks the older, and may date

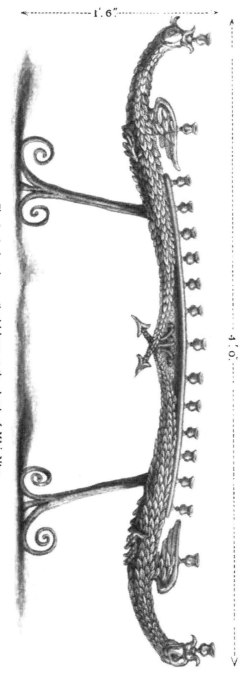

Fig. 2.—Ancient bronze Candelabrum at the church of Mâri Mîna.

from the fifteenth or sixteenth century. The haikal-screen is inlaid with plain ivory, a cross-in-square pattern, very pretty, though not remarkably fine. There is a detached Madonna above the central door, and the usual arrangement of pictures, seven in number. The centre is a Madonna; each of the six side pictures contains two apostles, and is divided into two arches with a pillar between. All the figures are seated, and half-face towards the Virgin, each upholding a cross; those to the north carry the cross in their left hand, those to the south in their right. The ground is of gold · in every case.

Five pictures in the same style are over the south iconostasis; Christ in the centre, and on each side two angels, separate.

On the screen outside near the haikal door, accord-ing to common practice, is fastened a small rude block of wood (4 in. by 4 about), hollowed out cup-like; it contains two little glass crewets, each holding less than a gill of wine. This is the wine used for the sacrament; it is unfermented, and made of dried grapes; it is sweet, thick, and opaque, never clear-coloured.

There follow five scenes on the south wall; above the screen dividing this end of the choir from the south aisle two others; and on the east wall a huge indecipherable Mâri Banai—a Syrian martyr.

The sanctuary or haikal is remarkable for an unusually lofty altar-canopy, which originally rested on four tall slender columns of wood, still standing at the four corners of the altar. But while the original columns remain, above them is now a larger and incongruous though handsome dome, supported on cross-beams running into the walls. The canopy shows fully from the choir above the screen; round the lower part outside is a wide border of painted arcading, and under every arch is a Greek cross, with the Coptic sacred letters between the branches; above each pillar too in the spandrels is a cross. Soft red and gold are the chief colours used: and the whole, as one glances from the sombre screen up to the line of apostles throned under golden skies beside the Virgin to the dome beyond, makes a picture in which the scale of colour is delightfully harmonious. The under part of the canopy is plain and unadorned. Although the interior of the apse is small, it contains a tribune, the steps of which are covered with plates of lead. The curved wall is panelled all round to a height of 12 ft., and painted with a design in three bands: lowest comes a sort of diaper filled with ugly flowers; next, six large figures of saints, three on each side of the central niche; above in circular medallions are six other smaller designs, two cherubs and an angel on each side. A figure of the throned Saviour, inscribed with the Arabic title ' King of kings,' is frescoed in the niche: and above it is painted a triptych-shaped fresco[1] of the seraphim and two angels, one in each of the open leaves. The work in detail has little merit, but the general effect is rich, especially when merely caught in glimpses from the nave or choir, as it would be to all but the priest and the few communicants. A doorway from the sanctuary southward communicates with the aisle-chapel, which has long been

---

[1] These Coptic wall-paintings are always in distemper, and are not technically frescoes; but the term is convenient.

disused, and lies in pitch darkness; it contains a few
decaying and worm-eaten paintings.

From the south end of the choir a door leads into
a long vaulted passage running east and west. At
the east end of the passage is a baptistery, with a
small font arranged in the usual fashion, i. e. a
round cauldron-like stone basin sunk in a bench
of masonry. The whole passage is vaulted, but
the baptistery is lighted by a small, oblong, open
shaft of brickwork, quite thirty feet high.   Three
old pictures, a small aumbry in the wall for oil
and incense, a bronze cross, and a gospel-stand, are
the only ornaments of this curious dim little recess.
The gospel-stand is a sort of high, four-legged,
oblong table; upon it in the centre a small frame
is nailed, making a lidless box, in which the silver
gospel rests during the baptismal service; and round
the outer edge is another frame, set with prickets for
tapers to give light at the ceremony. Details vary
a little, but the gospel-stand as here described is as
much an appanage of the baptistery as the lectern
is of the choir in Coptic churches.

Outside the baptistery in the passage one may
notice a rather curious picture of St. John greeting
the child Christ, and then pass on into the light
to the church of the martyr Mâri Banai, which lies
to the south of this passage, and is divided by it
from the main building.   The arrangement is rather
like that of the chapels of St. John and St. James at
Abu-'s-Sifain : for there are really two chapels side
by side, each chapel consisting of three parts—west,
middle, and east or haikal. Each of the west parts is
railed off for the women, and the two are divided
by an open screen ; the haikals are of course shut

out of view entirely by panel screens, and are divided
by a wall. The roofing is low : the west chambers
are covered each with its own groined vaulting ;
while two parallel wagon-vaultings run east and
west over the middle chambers and haikal. Each
chapel then has a single groined vaulting in the
western part, and an unbroken wagon-vaulting over
the middle and eastern parts. Over the haikal this
vaulting springs from the side wall and the partition
wall ; thence it is carried on beams laid from the end
of the partition wall to a heavy pier which stands
central for the four remaining contiguous chambers,
and which lends its support also to the two groined
vaultings. One enters into the north-west division,
where there is a picture of the Crucifixion ; passing
thence through the screen into the south-west chamber, one sees an ugly piece of modern upholstery
covered with flimsy embroidery—the patriarch's chair
—a strange contrast to the beautiful Arab thrones
of mushrablah work still abounding in these churches.
There is nothing else of interest here except a picture
of the patron saint, Mâri Banai. He is riding a
prancing horse and balancing a long spear. All
round him in the picture are by-scenes : below in
the right corner a man and woman talking before
a house, with a well between them : possibly Christ
and the woman of Samaria. Above this in the sky
is a squadron of Turkish horsemen led by a sultan.
Still higher on the same side is a saint preaching ;
then to the left a man chasing deer with hounds ;
and in the top left corner a woman being crowned
by two ecclesiastics. This picture is dated 1782 A.D.,
and if it may be taken as a fair index to the state of
art at that period, it shows the nadir of decline. The

drawing is rude and stiff; the colours, though mellowed by time, are vulgar; the faces are expressionless, and anatomy is unknown. The two middle chambers or choir are not separated by a screen; they contain together sixteen pictures, most of them dim with dust and dirt, some eaten into huge holes where they are painted on canvas, others on wood having the surface ploughed up or fretted away by insects, all presenting a melancholy spectacle of neglect and forlorn decay. The haikals of course have the usual hollow stone altar with a loose slab of wood let into a rectangular depression in the centre: in one are the remains of a very fine altar-canopy mouldering fast away. In the spandrels of this haikal door (the northernmost) is some pretty inlay work of ivory flowers: and above a curious little tablet, three inches square, with a design of the Virgin and Child in mother-of-pearl mosaic. The design is not very clear, but the Virgin seems to have open wings drooping. The date of this door is 1814 A.D., and the work is decidedly inferior in character.

The whole of this church of Mâri Banai is lighted by square holes in the roof. There is a special guest-room outside it, which is reached by mounting a short flight of steps to the level of the outer earth (see plan, p. 48), a low cold stone-vaulted room with stone benches on three sides, the fourth open. There is no door, but outside on the right a narrow angular passage leads back to the court-yard before the door of Mâri Mîna, enclosing some lumber-rooms, a sacristy, and perhaps the entrance to the burial vaults. But instead of returning by the passage one may mount to the left a flight of some twenty stone steps

and land upon the roof.   Here a strange scene presents itself.   Just in front, i.e. over the chapel of
Mâri Banai, is a stone floor hemmed in on three
sides by lofty irregular walls of brick, but open on
the west.   Against the walls piled in reckless confusion are broken relics of church furniture, mushra-
biah-work, screens, lecterns, taper-racks and all kinds
of odd timbers : and if these signs were doubtful, a
change in the level of the floor towards the east end
shows plainly enough that one is looking at the
débris of a ruined chapel.   It was called the church
of the Virgin.   Through an open grating here one
gets a view down into Mâri Banai, and one realizes
the dangers to which pictures and works of art are
exposed from the changes of weather, and the entrance of bats and owls.   The south and east walls
of this ruined chapel are boundary walls of the whole
dair, and they are finished off upwards in a very
curious and interesting way.   Even when the chapel
was entire, the walls rose some way above the roof ;
and instead of being capped with coping stones they
have great pitchers or jars of rather frail red pottery
embedded into the masonry and forming a parapet.
From outside one can count as many as six rows,
one above another.   The same construction may be
seen at Ḳaṣr-ash-Shamm'ah in the Arab masonry
built upon the Roman wall where it skirts the garden
of the Jewish synagogue.   From within, only two
rows are visible, one above the other ; in some places
only a single row ; and elsewhere the parapet of pots
has fallen.   The jars are about 3 ft. high, of course
hollow, and all have a hole broken in the shoulder,
apparently with the design of weakening the resistance.   For they are intended as a defence against

secret assaults and were arranged to break and give
the alarm in case a robber or other enemy tried
to scale the walls. At Imârat in Persia, as Mr.
Floyer tells me, walls are sometimes built tapering
to a thickness of three or four inches at the top,
and a yard from the top are set with a row of sticks
projecting horizontally: any ladder placed against
these would break them and bring down the wall
above.

On the same level with the floor of the ruined
chapel is another chapel, that of Mâri Girgis, which
has a flat timber roof rudely painted and blazoned
with stars. Railed off from the nave by a blue
cross-bar screen and running along the north wall
is a narrow baptistery, the font of which lies under
the nave pulpit. It contains a pitcher, cross and
gospel-stand. Two grated openings through the
wall show a view of the ambon in the nave of Mâri
Mîna below. In a little aumbry in the wall I found
four decayed pictures, one a mere board without a
trace of colour left, one a triptych of the Crucifixion
—Christ in the panel and a thief on each door. The
pulpit here is of commonplace design : and all over
the body of the chapel is the usual network of flying
spars or beams for hanging lamps, etc. The choir
is raised two steps above the nave floor : it contains
eight large pictures of small merit, though one is
unusual—John the Baptist greeting Christ. Christ
is represented as a child alone in the desert and the
child John is falling and kissing his feet : the absence
of the Virgin is remarkable. The scene too is surrounded by a curious sort of tasteless scroll work
embellished with festoons of flowers and fruit,—
grapes, roses and strangely enough English blue-

bells: above are two birds and a head wreathed in a garland of roses. In the air above Christ's head are five winged cherubs. The style of this work reminds one of English seventeenth century painting.

The east end of the chapel contains a sacristy as well as haikal or sanctuary. But the former is now a mere lumber-room and is fenced off only by an open screen instead of the high panel-screen that always veils an altar. The roof is stone wagon-vaulting. A dozen musty pictures hang about the walls or on shelves: and one or two of them, which at first looked mere dirty pieces of board, well repaid the trouble of dusting and washing, and proved really fine and ancient pictures. On the floor are tumbled broken planks—some with dabs of colour or fragments of Arabic inscriptions,— candlesticks, an altar-casket, a lectern and one or two disused coronae of ancient bronze. The latter are large crowns of pierced metal-work hung by chains; and though the design is plain and un-finished in detail, yet one could not help a feeling of anger against the men who could fling such an ornament into a dark hole full of dust and cob-webs and could set up in its place a Paris chandelier with hanging prisms and festoons of glass stars. The Copts are jealous of their treasures, or jealous of strangers meddling with them; but they care for them chiefly as fetishes or relics, objects of supersti-tious reverence and not of artistic value. In one corner of this (northern) sanctuary, after a pile of timber had been removed, I discovered a small door which led by a short passage into a dark chamber about 12 ft. square lying directly behind the haikal.

There were aumbries in the wall which excited
visions of hid treasures, but a short search proved
them empty and desolate. No doubt the place
was built as a strong-room for the church plate;
but its position behind the main altar is as far as
I know unique, though there is something of the
kind under the tribune steps at Abu Sargah. The
sanctuary has its iconostasis with the conventional
series of seven pictures—the Virgin and on each
side three pairs of apostles. The decoration inside
is elaborate and reminds one on a smaller scale of
the haikal at Abu-'s-Sifain. Over the altar is a
delicate little domed baldakyn, not supported on
four pillars, but differing from this arrangement
by resting on a pair of horizontal spars, which run
into the north and south walls. All round the apse
is an array of saints blazoned in panels. In the
niche is the figure of Christ robed and throned, and
on the wall above the niche a quaint design of the
Resurrection. Both these paintings and the screen
are rude in style. The Arabic characters over the
doorway are thick and unfinished, and the other
ivory work is clumsy. This is the more disappointing that the inlaid inscription on the lintel gives a
date corresponding to 1445 A.D. a time when certainly the arts were flourishing in Egypt although
decay had set in. But we cannot tell how hurriedly
the chapel was built or rebuilt, or what special pres-
sure of war or terror or want may have disabled the
builders from employing the best artists. Moreover
the very date may be misleading; the work may be
merely an inferior copy of older work, reproducing
the design without the spirit, and renewing the date
as it renewed a cross or a flower. So that in either

case, whether the date be true or false, it is not of much value in determining the state of art at any fixed epoch. One is driven more and more to the conclusion that anything like a history of the rise and fall of Coptic art is impossible : that the rise and fall are comparatively short periods of which little or nothing is known : that between the two there was no definite progression, no scale of merit mounting slowly on previous acquirement : but that at its best, art as it were crystallised into fixed forms, which were handed down for many centuries with little loss of excellence. Invention seems to have ceased early : but taste and skill of execution remained hereditary.

There are no more chapels attached to Mâri Mîna ; but quitting Mâri Girgis one may pass across into one of the three-storied houses which have been mentioned as forming three sides of the main courtyard. These houses—the old monastic buildings— are all united by corridors and staircases together, and one may wander from floor to floor and house to house at will. One desolate chamber succeeds another : the rooms are all bare and empty, ungarnished and unswept : and that is their normal state. But at a certain season of the year, at the festival of Mâri Mîna, these cold-looking cells are. thronged with families of pilgrims. Not that the tenants come generally from any great distance : but pious people belonging to the dair, or bound by special ties of gratitude or veneration to its patron saint, come and dwell here for three or four days to keep the feast.

Working round from the chapel of Mâri Girgis on the east side one reaches a balcony on the north

side, whence it is only a step on to the roof of
the main building.   One sees now that the curved
roof or vaulting of the nave is of brickwork and
the dome also is brick: there is however no clear-
cut design which one can call distinctly the roof.
The general impression despite the nave and the
dome is that of a flat-roofed building: but there is
the usual multitude of little roofs whose many levels
give the chaotic haphazard look peculiar to all Coptic
churches seen from above or outside.   For it seems
an unvarying canon, that in the outer shell of a
church strength alone was studied, not beauty.   But
pass along the dome and stand looking over the
eastern parapet: you will soon cease to think of the
ugliness of your standing-place.   In front opens one
of the grandest views in Egypt.   At the foot of the
wall lies an old graveyard resting amid ruins: the
tombs are flat, and English in form—not of the
Muslim type, which is a sort of stone altar on a
broader base with a short pillar at each end,—and
a tree here and there reminds one further of an
English churchyard.   Beyond the circuit-wall on
every side stretches or undulates a dark iron-looking
desert, sweeping away in broad levels or rising in
huge mounds,—not the mere barren sand or pebbly
plain that makes nature's desert, but a desert of
man's making, a desert formed out of and over the
ruins of a great and ancient city.   In a landscape of
this kind there is something even more desolate and
more hopeless than in all the sands of Sahara.   Well
in the foreground is a sheet of gleaming water:
round it stand a few stray palms, some of which cast
their shadow on the unbroken azure surface.   The
repose and beauty and brightness of this little lake

contrast strangely with the sombre melancholy of the
landscape around : one needs not the imagination of
an Arab to picture the banished spirit of the place
brooding on old-world memories in the depths below.
In the plain beyond the lake lies a small walled
village about which are scattered some drooping
tamarisks: and the minaret of the mosque of
Zainum al 'Abidîn rises picturesquely above the
houses. The background is formed by huge rubbish
mounds high enough to bound the horizon there,
save where a short fall lets in a glimpse of the far
white Muḳaṭṭam hills and the ancient ruined mosque
that crowns the ridge. To the north the line of
mounds is broken, and gives a view of the grand
citadel of Cairo shining in the sun : near its base
stand the ruined shrines and clustered minarets of
the Mamaluke kings. All the rest of Cairo is shut
out of view, but nothing could be more magnificent
than the part that is seen. Southward again lie
other pools of water and lower rubbish mounds,
beyond which stretches a nearly level plain spanned
by the long low aqueduct. In the far distance the
Muḳaṭṭam range comes again into view, faint, blue,
and mist-crowned,—if the word mist can be used to
denote that faint ethereal splendour in which the
mountain-tops are lost.

But abandoning the view one may notice that the
parapet of pots seems to have gone all round the
church. To the north of the nave roof one looks
down a huge open shaft into a space that was once
the north aisle but is unaccountably walled off the
church, and used it would seem as a mere outhouse
or store for filters and various utensils. Here also is
the oven for baking the ḳorbân or eucharistic bread,

which is always prepared by the sacristan in a place specially set apart for that purpose somewhere within the enclosure of the church.   The flat roof of the courtyard buildings is higher than the church roof, but a scramble up is rewarded only by the discovery of a small ancient bell hung in a cupola, in which the ringer stands.   Not many of the churches have bells or any instrument for calling the people to prayer. The bell here has no date or inscription.

HISTORICAL NOTE ON THE CHURCH OF

MÂRI MÎNA.

THE first foundation of this church was probably in the fourth century, but the solitary notice that I can find of it is given by Al Maḳrizi[1] to the effect that the building was restored in the time of Theodorus XLV, patriarch about the year 730 A.D. The saint belonged to Alexandria and the first church erected to his memory was nine miles from that city, at the place where his body is said to have been discovered. For at his death, according to the legend, he requested that his body might be placed upon a camel, and that the beast might be turned loose into the desert. The story of the finding of his remains will be given among the legends rendered from the Synaxar in another part of this work. There can be no doubt that churches were dedicated to St. Menas soon after his death in various parts of Egypt. His shrine near Alexandria was the resort of pilgrims from all parts of the East, and a similar pilgrimage is made even now to his church at Old Cairo. Very early and interesting evidence of his repute is afforded by the small bottles or cruses of grey earthenware which are found in large quantities at Alexandria and else-where. They are about four to six inches in height with flat circular body, neck, and double handle joining neck and body. These flasks are meant to

---

[1] History of the Copts, translated from the Arabic by Rev. S. C. Malan, p. 77.

be carried by strings as they will not remain upright unless suspended. The body has generally the figure of Mâri Mína with arms outstretched in prayer: low down on either side a camel or some other animal is represented, and higher up are two or three small Greek crosses. Sometimes, but not always, a Greek inscription is also found, either EVLOΓIA TOV AΓIOV MHNA or simply TOY AΓIOY MHNA or O AΓIOC MHNAC[1]. The whole of the work is in low relief and surrounded by a circular moulding. The British Museum and most of the continental museums contain examples of these pilgrim bottles, which may have been used as chrismatories[2]. Two in my possession have no inscription, but a double circular moulding with a band of small pellets between them.

---

[1] Menas or ⲘⲎⲚⲀ was a common Coptic name in the fourth century.

[2] v. De Rossi, Bulletino di Archæologia Cristiana, 1869, p. 31, 32, and 1872, pp. 25–30, where cuts are given.

CHAPTER III.

Dair Abu-'s-Sifain (ابو السيفين).

The Church of Abu-'s-Sifain.—The Nunnery called Dair al Banât.—
The Church of Anba Shanûdah.—The Church of Sitt Mariam.

HALF a mile beyond Mâri Mîna lies the walled enclosure or dair of Abu-'s-Sifain; so called after the principal though not the most ancient church within it. The high straggling windowless walls, propped by rude buttresses, give this dair a picturesque look on all sides; but the best view is from the south, where, above the varied lines of wall, clusters of palm are seen waving and half-concealing the white domes of the churches. The dair is only about a furlong in diameter: yet it contains the three churches of Al ʿAdra, Anba Shanûdah, and Abu-'s-Sifain, besides the nunnery called Dair al Banât.

At the low square doorway of the enclosure one sees, swung back on its hinges, a ponderous door, plated with bands of iron and studded over with flattened bolt-heads. This iron casing stands out six inches from the wooden frame or backing, and fits closely into the doorway. A short dim passage leads by a turn to the left to Al ʿAdra: straight onwards it emerges from a sort of tunnel into a street about eighty yards long, on one side of which are high dwelling-houses, on the other the churches of Anba Shanûdah and Abu-'s-Sifain separated by the ruins of an early mosque, the ķiblah or eastern recess of which is still visible.

The church of Abu-'s-Sifain dates from the tenth century; it is dedicated to St. Mercurius, who in Coptic paintings is represented as brandishing a sword in each hand over his fallen foe, the heathen king Julianus, and who is hence called in the vulgar Abu-'s-Sifain, i. e. 'the Father of Two Swords[1],' or 'the Master of Two Swords.' The legend of St. Mercurius and the legend of the building of the church will be found elsewhere.

The western façade aligning the street is built of small dark-coloured brick, and has no windows or pretence of ornament except six little oriels from the west triforium, which are covered with wood-work at a distance of twenty feet from the ground. The single door now existing is at the north aisle entrance: it is sheeted with iron, but quite modern; in fact, the doorway has been squared and enlarged within the last ten years. The ancient door was plated with crocodile scales, and part of it lies now in the narthex of the church, though scarcely a shred of the scales remains.

---

[1] The Arabic 'abu' often denotes a mere quality or characteristic: thus the Spanish dollar is called, from the pillars figured on it, 'abu madf'a,' i.e. the cannon piece: so a butterfly is called 'abu daķîk,' or 'master of flour,' from the dust on its wings. The term is, however, sometimes used as a prefix to the names of saints or other worthies, in its literal sense of 'father.'

The church is an oblong building, roughly about ninety feet long and fifty broad, but beset on the north side with various irregular chapels. The northern aisle is cut off from the body of the church, and serves merely as a passage. Just inside the doorway a space with a groined vaulting forms a sort of porch, northwards of which a door opens to the mandârah or guest-room, where worshippers meet after the service, talk, smoke, and take coffee together. Half of the guest-room is open to the sky, half roofed by cloven palm-trunks, over which are laid loose pieces of board, wattled palm-sticks, &c. Round the walls are ranged some old benches : overhead is the chapel of St. Mary—of which hereafter. It should be noticed that the guest-room lies outside the shell of the church. In the porch itself is another bench, and on the left the patriarchal throne, the high chair of lattice-work found in all Coptic churches. A little further on in the passage, still on the left, are seen double doors of open woodwork and above them a rude painting of an ancient anchorite. This is Barsûm al 'Ariân, and these are the doors at the head of a short steep staircase of stone by which one descends to his shrine—a small dark underground chapel. The chamber, roughly about ten feet square, is vaulted and the walls cemented, but the water oozes in when the Nile rises. There is no ornament of any kind, not even a niche eastward; the altar stands in the centre of the little chapel; it is of stone, but the altar-board is square instead of oblong as usual. The priest told me that Barsûm lived 400 years ago, that he abandoned great riches to become a hermit, and passed eighteen years on the roof of Abu-'s-Sifain without

shelter from the sun.   He seems to have dug some
sort of cave, where his shrine now is, after this
period of exposure.   Once a year a service is still
held in the chapel, and sick people resort there
with faith in the healing virtues of the altar which
probably encloses the saints' relics.   This chapel
can hardly perhaps be called a crypt or confessionary, because it lies outside the church walls,
and is also much later in date than the high altar,
from which it is far removed in position also : but
it is remarkable owing to the great rarity of subterranean altars in the churches of Egypt.

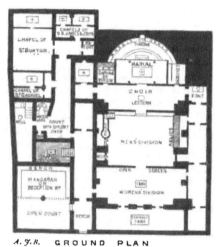

A. J. B.   G R O U N D   P L A N

Fig. 3.—The church of Abu-'s-Sifain, and the several adjoining chapels.

General Description.—The church is built of
small greyish brick, with scarcely a trace of stonework, but the pendentives of the large dome are
fashioned of stone, and marble is used for inner

decoration. Abu-'s-Sifain is distinguished from other churches by the absence of pillars. The aisles and narthex are marked off from the nave by enormous piers instead of. by columns, and the inner walls of the triforium are not broken by bays or relieved by pillars. The reason for this peculiarity is simple : the church was built in the tenth century—a period when the wrecks of Greek and Roman temples and palaces had vanished.

Of these piers the two eastward and the two westward are extremely massive. The former help to uphold a large and lofty dome which covers the haikal and choir. Halfway down the church, on either side, is a pair of heavy oblong piers close together, and each side of the pair a smaller pier. Advantage is taken of these piers to curve the walls on the north and south each into two wide and lofty arched recesses. The western or narthex wall remains straight, but is lightened by three pointed-arched openings covered with wooden grills.

Above the aisles and the narthex the usual gallery or triforium runs round the body of the church, and is divided into various corridors and chapels. Only from one or two points can even a narrow glimpse be seen of the church below ; a fact which unquestionably indicates that at the date of building women were allowed to worship in the body of the church and were not consigned to the gallery. For the present division of the nave into men's section and women's section is clearly unaltered from the original arrangement ; whereas in older churches, such as Abu Sargah, the nave-screens formed no part of the builder's plan, but were added as the custom arose for women to attend service in the nave. The men's section of course lies eastward of the two; beyond is the choir, and then the haikal.

The choir is only about eight feet long and the same width as the nave, thirty feet. Southward it is walled off from a baptistery which lies at the end of the aisle and may be entered by a door from the choir; northward a wing-wall, thrown out from the main pier, half divides it from a low dark chamber which forms a kind of choir to the northern aisle-chapel. This chamber is really part and parcel of the north aisle which, as was mentioned, is severed from the church.

The haikal is apsidal and has a very perfect tribune. There were, I think, originally two other apses. The northern aisle-chapel is not rounded, but the eastern wall may have been straightened when the exterior chapels were added on. There is, strangely enough, no southern aisle-chapel; the east wall of the aisle, against which the font is placed, aligns with the haikal-screen; but there must be a blocked chapel or space of some kind behind it, because the triforium above projects eastward beyond it and ends in an apse. It is almost certain therefore that there was an apse below on the ground floor; and the south aisle, like the north, terminated in a chapel.

The western wall shows no sign of having been pierced with three doorways: but it is said to have been rebuilt—probably in turbulent times, when it was felt that a triple entrance seriously weakened the defensive powers of the fabric.

The nave is covered with a pointed wooden roof, of the kind known as a 'pair of principals.' It has tie-beam and collar-beam, king-post and queen-posts, which are held together by braces, struts, and straining-piece. The peculiarity is that the small rafters run longitudinally: there are no purlins. The triforium is flat-roofed.

Details.—It will be convenient to take the details in the following order: i. narthex: ii. women's section: iii. men's section: iv. choir and choir north: v. north aisle-chapel: vi. haikal: vii. south aisle.

i. The narthex is a gloomy place unillumined by a single window, and unless it had originally a western entrance, it can have been designed for use only at the Epiphany ceremony. The tank still remains, but the custom of plunging in the waters has been for some years abolished. The old door-leaves, once plated with crocodile scales, which now lie on the ground there have been already mentioned. Here too may be seen lying part of a white marble column with an Arabic version of the Trisagion— the legend that is printed on the eucharistic bread— sculptured in high relief. The original place and purpose of the column are not known; but as the writing is ordinary Arabic, not Cufic, it can scarcely be coeval with the church.

ii. The entry for worshippers is by a door between the outer passage and the women's section. In the middle of the floor is a small tank, edged with marble, where, following the ancient usage, the priest once a year, after the consecration of the holy oils, washes the feet of sundry poor folk. On the walls hang five pictures. Of the three on the narthex wall, one in the centre, representing the Baptism of Christ, is old and interesting. The perspective is rude, and the river, full of the conventional fishes, is

shown in section half-submerging the figure of our
Lord; but the faces are well drawn and expressive.
The paintings of St. Michael and St. Menas, on the
same wall, are very poor. The other two subjects
face each other on opposite piers near the screen.
On the north side is the Coronation of the Virgin.
This picture is mounted in a frame which holds it six
inches clear of the wall; before it is fixed a little
beam set with a row of prickets for candles. The
Virgin is a three-quarter length figure, robed in a
dark mantle that forms a hood over the head. In
front a dim red dress shows under the mantle, but
both are thickly covered with golden stars, or rather
star-like crosses. The child is held on the left arm,
the Virgin's fore-arm falling, and the hands crossing
at the wrist. A flying angel at each side above is
holding a golden crown; and six cherub-faces peer
dimly from the gold background round the head and
shoulders. The Virgin has a fixed look, perhaps
too apathetic to be called pensive. Still, the picture
is pleasing, and recalls Albert Durer's treatment of
the same subject. The Arabic title upon it runs as
follows: 'Peace on Mary, the Mother of our Lord
Jesus.' It may be noticed that even Muslim writers,
when they have occasion to mention Christ or Mary,
add after the name, 'on whom be peace.' The other
painting represents one St. Kultah, apparently a
notable physician. In his right hand he holds
a wand pointing to a casket in his left hand; the
lid of the casket is raised, and shows six little compartments for drugs. On the dexter side in mid air
is a fine gold cross; on the sinister a long gold staff
or crozier. Many of the patriarchs were renowned
for their skill in medicine.

Abu-'s-Sifain is so very rich in pictures that I think it worth while to give a complete list of them as they stand, choosing the more remarkable for special description.

iii. Passing now from the bare and cold division for the women, one is at once struck by the magnificence of ornament lavished on the men's section. The screen between the two is heavy, and of plain bar-work, but the spandrels of the screen-door are very delicately carved, and very beautiful. But the screen between the men's section and the choir—the choir-screen—is a most superb and sumptuous piece of work. It is a solid partition of ebony, inlaid with carved ivories of the most exquisite workmanship. The south side of this section, and the north side from the women's screen to the ambon, or pulpit, are also bounded by lofty screens. The result is a beautiful chamber, thirty-one feet long and twenty-three broad, shut in on all sides with screens. A continuous band of little pictures mounted on the screens runs round the chamber; and other pictures are set above and below, save when the line is broken for about twelve feet by the ambon, which stands at the north-east of the nave.

At the south-west corner of the men's section, whence it is well to start, a little room that is railed off and placed between two piers is used as a sacristy. Here the principal vestments are kept. Between this and the ambon comes the shrine of Abu-'s-Sifain,—an arched recess of gaudily painted woodwork. The top is square, and mounted with gilt plates of pierced metal-work. In front hangs a curtain of the silk and velvet tissue once woven at Rosetta. The whole reminds one of a small theatre, or peep-show. At the back of the recess is the picture of St. Mercurius slaying Julian—like the shrine, a poor performance. A metal glory has been nailed over the head of the saint. Under the picture is a locker containing relics of St. Mercurius enclosed in the usual silk bolster. A small pendant lamp burns before the shrine, and there stands also on the ground a very curious and ancient candlestick of iron, with three prickets. The shrine is quite recent, and unfortunately obscures part of the ambon. Many chains for lamps hang from the roof, but are used only at great festivals.

The ambon is built of marble. At the foot of the choir-screen lies a narrow stone platform, probably the solea. Thence a staircase leads through a carved doorway, with lintel and posts of marble, up to the ambon. This consists, as at Mâri Mîna, of a balcony and pulpit proper. The balcony is faced with an oblong panel inlaid with the most beautiful and elaborate marble mosaic. On each side of the panel is a little pillar of white marble, sculptured with scroll-work, and finished with an oval cap. Along the top of the panel and down the balustrade runs a broken Coptic inscription carved in high relief. The pulpit proper is circular, and set round with five semi-columns alternated with wedge-shaped projections. These pillars and wedges are covered with a minute mosaic of coloured marble and shell-pearl; but the full arrangement can only be seen from inside the pulpit, because three of the pillars and three of the wedges are quite hidden by the shrine, which is thrust up against the ambon.

Behind the ambon, the arched recess, across the chord of which it stands, is filled up nearly to the

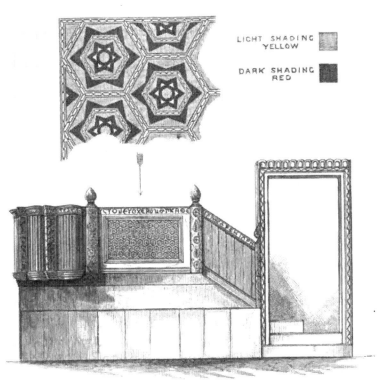

LIGHT SHADING
YELLOW

DARK SHADING
RED

ELEVATION.

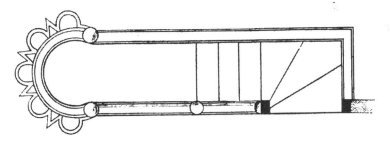

A. J. BUTLER.

PLAN.

SCALE OF FEET.

0   1   2   4   6   8   10   12

Fig. 4.—Marble Ambon at Abu-'s-Sifain (tenth century).

level of the pulpit-top with a platform of masonry, beneath which are said to rest the remains of a patriarch. There is of course no inscription to record the name.

On the south side of this section is a solid wooden partition, drawn in front of and therefore hiding the somewhat ungainly piers. Most of this partition is occupied by three arched recesses of carved and painted woodwork, decked with small pillars at the corners. In the back of each recess is a picture— Elias, Barsûm al 'Ariân—and between them a curious painting of the Virgin in triumph. She occupies a small arched panel in the centre of the piece, and round it twenty small oblong panels are marked off by lines of colour. She is seated on a high-backed Byzantine-looking throne, holding a cross in her right hand and a palm in her left. Over her head are two flying angels, one carrying a cross, the other a palm, and above the angels in the middle is a winged cherub-head. Each of the twenty small panels contains two half-length figures of angels robed and crowned; and every figure carries a cross and a palm-branch sloped together so as to touch over the angel's breast. The ground of the whole picture is gold, but the Arabic date proves that it is nineteenth-century work.

The choir-screen is worth a journey to Egypt to see. It is a massive partition of ebony, divided into three large panels—doorway and two side panels— which are framed in masonry. At each side of the doorway is a square pillar, plastered and painted; on the left is portrayed the Crucifixion, and over it the sun shining full; on the right, the Taking down from the Cross, and over it the sun eclipsed. Each of the

three panels is about six feet wide and eight high.
In the centre a double door, opening choirwards, is
covered with elaborate mouldings, enclosing ivory
crosses carved in high relief. All round the framing
of the doors tablets of solid ivory chased with
arabesques are inlet, and the topmost part of each
panel is marked off for an even richer display of
chased tablets and crosses. Each of the side-panels
of the screen is one mass of superbly cut crosses of
ivory, inlaid in even lines, so as to form a kind of
broken trellis-work in the ebony background. The
spaces between the crosses are filled with little
squares, pentagons, hexagons, and other figures of
ivory, variously designed, and chiselled with exquisite skill. This order is only broken in the
centre of the panel, where a small sliding window,
fourteen inches square, is fitted; on the slide a
single large cross is inlaid, above and below which
is an ivory tablet containing an Arabic inscription
interlaced with scroll-work. In these ivories there
is no through-carving; the block is first shaped
in the form required—cross, square, or the like;
next, the design is chased in high relief, retaining
the ivory ground and a raised border; and the piece
is then set in the woodwork and framed round with
mouldings of ebony, or ebony and ivory alternately.
It is difficult to give any idea of the extraordinary
richness and delicacy of the details or the splendour
of the whole effect. The priest told me that this
screen was 953 years old, i. e. dates from 927 A. D.,
which seems to be the year of the church's foundation. The tradition is doubtless right: work of
exactly the same style may be seen on the mumbâr
at the mosque of Ibn Ṭulûn, built in 879 A. D. Many

Fig. 5.—Blocks of solid ivory carved in relief: from the choir-screen at Abu-'s-Sifain (tenth century).
SCALE ⅜

of the designs there are absolutely identical with
those at Abu-'s-Sifain, though neglect and exposure
have half ruined them.   It may be remarked that
the Ibn Ṭulûn was built by a Copt.

Over the doorway of the screen a small beam
projects on brackets; it was meant to uphold a
curtain, no longer used, and is painted with a Coptic
text too dim to be decipherable.   The screen is
carried upwards flush with the masonry setting or
framing of the large panels by some beautiful
woodwork which serves as mounting for a great
number of pictures.   First comes a band of golden
texts with large letters carved in relief—on the
dexter side Coptic and on the other Arabic writing;
then a row of small pictures set in a continuous
framing or arcading of woodwork; above this a
second band of golden texts in Coptic and Arabic;
then twelve small painted beams, projecting about
a cubit and fitted each with an iron ring long disused but meant to hold a pendant lamp.   Above the
beams a third band of golden letters—all Arabic;
and lastly, a row of eleven separate large pictures.
The series of large pictures is continued round
nearly the length of the south wall; while the series
of little pictures runs between its bands of golden
texts without change or break all along the four
sides of the men's section, stopping only at the
shrine of Abu-'s-Sifain by the pulpit.

To take the upper row first.   Each picture is
about 30 in. by 20.   In the centre is Christ, robed
with cross-embroidered pall and dalmatic.   The right
hand is uplifted in the attitude of benediction: in the
left hand is a book of the gospels drooping downwards.   The type of countenance with small oval

outline, arched eyebrows, and short pointed beard, is unusual and scarcely eastern. All the figures in this series are three-quarter length : those at the side all turn toward the central figure, but show nearly full face. The features are bold, powerful, and dignified, but decidedly Jewish in cast. The subjects are : (1) St. Paul, (2) St. Peter, (3) St. John, (4) The Angel Michael, (5) The Virgin, (6) Christ, (7) John the Baptist, (8) The Angel Gabriel, (9) St. Matthew, (10) St. Mark, (11) St. Luke. All the figures are nimbed and carry open gospels, except the Virgin, the two angels, and St. Peter, who bears instead two long golden keys. The picture of Gabriel is exceptional. The angel's right hand is uplifted, palm outwards; in the left are two large lilies, which part at a wide angle from his hand; the lilies blossoming with red and white flowers, alternated on each side of the stalk and divided by leaves, are rendered with exquisite colouring.

On the south side are nine pictures of the same series. Here also the central figure is Christ, and the others face towards it. They are : (1) St. James, (2) Thaddaeus, (3) Simon the Canaanite, (4) St. Michael, (5) Christ with glory lettered *O ΩN*, i. e. ὁ ὢν 'The Being,' or, 'He that Is.' This title is common in the Greek Church, but according to the 'Guide to Painting'—an ancient MS. brought by Didron from Mount Athos—it should be used only for the Trinity. The Copts, however, while they rarely if ever represent the Father, ascribe all his attributes to the Son. (6) St. James, Son of Alphaeus, (7) St. Gabriel, (8) St. Andrew, (9) St. Jude.

Here the series ceases, but in the same line, between St. Jude and the western screen, is a panel

5 ft. long and 1 ft. high, containing seven half-figures of saints on a gold background, each in its own division.

Of the under row or small pictures running all round the men's section there are no less than 65, all on a gold ground; viz. 21 on the east screen, 20 on the south screen, 17 on the west screen, 7 on the north wall. Starting from the north end of the choir-screen they are as follows :—

1. The Annunciation. The angel is crossing a courtyard to the Virgin, who stands facing the spectator; she has risen from a bench and is lifting her right hand in a deprecating attitude.

2. The Nativity. In the foreground is a kind of cradle or crib into which two oxen are gazing as the child is being taken out of it. Farther back the Virgin is seen sitting up in a kind of couch; the child, wound arms, legs and body with a mummy-like swathing, lies on his back at a little distance above the Virgin in mid-air. At the sides and in the background crowned kings are kneeling and offering vessels of gold and silver.

3. The Presentation in the Temple. In the background is a red-coloured altar-canopy.

4. The Flight into Egypt.

5. The Resurrection of Lazarus. A very curious painting. Lazarus is standing upright swathed from head to foot in bands of linen like a mummy, while over his head and falling behind is a dark heavy robe which forms a head-dress or hood, precisely like the arrangement seen on mummy-cases. Two

men are represented unwinding the strips of linen.

It is quite probable that ancient Egyptian forms of burial survived among wealthy people even into Christian times, though nothing of the kind is known now[1]; and it is very singular to remark that the same kind of wrapping is common in early Italian frescoes or paintings in the late third and following centuries[2]. It may be seen, if I remember rightly, in the mosaics of the porch of St. Mark's at Venice; and the 'swathed mummy-like figures of Christ' found in early Celtic work are quoted, though wrongly, by Mr. Warren in distinctive evidence of a connexion between the Celtic and eastern Churches[3].

6. The Marriage at Cana.

7. The Baptism of Christ.

---

[1] Embalming was still common as late as the middle of the fourth century: for we read that St. Antony's dread of the process was the chief reason why his followers concealed the place of his burial. But the whole subject of the transition from ancient Egyptian to Christian rites awaits investigation.

The Mohammedan custom as described to me by a native, and as I have witnessed it, is to lay the body on a white shroud which is then loosely folded over it. Round this a winding-sheet is wrapped, of a material varying with the wealth of the deceased's family: rich people use silk, and red silk for a maiden. Three loose bands are then tied round the sheet—one at the neck, one at the waist, and one at the knees or feet. When the body is placed in the tomb these bands are further loosened or removed.

The present Coptic custom is to dress the deceased in his best dress, and to lay over this a sheet of cloth, silk, or cashmere. They do not swathe the body in bands, and they use a coffin.

[2] Roma Sotteranea, vol. ii. p. 99.

[3] Liturgy and Ritual of the Celtic Church, p. 51.

8. The Transfiguration.

9. Christ and the Eleven; the Temple in the background is represented by a stiff Byzantine building with three domes and oblong windows.

10. Christ blessing two children.

11. (Centre) The Resurrection. Christ standing on the tomb and holding a flag of victory; at each side an angel sitting.

12. The Crucifixion.

13. The Last Supper.

14. The Entry into Jerusalem.

15. Christ in Glory, or the Transfiguration. An aureole with rays, and at the four corners the apocalyptic symbols. This somewhat resembles a fresco in the apse of the crypt of the cathedral at Auxerre—twelfth century[1].

16. The Ascension. Christ in an azure medallion upheld by two flying angels; the disciples below gazing upwards.

17. Christ with a boy who carries balanced on his head a sort of cradle surrounded by an open railing. The subject is doubtful, but it may be the sick of the palsy carrying his bed, our Lord being drawn on a larger scale, as was the custom sometimes in the West.

18. The woman of Samaria. In the foreground is the well with a coping round it. A horizontal rope slung between two tree-tops upholds another rope from which the pitcher hangs by a pulley. One of the trees is beside the well, the other behind in the

---

[1] Didron's Christian Iconography, tr. by Millington, vol. i. p. 108.

distance, so that a line joining them would pass nowhere near the well. The trees are large sycamores, but bend under the strain of the rope. Perspective is not much regarded in these pictures.

19. Christ healing the blind and halt. The man is kneeling and our Lord touching his eyes.

20. Christ and the man who 'had great possessions.' The latter wears a crown.

21. Christ raising the widow of Nain's son. The body lies on its back and is being carried head foremost on a bier with four corner-poles. The body is swathed in the same mummy-like fashion as Lazarus in (5).

This ends the pictures over the choir-screen, eastern side. The following twenty on the south side are chiefly Old Testament subjects :—

22. The Three Children in the furnace. Towards the top of the picture in the background is a golden image, and each side of it a man falling in worship. In the foreground to the left is Nebuchadnezzar crowned and robed in ermine; to the right is a dome-shaped furnace of brick, one side of which is broken open; it resembles the ordinary lime-kiln of the country. Flames issue from the top; inside are the three children, and with them an angel.

23. Moses and the burning bush. The painter clearly had no idea of a bush or thicket, (cf. No. 33 infra), only of trees with bare trunks and branches above. So he represents a group of sycamores with their tops alone on fire and their stems showing under-

neath. An angel leans out of the flames looking downwards. From the left of the picture a piece of ruined wall projects without apparent purpose.

24. Ascent of Elijah.
25. David bringing the Ark from the house of Obed-edom. David in front is playing the harp; behind him walk a man playing a lute (the Arab *'aûd*) and some other figures. The Ark is a large coffer on wheels drawn by oxen; soldiers bring up the rear.
26. Jonah being cast up by the fish.
27. Jacob's Vision. A short Arab ladder resting on low clouds; one angel ascending, one descending.
28. The angel appearing to Zacharias in the Temple. The Temple is represented by a short arcade in the background; Zacharias is robed as priest and swinging a thurible.
29. The miracle of the loaves and fishes.
30. The finding of Moses. In the background are shown the Pyramids, and a sort of castellated wall runs up to them from near the river. Pharaoh's daughter has ridden down on a handsome donkey.
31. The meeting of Mary and Elizabeth.
32. Christ at Bethany. Arab spoons and tumblers are on the table, and beside it an Arab ewer and basin for hand-washing.
33. The sacrifice of Isaac. The ram 'caught in a thicket' is shown hung in mid-air by his horns to the top of a tree which has no lower branches. Yet the ram is nearly as large as the tree.

34. The Ark resting upon Mount Ararat. The Ark is on a slope and shored up by wooden props; a raised causeway of wood leads up to it. Noah and animals in the foreground.

35. Pharaoh and his host overwhelmed in the Red Sea. Heads of men and spear-tops are showing between all the waves. Pharaoh's chariot is on the water but sinking.

36. Samuel anointing Saul.

37. Isaiah. An angel flying above a flaming altar holds between a pair of tongs a live coal with which he is touching the prophet's lips.

38. Moses on Sinai receiving the tables of the law from a cloud.

39. Aaron in the Tabernacle. With both hands he is swinging a thurible hanging by three chains; in his right hand he holds a branch, like olive, budding; on the altar is a book with golden clasps and a pair of golden candlesticks.

I have never seen a Coptic book with clasps; the altar books are always sealed in metal cases. Probably clasps are earlier.

40. Peter walking on the water,

41. Peter receiving the keys.

The seventeen pictures on the west side are these:

42. The Temptation of Christ. The devil in golden air is flying away from the mountain.

43. The devil being cast out of Mary Magdalene.

44. The man with a withered hand.

45. The healing of the lame man (?).

46. The sick of the palsy. He is being let down, not through a roof, but from the housetop into an open courtyard.

47. Mary anointing Christ's feet.
48. Christ arguing with the doctors.
49. The healing of the man whom Satan had bound thirty-eight years.
50. The Crucifixion. The cross stands between two heavy Byzantine buildings.
51. The Syro-Phœnician woman.
52. Christ casting out a devil.
53. Christ cursing the fig-tree.
54. Christ on the sea of Tiberias rebuking the storm. ' Peace, be still.'
55. Christ asleep in the storm. ' Save us : we perish.'
56. Christ and the disciples walking through the cornfields.
57. The woman with the issue of blood.
58. The raising of Jairus' daughter.

There remain on the north side seven of the same series :—

59. The widow casting her two mites into the Treasury.
60. The man among the tombs from whom Christ is casting out a devil.
61. The healing of the centurion's servant.
62. Constantine.
63. A plain white cross of Greek form.
64. Helena.
65. Christ sending forth the Apostles.

The figures of Constantine and Helena, and the cross between them, commemorate of course the finding of the cross. The legend is well told in Curzon's Monasteries[1]. The emperor and empress

---

[1] Monasteries of the Levant, p. 164.

are both crowned and robed in sacerdotal vestments — chasuble, dalmatic, alb, and stole. The
stole is the single epitrachelion and hangs between
chasuble and dalmatic. The dalmatic is short,
reaching only a little below the waist; it is cut
so as to leave a curve at the bottom : the chasuble
also has a very short curve in front, but seems to
be very full behind and at the sides.

This ends the somewhat lengthy catalogue of
pictures in the men's section. They were perhaps
painted in the fifteenth and sixteenth century, but
the date must be quite conjectural. In drawing
and perspective they are very rude if closely examined, but seen, as they are meant to be seen,
at a distance they have their own enchantment.
The colours are very soft and harmonious, and the
figures have all a freedom and even grandeur of
outline that redeems the want of technical finish.
The whole tone is one of unmistakable splendour;
and the contrast between the dark screen below,
starred over with ivory crosses, and the space above
divided by bands of golden writing and set with
panels in which haloed saints and sacred scenes
glow under golden skies, is something admirable
and delightful. And when in olden times the twelve
silver lamps that hung before the screen were burning at night and throwing a mellow light upon it,
the beauty and richness of the view with all its
sacred memories and suggestions must have deeply
moved the worshippers, and helped, with the odour
of frankincense and the sound of chaunt and cymbals,
to create an impression of ritual splendour now quite
unrivalled.

iv. The choir is raised 2 ft. above the nave, and

is very long from north, to south but narrow.
Passing inside, one remarks that the inner as well
as the outer face of the screen is inlaid with
ivory: and a bridge of masonry, invisible from the
nave, is seen to join the two great piers between
which the screen stands, and from which the wide
dome springs to cover the choir and apse. This
bridge (about 2 ft. high) is lightened by five drop-
arched openings, on the spandrels of which six-winged
cherubim are painted in dusky red colours. On this
side of the screen too are many pictures and some
Coptic writing.

The lectern which stands in the centre of the
choir is quite plain, adorned only with geometrical
mouldings. A fifteenth century book of prayers
lying upon it has some good illuminations. The tall
standard bronze candlestick beside the lectern, and
the silver censer hanging on the candlestick, are both
ancient and fine pieces of work. Several silver
lamps, lamps of plain glass, and silver-mounted
ostrich eggs depend from a lofty beam before the
haikal-screen.

The centre part of this, the iconostasis, resembles
in style the choir-screen, and is doubtless of the same
period. It is made of ebony inlaid with thin plates
of ivory variously shaped and carved in relief, and
with carved blocks of ebony marked off by ivory
borders. The side-pieces are of a lighter-coloured
wood, perhaps cedar, inlaid with crosses and other
patterns of plain flat ivory. All the doors however—
there is one on each side of the haikal-door—are very
fine, having their spandrels inlaid with flowers. Moreover at each side of the haikal door is a little square
slide-window, as in the choir-screen. A silk curtain

Fig. 6.—Ivory-inlaid doorway of the Haikal at Abu-'s-Sifain.
(Designs in geometrical mouldings merely indicated : design of framing facsimile).

embroidered with a gold cross hangs before the entrance : just over it is a splendid ivory cross inlaid, and on each side of the cross a superb panel of open ebony carving.   The screen of course ends upwards with a row of pictures.   The central doorway closes by folding doors beautifully inlaid : on each is a delicate bronze knocker, a ring resting on a scutcheon with open work above and below and shapely bosses. The horse-shoe arch of the doorway is followed round by a sort of baluster pattern in ivory : each spandrel is inlaid with an eight-branched flower springing from a vase and curving towards the centre, where a dove meets it.   The vacant spaces are filled with stars, and at each corner is a tablet with an inlaid inscription of dedication in Arabic— the usual 'Reward, O Lord.'   Across the lintel is a band with Coptic writing inlaid on the dexter, and Arabic on the other side.   The Coptic means 'Glory to God in the highest,' while the Arabic is a verse from the psalms, 'Lift up, O kings, your gates; and be ye lift up, ye everlasting doors.' Exactly the same variation from the better known rendering occurs in the Ecgbert Pontifical[1].   The illustration will give some idea of this beautiful door.

The choir is strewn with Turkey and Persian carpets much worn.   Round the walls on shelves are a number of pictures.

   1. On the north pier but facing south the twenty-four priests of the Levitical courses : the figures are painted in two rows of twelve, one above the other, on a gold ground.

---

[1] Ecgbert Pontifical, ed. Surtees Society, p. 31.

On the back of the choir-screen are these :

2. The Three Children in the burning fiery furnace. Christ is seated blowing on the fire to quench it.

3. John the Baptist's head being brought to Herod on a charger.

4. St. George and the Dragon.

5. The anchorites St. Antony and St. Paul.

6 and 7. St. George and the Dragon.

8. Abu Iskharûn—a native saint as indicated by the camels in the scene. In the background of this picture is a church or chapel like a doll's house with open doors. On the ground floor inside are six little figures standing in a row : in the upper story an altar is seen with the arca or altar-casket upon it, two golden candlesticks and three golden thuribles.

The average size of the above paintings is 30 in. by 20.

This brings us to the doorway of the screen, over which are three glazed pictures—the only glazed pictures I have seen in a Coptic church—set in a single frame. They are about 10 in. by 7, and represent—

9. The angel Michael triumphing over Death. Death is a bearded man lying with closed eyes and resting his head on a pillow. The angel is standing upon him.

10. The Baptism of Christ.

11. St. Mark.

The glass of the two latter was so dingy that I could not distinguish them, but took the titles on trust from the priest.

Thence the larger series continues:

12. Mary and Martha, both full-face. Mary in her left hand carries a palm-branch with which she touches Martha's right.

13. Abu-'s-Sifain and his father.

14. Mary finding Christ among the doctors. Silver crescents are nailed on for glories.

15. St. Julius.

16. St. Stephen (?) crowned, swinging a thurible in his right hand and carrying a model of a church in his left.

17. St. James the martyr.

18. Anba Rûais: a Coptic martyr. There is a church dedicated to him at the Coptic cemetery near the 'Abbasîah road, Cairo.

On the south wall of the choir are three:

19. Anba Barsûm al 'Ariân.

20. Baptism of Christ.

21. Virgin and Child.

22—30. The icons or pictures over the haikal-screen are no less than twenty-nine in number, all about 10 in. by 7. Over the central part, i.e. before the high altar, are nine—three panels each with three arches.

 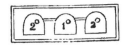 

In the middle is the Virgin and Child, 1°: on each side of her an angel, 2°: under each of the remaining six arches are two apostles, 3°—5°. The icons therefore consist of Christ and his Mother, two angels, and the twelve apostles.

On the north part of the screen is a single panel containing nine pictures (31—39):—

The central figure is Christ 1°.

On each side are two angels, 2° and 3°, and beyond them two evangelists, 4° and 5°. Each of the four angels carries a patriarchal cross (with three transoms) in his right hand, except Gabriel, who carries the cross in his left and a trumpet in his right.

40—50. On the south part of the screen are eleven pictures on two panels:—

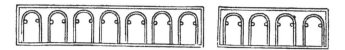

In the longer panel each division contains a group of three figures: in the shorter are four horsemen. But all are dim with age and indistinguishable. The icons generally speaking are ancient and well executed.

The choir north contains nothing except some paintings. On each of the buttresses dividing the choir from the choir north is a picture—the Crucifixion and St. Michael respectively (51 and 52). On the north side, in a broad carved frame let into the wall, is a figure of Raphael (53). The angel has a red robe with white wings outspread: a stole is crossed diagonally over his breast. On the west wall is a large panel (54) about 5 ft. by 2 ft. 6 in., containing twelve scenes, which are among the best and the most interesting paintings in any of the churches of Egypt. As usual in ancient Coptic pictures, the wood panel has been overlaid with a thin coating of plaster or 'gesso': the plaster was then washed all over with gilt, and on the gilt the colours were laid. The early Italian painters, in employing the same method, were careful to paste strips of parchment across the joinings of the wood at the back, to prevent it starting. The Coptic artist took no such precaution, and his picture is now disfigured by narrow rifts that run from top to bottom. Neglect and wanton damage have further injured it: but not so far that its value as a work of art is seriously diminished. Its age cannot be less than 500 years: I think it may date as far back as the eleventh century. The choir north is so dark that candles are required to see the picture: but its position may have saved it when others more exposed have been broken in pieces.

1º	2º	3º	4º	5º
6º	7º	8º	9º	10º

Starting from the top dexter corner, the subjects are :—

1º. The Annunciation. This is a most beautiful picture. An angel with outspread wings is advancing across a courtyard; his right hand is outstretched, and his left holds the gathered folds of his robe. Mary stands at the other side (where she has risen from a bench) with face half averted, sideways to the angel. Her right arm is bent, and hand held up palm outwards, with a gesture of deprecation. Her face has been injured by some malicious person, who has picked out the eyes: but there is a look of sorrow and fear upon it, not of rejoicing. The angel, too, has an almost pained expression of solemnity: the eyebrows are drawn together, and lips half open. The treatment, in point of expression, reminds one very curiously of Mr. Burne Jones' picture of the same subject, though the scale is much smaller. The angel's wings are a soft green with rich red underwings. A shaft of deep green light is slanting down on the Virgin's head. In the background is an arcade of Corinthian pillars supporting a Byzantine building. Here the drawing is rude and careless, although the figures are modelled and coloured with all the skill of a master's hand.

2°. The Nativity. The Virgin is lying on a couch in the centre; below, a desert pastoral scene, amid which the Child is being washed in a large brass vessel. Higher up on the dexter side are the Magi bringing gifts; and above the Virgin, in another scene, the Child is lying in a manger. This is the conventional composition as found also in all the western Churches.

3°. Christ in Glory. This is the central picture of the upper row. The background in gold; at the four corners are the apocalyptic symbols; in the midst an orb of dark yet faint green colour, in which Christ is seated with outspread hands. The hair of the face is full, but short, and the type quite unusual. The expression is severe but powerful. The drapery, particularly the folds falling from the knees, is beautifully rendered.

4°. The Presentation in the Temple. Simeon has just taken the Child in his arms from the Mother : at each side is a figure, one of whom, Joseph, carries a pair of turtle-doves.

5°. The Baptism of our Lord. Christ wears no loin-cloth. The angels stand on Christ's left hand instead of the right. Fishes are swimming in the water, and uncouth little figures riding on strange beasts like dwarf hippopotami. These figures denote probably the evil spirits which reside in the Nile, and which are exorcised at the consecration of the water for baptism in the Coptic service. In this picture, as in that at Mâri Mîna, Christ is standing upon a serpent.

6°. The Transfiguration. Of the three figures, Peter, James, and John, two are falling headlong on their faces, down the mountain side : one is seated burying his face in his hands. Christ stands in an orb, from which shoot out curious wing-like or feathered rays of glory. At each side is a figure in clouds—Moses and Elias.

7°. The Entry into Jerusalem. The faces here are very finely modelled, and surprisingly powerful in expression : but the drawing of the ass is almost ludicrous. The painter's indifference to all the *accessories* in these pictures is very remarkable.

8°. The Ascension. Christ rising is upheld by two ascending angels. Below are two holy women with glories, and the apostles gazing up with shaded eyes.

9°. Pentecost. The twelve are seated on a large horseshoe bench, and rays are falling upon them. The treatment is clearly suggested by the ring of presbyters seated in the apse.

10⁰. The Death of the Virgin. This subject is so rare in the Coptic paintings that I know no other instance of it. In the western Churches it was common. The Virgin lies on a high altar-like couch, behind which Christ is standing and receiving in his arms a little swathed figure, which represents Mary's soul. On each side of our Lord is an angel holding, and sloping towards him, a large golden candlestick. Round about the bier are twelve figures—the apostles —who wear the episcopal omophorion. One carries a pyx, or a vessel of chrism, and a swinging censer : one is reverently touching the bier : and another wears a most pathetic look of sorrow as bending down over the bier with forward-leaning face, and hand laid gently on the coverlet, he gazes sadly and enquiringly on the closed eyes and still face of Mary. Of these twelve figures only the three highest up in the picture, whose heads show against the sky, wear the nimbus : the others have none, perhaps because the close grouping made it difficult to render. The whole composition is almost precisely identical, even in detail, with the bas-relief of the same subject at Or-san-Michele in Florence.

It will be noticed that the events depicted were in chronological order, showing the unity of design. The titles are given in Coptic only—not in Arabic— which is generally a proof of great age, if proof were wanted.

v. The north aisle-chapel is completely walled off from the haikal. It has its own screen : the roof is low, as there is a chapel above it, and the interior is very dark. Yet there is perhaps less sign of neglect than usual in these side-chapels. In the eastern wall, which is straight, not apsidal, there is a niche covered

with fine Damascus tiles.   The altar candlesticks, of
bronze, are of a simple but good design : but the most
interesting thing in this chapel is the ark or altar-
casket, which I found lying in darkness, and smothered
in rubbish and dust, on the ground in the corner of
one of the outer chapels, and which apparently had
long fallen into disuse.   The priest was unaware of its
existence, but has had the good sense to remove it
into the church.   This box is more than *six hundred
years old:* for it bears the Coptic date 996, corresponding to 1280 A.D.   The form is cubical, with a
round hole at the top: the sides are covered with
paintings.   If one imagines the box in its position
for the celebration of the ķorbân, the order will be
as follows : On the east side : The Redeemer.   This
is an exceedingly fine picture, quite Rembrandt-like
in tone, in its splendid depths of shadow and play of
light, and almost worthy of the master.   Christ, half-
turning to the left, is walking with earnest luminous
eyes fixed before him, and lips half-parted.   In his
left hand a golden chalice is held outstretched :
two fingers of the right hand are uplifted in benediction.   Under his feet is an eagle flying reversed,
i.e. with the under parts uppermost, and head
curved over the breast.   The face of Christ is full-
bearded, resembling the type traditional in the
western Churches : and the rich umber shadows
round it deepen the impression, which is one of
fascinating solemnity.   This is among the most
powerful pictures I have ever seen.

Southward.   Virgin and Child.   The background
is gold, and the nimbs are covered with patterns of
stippled or dotted work.   The Child rests on the
Virgin's right arm : her right hand is holding his

fore-arm.   Christ carries an open scroll.   On either side is a red-robed angel with arms crossed upon the breast.

Westward.   The Annunciation.   The subject is treated in the conventional manner: but the angel bears a lily in his left hand, more after the type found in the western Churches.   The angel's wings, the two glories, and the whole sky are covered with stars, each star consisting of a cluster of seven dots, or shallow dents; and the whole scene is worked over with conventional flowers and scrolls traced in red dotting.   This style of work is found also in early Italian painting.

Northward.   The picture here is sunk in a frame instead of being flush with the edges, like the other three.   The execution is ruder and stiffer—probably later, and the work of a feebler hand.   It represents a priest administering the eucharist to a Coptic martyr called Mariam-as-Saiah (the Wanderer)—a hideous naked famished-looking figure, such as is generally drawn to depict an anchorite.   The priest holds in his left hand a golden chalice, and over the chalice, with his right, a golden spoon containing a wafer, which is stamped with a single cross, such as may be seen in mediaeval Latin illuminations, or the mosaics of St. Mark at Venice[1].

The northermost of the three doors in the haikal-screen opens into a tiny room, shut off by heavy

---

[1] I much regret to state that on a visit to the church of Abu-'s-Sifain in the early part of this year (1884), since the above was written, I could neither see nor hear of this beautiful altar-casket. It is only fair, however, to state that the priest of the church was absent.

woodwork from the sanctuary. This is the shrine
of the Virgin, whose picture is set in the back of
a deep wooden niche carved and painted. She is
seated on a Byzantine throne, and above her two
flying angels are holding a crown. The treatment
is singularly free from convention. On the wall are
three other pictures :—

1. Tikla Himanût, the Abyssinian. Here is a
large palm laden with purple dates, and at either side
canopied by the branches stands a saint.

2. A good painting of the first monk, St. Antony,
which the priest declares to be 900 years old : but he
seems mistaken by some centuries.

3. Abu-'s-Sifain. The southermost door opens
into a similar little room, railed off from the sanctuary,
and used as a sacristy. Here are some books and
vestments.

vi. The haikal or sanctuary is of course entered
by the central door. It is raised one step above the
choir and therefore three above the nave : and is
remarkable for a singularly fine tribune in the apse,
the wide arc of which spans not only the sanctuary
but also the two side chambers which are railed off
from it by crossbar woodwork. The floor of the
haikal is oblong and the altar stands nearly in the
midst : eastward the tribune rises in two stages
filling the area of the arc. Three narrow straight
steps, faced with red and white marble alternately,
lead up to the first stage or landing, which is semicircular : thence two curved steps which follow it
round lead to a broader landing bounded only by
the apse wall, or rather by the wide marble bench
which runs round the apse wall forming the seat
for the presbyters. This bench is divided in the

midst by the patriarch's throne which like all the tribune is of marble. At the back of the throne, before which is a single step, a niche is hollowed in the wall: the sides of the seat are of white marble and slope downwards between marble posts. These posts or pillars have oval caps resembling those on early Muslim tombs.

In the niche is a fresco representing our Lord: and over the arch of the niche another wall-painting in form of a triptych, which contains in the centre panel a head girt with six wings crossed in pairs representing the seraphim: and in each side panel the figure of an angel. This triptych is about 2 ft. high and cuts into an oblong space of wall, some 12 ft. by 4, overlaid with fine blue and green porcelain tiles, which enclose also two panels of plain colour. On each side of the tiles is a row of six large pictures, or rather a continuous wooden panel with painted arcading, containing figures of the twelve apostles. Here the perpendicular wall ends and the curve of the dome begins. Upon this curve directly above the tiles is a semicircular fresco representing Christ in glory upheld by two angels. A conventional border encloses this painting, and at its highest point is the figure of an eagle with outspread wings slaying a serpent. The rest of the dome is plain whitewash.

Below the row of apostles the wall is painted with a large diaper pattern in flat colours.

To the left of the lowest steps, in the wall that forms the chord of the arc, is a small recess or aumbry. Within it is a curious little wooden stand, for a vessel of chrism which is used to anoint the steps

ere the patriarch mounts his throne. In the same
aumbry may be seen an ancient iron or bronze lamp
of very unusual design—a kind of low-rimmed bowl
with seven lips for as many wicks, and a flat raised
handle at the back. It is made of a single piece of
metal. The iron stand on which the lamp is placed
when kindled is also a singular and pretty piece of
rude work, and may be seen resting and rusting òn
the tribune. This lamp is used only once a year,
at the festival of Abu-'s-Sifain. The bronze ewer
mentioned by Murray seems to have disappeared :
for in answer to my questions the sacristan always
replied that it was under repair. The basin 'in blue
and green enamel' still exists in very filthy condition,
but the description is scarcely accurate. Six little
bosses round the bowl inside are enamelled, but
otherwise the basin is quite plain, and by no means
specially beautiful. The altar, standing nearly in
the midst of the sanctuary and overshadowed by a
canopy, is 3 ft. 4 in. high, 7 ft. 1 in. long from north
to south, and 4 ft. 3 in. broad from east to west. It
has the usual depression for the altar-board on top,
and the cavity for relics; but though built of masonry in the orthodox manner, it is cased in wood,
for some reason unknown. Over the wood is the
usual tight-fitting covering of brocade.

The altar-canopy or baldacchino is a dome resting
on woodwork with four open pointed arches, which
spring from four marble pillars. The two eastern
pillars stand at a distance of 2 ft. from the nearest
corner of the altar : the two western at a distance
of 2 ft. 8 in., close against the screen. The canopy
projects on all sides over the altar and the pillars
stand clear, so that the celebrant can move round

the altar without passing from under the canopy:
but the centre of the canopy is not quite over
the centre of the altar.

The whole underpart of the dome is richly painted.
At each of the four corners inside, where the arches
spring from the pillars, is a large figure of an angel
kneeling: a glory shines round his head; his wings
are raised and outspread to the utmost on each side,
so that they follow the curve of the arch. Thus the
tips of the wings of the four angels meet together.
Just underneath the meeting tips of the wings, i.e.
at the point of every arch, a small circle is painted
enclosing a cross in red and gold colours. All the
four angels with uplifted hands grasp and hold above
their heads a golden circle. Within this circle is
another golden ring concentric with it, and in the
space between stand the four apocalyptic symbols,
each bearing a golden gospel and crowned with a
glory. They are divided one from another by circles—
one circle at each cardinal point of the compass: in
the eastern and western circles is an eight-rayed
star; north and south are two suns or sun-like faces,
one eclipsed, one shining in strength. The inner
golden ring, or the centre of the dome, is charged
with a half-length figure of the Redeemer. The nimb
is lettered 'O ΩN: the right hand is raised in benediction; the left carries the book of the gospel. On
the dexter side of the head are the letters CX, on the
sinister CI, curiously written backwards, instead of
IC XC, or Jesus Christ. The line of the figure
runs east and west, the head lying towards the
western star.

Each spandrel of the canopy *outside*, fronting the
choir and visible from it, is decked with a haloed

angel holding a palm. All the arches are pointed as mentioned above, and from each point an ostrich egg hangs down by a short chain. The caps of the four pillars are joined by spars on which rings are fastened, doubtless used in ancient times to suspend the curtains that veiled the altar. These spars are joined by cross-beams which form a cross above the altar, thus ⛢. High above the ground the whole sanctuary is covered with a network of flying spars, crossing each other, and used for hanging lamps.

Before quitting the haikal one may notice that the back part or inside of the screen, the choirward face of which is so magnificent, shows nothing but the rude skeleton framework without any pretence of concealment or adornment. This contrast however is usual, not exceptional.

vii. The south aisle of Abu-'s-Sifain extends the whole length of the church except the sanctuary: it is divided by three rough screens into four sections, the easternmost of which contains a font; for the whole aisle is used as a baptistery. The font is a round basin 3 ft. deep, embedded in masonry, enclosed by a sort of wooden cupboard and surmounted by a little wooden canopy. The doors of the cupboard are very rudely painted with flowers. From the second division of this baptistery one may get behind the south screen of the men's section. There, lying disused and forgotten on the ground, are two coronae—one of bronze circular, and one of wood octagonal, tapering in stages pierced with holes for glass lamps.

One other object of interest remains to be noted— the curious ancient winepress of rough woodwork, which ordinarily lies in the western division of the baptistery. Every year, however, in the spring, it is transported to the chapel of Abu-'s-Sifain next the church of Ḥârat-az-Zuailah in Cairo. The grapes, or rather raisins, are placed in rush mats between two round wooden trays, the lower of which is fixed, the upper moveable and worked by a screw lever. The whole is mounted on a heavy wooden frame.

THE EXTERIOR CHAPELS OF ABU-'S-SIFAIN.

Just beyond the doorway leading down to the chapel of Barsûm al 'Ariân is another on the same side, leading out of the church and into a courtyard roofed with palm-beams. In the left corner of the courtyard is the door of the bakehouse, where the eucharistic breads are made, and where the wooden die for stamping them is kept. Opposite, in a recess, are six or seven large waterpots in a masonry setting: close by is a well, and a staircase for mounting to the upper chapels.

From the courtyard a roofed passage leads eastward to a cluster of tiny chapels, more resembling dungeons than shrines or places of worship. First on the left comes

The Chapel of St. Gabriel.

Here a scanty light falls through a small open grating in the roof, which a solitary Corinthian column upholds. The chapel consists merely of choir and haikal, but there is a curious side section for the women, very narrow, but aligning the sanctuary as well as the choir. The woodwork of the haikal screen is very rude, and the icons above it—Christ and the twelve Apostles—are . mere daubs. Rude painting replaces inlaying in the spandrels of the doorway.

At the end of the passage, candles must be lighted to show the way. Turning to the right, one passes through two heavy open screens into a small *baptistery*, where there is a font, or rather large basin of stone, built up in masonry. The basin is circular, with a square enlargement east and west, at the bottom of which are two steps, obviously adapted for immersion, although the font is not more than about four feet in depth. It was in this font, according to the legend of the priest, that the Sultan Mu'azz was baptized on his conversion to Christianity.

Leaving the baptistery, one passes under an archway into

The Chapel of St. John the Baptist,

consisting merely of choir and sanctuary. It was in the haikal of this chapel that I found, lying unknown in dust and darkness, the beautiful altar-casket, now in the north aisle-chapel of Abu-'s-Sifain. An archway separates St. John from the adjoining

Chapel of St. James,

but the same screen is continued, and serves for both sanctuaries. The work is poor : so are the paintings. Both these chapels, built in dark, low, vaulted recesses, with round arches springing here and there, are very crypt-like.

Returning towards the doorway of the passage facing north one sees in front a thick open screen, beyond which lies

The Chapel of Mâri Buktor.

This is larger than St. John and St. James, and the haikal is more artistic. The pictures are worthless. Over the sanctuary door, Mâri Buktor is represented in a large painting, on horseback. The altar here is remarkable for a curious variation. It has no altar-board, but a large slab of marble is inlet into the top, and is carved with a horse-shoe depression to the depth of two inches: within this depression is another of like form, but shallower, and with a channel or groove tending westward, but blocked by a ridge at the outlet. This altar-top resembles one at Al Mu'allakah.

Buktor, it may be noted, is the Arabic form of Victor.

THE UPPER CHAPELS OF ABU-'S-SIFAIN.

Mounting now the staircase, one arrives in the open air, on a flat roof. This story is about half the height of the main building: on it the triforium runs round the church : and outside is another cluster of chapels, over those in the crypt-like buildings below.

East of the landing is a small roofless enclosure: a door in the farthest wall opens with a wooden key, and shows beyond

The Chapel of St. Antony,

in three divisions. Between the women's section
and the choir (which serves also for the men) is an
open screen, surmounted by a plain wooden cross—
an uncommon arrangement. The haikal-screen is of
an ordinary geometrical design. The altar-canopy

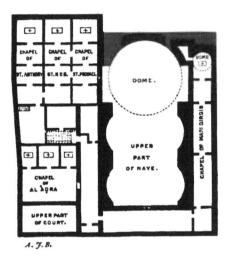

Fig. 7.—The Upper Chapels of Abu-'s-Sifain.

is painted, and has been extremely beautiful, but is
now rotting to pieces. Behind the altar, in the
niche, is a dim fresco of the Virgin and Child, a
very unusual subject for this position, which is
nearly always occupied by a pourtrayal of our
Lord in glory. The whole of this chapel, except
the haikal, is roofless, and answers the purpose of
a fowl-house.

Returning and passing through another door, one enters a double chapel—two similar chapels side by side, divided only by an open screen : each of them has a place for women and for men, besides choir and haikal.   In the first, called

The Chapel of Abba Nûb,

the sanctuary screen is of very intricate and graceful workmanship, though the icons are very rustic-looking.   Within the haikal is a fine niche, faced with little Damascus tiles of rich colour.

The other, called

. The Chapel of St. Michael,

is also remarkable for a good screen, and a very pleasing picture of the angel Michael holding a sword in his right hand and a balance in his left. Other decayed and battered paintings stand about the walls on shelves.   From this chapel a window, or rather shutter, opens, giving a view of the sanctuary of Abu-'s-Sifain below.   One sees that the roof of the altar-canopy is painted with bands of colour, and is surmounted by a cross of gilt metal.

Leaving these chapels, and returning to the landing, one passes now along beside a low coping, over which, through a huge grating of palm beams, may be seen the courtyard below, near the bakehouse.   A doorway now leads from the open air into a corridor, which corresponds to and lies over the entrance passage or north aisle below, and therefore belongs to the triforium of the church.   A few paces forward one discovers on the right,

The Church of Al' Adra.

This is not in the triforium, but quite outside the walls of Abu-'s-Sifain, built in fact over that half of the guest-room which was described as being roofed in, but projecting further eastward, not coextensive with it. The western wall of this chapel is merely an open screen, through which one may look down upon the floor of the guest-room. This little church is divided into women's section, choir, and haikal: but it contains three altars, in three separate sanctuaries at the east end. The roof alone shows indications of a former division into nave and aisles: for while at each side it is low and horizontal, in the centre it is arched into a semi-decagon. The eastern gable is filled with a window, in which are some quarries of coloured glass.

In the nave is a large picture of the Virgin and Child, noticeable only for the fact that Christ is holding a regal orb. A St. George, a pair of unknown saints, and the icons, are all clownish performances.

The canopy over the central altar, upheld on four horizontal beams, shows now only dim traces of its former splendour, but some figures of lions are distinguishable. The niche in the eastern wall is unusual in size and in structure. It is nine feet high, and six feet broad, and covered with most beautiful old Persian or Damascus tiles, of a design and colour which seem to be unique: the ground of the tiles is an extremely delicate olive hue, upon which clusters of marigolds are figured in very dark green.

The adjacent chapel on the south contains in the wall-niche a dim monochrome fresco of the baptism of our Lord. St. John is standing on a high rock by the river-side, and pouring water on Christ's head: above, a dove is descending, and sending down three rays : at each side is a tree laden with fruit—perhaps pomegranate—and another very curious shrub, possibly an aloe, but exactly like a Gothic pinnacle on a Gothic turret. It is probable that the whole of this chapel, indeed the whole building of Abu-'s-Sifain, was once painted where now the walls are merely white-washed: here for instance, where a piece of plaster is broken away beside the niche, bands of colour are visible below. Certainly the contrast between the bare white walls which form the shell of the building, and the magnificence of the fittings, is singular.

The end of the corridor is screened off, making a dim empty chamber. Turning now into the western part of the triforium, which lies over the narthex, one finds it quite devoid of ornament. In the right-hand wall are a number of blocked window-bays, but no windows, save the little oriels noticed outside. The eastern wall, however, is pierced with an opening, eight feet by six feet, from which a mushrablah framework projects into the nave. This opening is so high above the floor, that no one standing in the triforium can see into the church below: it cannot therefore have been meant for women. The view from this point, as one looks down over the golden-pictured nave to the choir, and the haikal beyond, with its painted canopy, is surprising, and admirable in its tone of dim religious splendour.

Where the plaster has fallen from this corridor wall, one sees that it is built of small brick, laid in fine hard cement. The priest said this wall has stood since the church was built.

At the end of this passage, as in the corresponding corner of the church below, are the latrines.

The third corridor, i. e. the south triforium, is walled off, and forms by itself a single long chapel called

The Chapel of Mâri Girgis.

Three transverse screens of plain design divide it into women's section, men's section, choir, and sanctuary. In the second division is a very curious wooden ambon, or pulpit, let into the north wall. It is merely a little box adorned in front with geometrical designs. The stone staircase is cut off abruptly, the lowest step being four feet above the ground, so that it cannot be mounted without the aid of a ladder. The choir of this chapel retains part of the ancient panelled roof which probably once covered the whole triforium. The beams and coffers are sumptuously gilt and coloured in the style of the thirteenth century: but only faint relics of its former beauty remain. Such work is distinctively Arabian, not Byzantine. The pictures here—St. Michael, mounted with a projecting frame and a candlebeam on brackets in front, the Virgin, and Abu-'s-Sifain,—are old but rude, and in ruinous condition.

The haikal-screen is exceptional, differing from all others in the church in its unconventional, un-geometric character. It is made up of a number of small oblong panels set in mouldings, and variously carved with vine-leaves, crosses, and figures of saints.

The cedar-wood of which it is composed is unfortunately so much decayed that the figures cannot
easily be identified. The haikal is entirely roofed
with a small dome, the south dome of the main
building as seen from without. The wall-niche
behind the altar contains a fresco of Christ in an
aureole [1] throned, holding a gospel in the left, and
raising the right hand in benediction. North of the
altar, in a small irregular chamber which opens out of
the sanctuary, and may have been used to guard the
sacred vessels, the curved wall of the main apse
may be seen starting.

Historical Note on the Church of
Abu-'s-Sifain.

The materials for the history of Abu-'s-Sifain are
very scanty, and to separate the true from the
legendary would require much fine winnowing. But
there can be little doubt that Makrîzi is mistaken in
stating that the church was built by the patriarch
Christodulus [2], c. 1060 A.D. A very strong tradition
assigns to it an earlier origin, and connects its
foundation with the Sultan Mu'azz, the builder of
Cairo, in the tenth century. Here is the legend as
given by Renaudot [3].

---

[1] I avoid the word 'vesica' as both ugly and inappropriate.
[2] Malan's History of the Copts, p. 92.
[3] Hist. Pat. Alex. p. 369 seq.

The khalíf having heard that it was written in the
gospel of the Christians that if a man had faith he
could by his word remove a mountain, sent for the
patriarch Ephraim, and asked if this strange story
were true.   On the patriarch answering that it was
indeed so written, the khalíf replied, 'Then do this
thing before mine eyes; else I will wipe out the very
name of Christian.'   When the tidings spread, great
was the consternation among all the churches : a
solemn assembly of clergy and monks was held, and
prayers with fasting were continued for three days,
without ceasing, in Al Mu'allakah.   On the third
morning the patriarch, worn out with watching and
fasting, fell asleep, and saw in a dream the Blessed
Virgin, to whom he told the matter, and was bidden
to be of good cheer, and to go out into the street
where he would find a one-eyed man carrying a
vessel of water.

So the patriarch went out, and meeting a man
bearing a pitcher, bade him kiss the cross and tell
the story of his life.   Thereon the water-carrier said,
'I was born with two eyes even as other men : but
according to the scripture, I plucked out one eye to
enter the kingdom of heaven, rather than have two
and go to hell-fire.   All day long, from morning till
night, I work as a dyer of wool; I eat nought but
bread; the rest of my wages I give in alms to the
poor, and by night I draw water for the poor.'   Then
hearing of the patriarch's vision, he told him to go
without fear to the khalíf, bearing in procession
crosses and gospels and censers, and his faith should
prevail.

Then a great multitude of Christians went to the
place appointed, where the khalíf and his court

were assembled before a mountain: and when the patriarch had made solemn prayers, crosses and gospels were lifted on high amid the smoke of burning incense, and as all the people shouted together ' Kyrie Eleëson,' the mountain trembled and removed.

Thereon Mu'azz promised to grant Ephraim whatsoever he might desire: and the patriarch demanded the rebuilding of the church of Abu-'s-Sifain. So the church was rebuilt.

It is to be noticed that in this legend only restoration is spoken of, as if an earlier church on the same site had suffered destruction. It is curious to find the legend surviving to this day, though in a somewhat changed form. The story, as related to me by the present priest of Abu-'s-Sifain, is briefly as follows:—The khalîf Mu'azz, founder of Cairo, hearing much of the godly life of the Christians, their devotion to their prophet, and the wonderful things written in their scripture, sent for the chief among the Christians and the chief among the elders of his own people, and commanded a solemn reading first of the Gospel of Christ, then of the Kurân. After hearing both with great attention, he decided very resolutely 'Muḥammad ma fîsh'— Mohammed is nothing, nobody, or nowhere,—ordered the mosque against the church of Anba Shanûdah to be pulled down, and the church of Abu-'s-Sifain to be rebuilt or enlarged in its place. The ruins of this mosque still remain between the two churches. The priest added that the khalîf Mu'azz became a Christian, and was afterwards baptized in the baptistery beside the chapel of St. John.

The coincidence of the two legends—the one

written down from hearsay by Al Makīn in the fourteenth century, the other current among the Copts
of to-day—is enough I think to establish the fact
that the church was either built or rebuilt in the
time of Mu'azz, that is, c. 980 A. D. The traditions
of the church fix the date of its foundation very
precisely at 927 A. D., and I see no reason to doubt it.

There is another early legend [1] which assumes
the existence of the church a little later than Mu'azz
—in the time of the XLIII patriarch Philotheus, who
reigned from about 981 to 1002 A. D. The story is
that once a certain Wazah, a Mohammedan, seeing a
Christian convert being dragged to execution in Old
Cairo, reviled him and beat him with his shoe. Some
time later Wazah, returning through the desert from
a pilgrimage to Mecca, strayed from his companions
and lost his way. While wandering about the mountains, he saw a vision of a horseman clad in shining
armour, and girt with a golden girdle. The horseman questioned him, and hearing his case bade him
mount behind him. In a moment they were caught up
through the air to the church of Abu-'s-Sifain, where
the horseman vanished. Next morning Wazah was
found in the church by the doorkeeper, who at first
thought him mad, but on learning what had happened
pointed out the picture of Abu-'s-Sifain, whom
Wazah now recognised from the golden girdle.
Wazah believed, was baptized, and retired as a
monk to the monasteries of the Natrun desert.
Thence he returned to Old Cairo, was thrown into
prison and starved by his family, but relieved by
St. Mercurius: then he was accused before the

---

[1] Renaudot, Hist. Pat. Alex. 374 seq.

Sultan but pardoned, and became a great writer of Christian books.

It seems then that the claims of Christodulus may be dismissed. The only other notices of the church that I have found are later. The LXX patriarch, Gabriel Ibn Tarĭkh, was a deacon of Abu-'s-Sifain [1], elected 1131 A.D. The church is stated by Maḳrĭzi to have been burnt down about the year 1170 A.D., 'in the fire of Shauer the Vizier'[2] on the 18th day of Hator. But towards the middle of the next century the scandalous Cyril, the LXXV patriarch, after his second imprisonment, celebrated with great pomp in the church on the feast of the patron saint[3]. It may be mentioned that the festival of St. Mercurius is the 15th day of the month Hator, corresponding to our 21st of November[4].

THE NUNNERY CALLED DAIR AL BANÂT,

OR THE CONVENT OF THE MAIDENS, IN DAIR ABU-'S-SIFAIN.

It was only after many visits to Abu-'s-Sifain that I had the good fortune to discover the Convent of the Maidens[5]. Guide-books know nothing about it, and I never met a Cairene, at least a European,

---

[1] Malan's History of the Copts, p. 93.

[2] Id. p. 95.   [3] Renaudot, Hist. Pat. Alex. p. 582.

[4] Malan's Calendar of the Coptic Church, p. 12.

[5] Sir Gardner Wilkinson is of course wrong in stating that 'Egypt is entirely destitute of nunneries' (Modern Egypt and Thebes, vol. i. p. 392 : London, 1843). Besides Dair al Banât there are two others in Cairo.

who had heard of it. The patriarch and some few other Copts are perhaps aware of its existence: but the idea that it possesses any special interest or beauty would probably strike them with astonishment. It is one of the most out-of-the-world and picturesque places imaginable: and if the inmates resort there in search of tranquillity, they have it to perfection in their surroundings. Dair Abu-'s-Sifain itself stands like a walled oasis in the desert of dust and potsherds which stretches for miles south of Cairo: no wheeled thing ever enters there, and its peace is unbroken by any stir and clamour of life or noise of the world. In old times the clash of swords and the shouts of battle were often heard under the walls and in the narrow streets: now its stillness is almost unearthly.

The lane in which the churches of Anba Shanûdah and Abu-'s-Sifain stand seems a cul-de-sac, but a little way beyond the latter church it really opens out by a narrow passage: a few turns at sharp angles, still between high walls, bring one to the outer convent door. Thence a straight dark passage of twenty yards, and another door which is barred and bolted. There is no knocker, though the knocker is seldom missing from an old Arab house, and many of the designs in plain ironwork are of great beauty. But a few gentle taps will bring the porteress. 'Who is there?' and 'open' are the usual question and answer: she opens and stands shyly with a corner of her veil drawn over her mouth. Permission to enter is readily given by the mother superior—a tall and rather comely matron, who receives one with a frank smile of welcome.

Just at the entrance in a recess to the right lies a

very pretty well with a windlass above, and pitchers
and other water-vessels scattered about in charming
disorder.   To the left is the small but beautiful
courtyard of the convent overshadowed by a fine
tall nabuk or zizyphus tree, which rises near the
well and mounts in a sweeping curve into the midst
of the court: higher up its branches spread out,
and their graceful leaves brush against the upper
windows.   The east face of the court is formed
by a large open screen of woodwork, with two
circular steps leading up to an open doorway with
tall folding doors in the centre.   Inside is a long
shallow room, 15 ft. by 7, with a kuramâni carpet
and some cushions or pillows against the wall.   Here
the nuns recline at their ease, and on feast days their
friends are regaled with such good things as the
convent provides.   It is in fact the mandârah or
reception-room.   It opens to the north by a high
pierced wooden screen into a tiny oratory, 10 ft. by
6, which has a low niche eastward containing a
picture of the Virgin, and a shelf running round the
wall with several other paintings.   There is also a
curious wooden candlestick in the form of a cross
with an iron pricket on each of the three branches.
Of the pictures two or three are noticeable.   There
is an old picture of the Virgin and Child, in which
the Child is seated on the Virgin's right arm, and is
clasping her neck: he wears a golden dress, and the
background of the painting is gold.   There is also
a curious sixteenth-century picture with a background
the lower half of which is pale green, the upper half
gold (as in the series at Sitt Mariam).   It shows two
figures, who wear glories edged with a red margin:
leftward St. Anthony robed as a priest, with staff and

scroll : rightward St. Paul the anchorite, dressed in sackcloth, and wearing a rosary hung at his girdle. His long beard falls down in front; his open angular arms are half raised; and a raven in the air is bringing him food : at his feet are two lions, his usual symbol.   The other paintings call for no remark.

So much for the east side of the courtyard.   The north consists of a large rude whitewashed balcony supported on two piers of masonry, and backed by a high wall.   A small bell pulled by a rope from below hangs at one corner, and underneath is a stone bench. But it is the eastern wall that moves one most to admiration.   This is the front of the house in which the nuns live, a fine, tall, three-storied house in good Arab style.   The topmost story has a large panel of mushrabiah work framed into the wall.   Below this comes a true mushrabiah or projecting bay-window of carved woodwork, not glazed but covered with extremely fine and delicate grills of wood.   This first story as usual in old Arab houses projects some three feet beyond the ground story.   There are two doors below, one in each corner, and the space between is lightened in a singular manner.   Half is walled : half occupied by an open screen of woodwork, divided horizontally into belts or sections, and the sections again into panels, each of which has its own design.   The effect is charming from the ingenious variety of pattern and the light airy look of the whole, in contrast with the solid walls beside and above.

But the mother superior comes to say coffee is ready.   We re-enter the reception-room, and sit down on the carpet in oriental fashion, or recline against a cushion. A nun hands each of us a tiny china cup resting in a brass zarf or holder. We drink, making many salâms to the mother superior, who does not disdain the formality of a cigarette: though the nuns apparently are not given to the practice of smoking. Against the wall opposite is a large and beautiful old bench; on this three or four damsels are sitting, or squatting, with modest eyes downcast on their embroidery. They are clad in the ordinary black Arab dress, but wear no veils; their wrists are circled with bangles or bracelets of massive silver; they wear also necklets of silver or gold, beads or brass, and earrings and anklets. Their quiet, shy, incurious manner, and the tranquil smile about their lips denote admirably the peaceful anchorite retirement of their lives. Under the bench lie scattered about crocks and pitchers and millstones; close by is an old brass mortar, and near the door an exquisitely designed little brazier of octagon shape with legs and pinnacles; its sides are finely chased and engraved with Arabic characters. Charcoal embers are glowing in it, and on them a coffee-jug is simmering as one of the maidens, kneeling, fans the fire with a fan of falcon feathers. High over all the nabuḳ tree is lazily waving its branches, across which the sun is striking: and the blue above seems deeper and more dazzling than ever, as the eye follows up the sombre colours of the wall.

But the scene varies from day to day. Sometimes the maidens are busy with needlework, sometimes tidying and cleaning the house or the vessels; and another time one may see a group sitting in the middle of the courtyard sifting and

winnowing corn, while close by a crone is grinding
beans, turning the handle of the millstone with her
left, and feeding the mill continually with her right
hand. The pigeons know when it is a corn-day;
and their ceaseless cooing as they perch about the .
mills, and the noise of their beating wings as they
sweep down and up again, add not a little to the
charm of the scene.

Out of the courtyard, round behind the mandârah,
is an open stable, where the convent cow is stalled
which supplies milk and butter to the inmates. On
occasion too she turns the flour-mill, which is a
curious antique structure in a room adjoining.
There is a brick-walled pit about 3 ft. deep and
12 across; in the middle a big cogwheel revolves
on a heavy wooden pivot, which turns above at a
height of 8 ft. in a solid beam running into the
north and south walls of the mill-room. From the
pivot a thick crooked pole rises and projects beyond
the edge of the pit to receive the yoke of the ox.
The millstones which are turned by wheels in connexion with the large cogwheel, are not in the pit
but sunk beside it: above them is a wooden frame
to hold the corn, and below a receptacle for the
flour. There is an Arabic inscription on this frame
rudely carved, with date 1480 A.D. On the transverse beam between the two walls are cut the
triangular symbol of the Trinity in a border, and
the 'svastica' or revolving wheel of light, the
original symbol of the worship of the sun in the
East, and the earliest known ornament. It is a
mere coincidence: but not without its significance.
From the stable a rough stone staircase leads up
to a flat roof, on which there are two little streets

or corridors of cells. Each cell has its own door,
but no window; all seem disused, containing
only palm-fibres for ropes, some baskets, broken
pitchers, and two little lamps of the old Arabic
pottery, thickly glazed in very beautiful colours,
turquoise blue and emerald green. One finds fragments of such lamps at all depths in the rubbish
heaps at Old Cairo. There is nothing else here
to notice except a small but curious wooden cross,
of Latin form, with a leathern bag attached to the
branches, the use of which is to collect alms. It is
evidently ancient and long disused, and is the only
example I have seen of this instrument.

There are fifteen inmates in all—ten besides the
mother superior and four servants. Admission is
granted by the patriarch to any young girl left
resourceless and helpless, or even to a widow.
Indeed the refuge is rather an almshouse than a
nunnery. The inmates are allowed to receive their
friends sometimes, or even to go to Cairo for a day
to pay visits. No conventual vows are required.
There is no veil to be taken; rather in the convent
the veil is laid aside; so far out of the world it is
not needed. Nor is marriage forbidden. If a girl
discovers relations who will receive her, or if she
finds a husband, she may open the door and walk
out. Their life is very quiet and simple. A bell
rings at dawn to arouse them; they all rise and
pray together; then they busy themselves in household work, cleansing, cooking, embroidery, and the
like; and when there is nothing special to do,—as
the priest naively put it,—they read the gospel and
pray again. Every Saturday evening the priest
holds a service in their little oratory. They have,

however, in theory at least, their seven daily offices or hours. The psalms form a large part of their devotional exercises; and I have seen manuscript books of psalms and other service-books in Coptic and Arabic written by present inmates of the convents with very considerable skill and finish.

THE CHURCH OF ANBA SHANÛDAH (انبا شنوده),

IN DAIR ABU-'S-SIFAIN.

ANBA Shanûdah stands close to Abu-'s-Sifain, as was before mentioned; their western walls are in a line, with a distance of some twenty yards dividing them. But the plain modernised stone front of Anba Shanûdah is neither curious in structure nor pleasing in colour, like the blind high wall of ancient brick that fronts Abu-'s-Sifain. The doorway is at the north-west corner and opens into a dim broad passage, the latter end of which is cut out of the north aisle of the church. But about the middle of the passage there is a door on the right through which one sees the ancient and very pretty well of the church. Water is drawn by means of a pulley suspended on a beam above; the well is set round with a low cone-like coping of stone, and is most picturesquely placed between rude lofty walls and doorless unillumined chambers, some of which are entrances to vaults of departed worthies of the church. In the background is a rough stone stair-

case, and troughs, pitchers, and water-jars are lying
at random about the stone-floor. In these little
scenes everything is so uniformly picturesque that
only the naturalness of the result saves it from the
suggestion of studied arrangement. The well lies
outside the west end of the church; the entrance
is on the north, near the end of the passage, and
leads into the women's section. For there is no
narthex at Anba Shanûdah, and consequently no

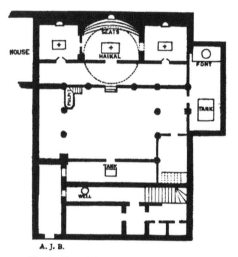

Fig. 8.—Plan of the Church of Anba Shanûdah.

western triforium. The women's section, if ever it
were intended for women, which is very doubtful,
is only about 6 ft. wide (east to west), and is railed
off by a heavy railing of rectangular pattern only
4 ft. high. It contains a small tank for ablution or
for the mandatum.

The church consists of nave,—which is divided
into men's section and women's section, and is
covered with a high-pitched roof like that at Abu-'s-

Sifain,—north and south aisles, and an outer aisle southward, choir, and the usual three chapels side by side at the east end. The nave is marked off from the two aisles by marble pillars, most of which have classical capitals, and stood once in some Greek or Roman building. A continuous wooden architrave rests on the pillars to support the nave walls, which are lightened above by drop-arched openings, highly stilted, one between every two columns. These relieving arches are curiously varied on the south wall; for while on the naveward side they are pointed, half way through they change form, and as seen from the south aisle, are round-headed. There is no such change on the north side. The architrave bears traces of magnificent colours and Coptic letters, and is carved with crosses in relief, one between each pair of pillars. These may possibly be consecration crosses, although they are too high for the bishop to have anointed the places without a ladder.

The pulpit in the nave is a good piece of Arab carving in rosewood: the design is composed of crosses, which are made up of minute ivory scroll-work, like the ivory carvings at Abu-'s-Sifain. The angles of the pulpit are bound with small bronze clamps.

The screen between nave and choir is divided by two ancient columns into central and two side portions; and in each side portion is an ancient panel of cedar, framed by open wooden grills. These panels are beautifully inlaid with little blocks and crosses of ivory. The first time I visited this church a boy who was showing me round coolly took out a penknife and would have hacked at one of these crosses to get a piece of ivory.

The north aisle is only about 6 ft. deep, but the south aisle is itself much broader, and opens out again southward into an outer aisle, the western half of which contains a large Epiphany tank, the other a baptistery with stone font or basin under a wooden dome; a mushrabîah screen divides them.

In the choir is the usual lectern, draped in an embroidered cloth which covers the top and falls in front; a tall bronze candelabrum with silver censer swinging from the plate; a tongueless bell, cymbals, and a pair of coloured cloth alms-trays on the shelf of the lectern underneath. The easternmost screen is curious. To the right, before the south aisle-chapel, is a magnificent piece of work inlaid with ivories superbly carved. The style is the same as that at Abu-'s-Sifain. The back of the screen, as seen inside the chapel, is covered with rude flower paintings. Originally this was the iconostasis of the sanctuary or central chapel; but in true churchwarden fashion it was judged ugly and antiquated, and was degraded to a lower position in favour of a modern screen of red cedar plainly inlaid with a wheel-and-cross pattern of unchased ivory. The north iconostasis is again different. It is quite black, and consists of a number of tiny panels, each painted with a rude flower or branch in white. Exactly similar screenwork may be seen in the mosque of Sultan Barkûk, among the tombs of the khalîfs at Cairo, dating about 1400 A.D.

The structure of the dome, with its lofty arch springing from the choir piers to support it, re-

sembles that at Abu-'s-Sifain. One of the marble
columns against the choir-screen bears clear traces
of an ancient distemper painting—the figure of an
angel 4 ft. high; under it are worn Coptic letters.
But all through the church the surface of the
columns is fretted and frayed; at a mere touch of
the finger there falls off a fine white powder like
salt or snow crystals.

All round the choir, ranged on shelves, set in
niches, or mounted on mushrabíah frames, are
paintings of saints and angels. On the north wall
the most interesting is a figure of the patron saint,
Anba Shanûdah. He appears as a long-bearded
stumpy little man, with huddled shoulders and a
sad wistful look in his large eyes, as he clasps
a cross with folded hands before his breast. His
vestments are of singular splendour. A black
hood covers his head, but on the margin over the
forehead are three white crosses. The cope and
dalmatic are decked all over with the richest embroidery of flowers and crosses. He wears the
patrashîl with the twelve apostles figured in pairs—
six little pictures one above the other finely coloured.
There is a touch and tone about this painting which
suffice to mark it as fairly early, probably about the
sixteenth century. Later work is never so fine, or
so careful in detail.

Next comes the angel Gabriel holding a triple
cross and a pair of scales; he is standing on a red
bolster of relics.

On the screen are five pictures:

1. Michael the archangel carrying a scroll and
   holding in his left hand a round medallion
   enclosing a bust of the Redeemer.

2. Virgin and Child. The attitude is just that of the Sta. Maria of Cimabue. The Virgin has a typical Syrian face—half Greek and half Jew—and shows unusual emotion. But both faces are of an ugly brickdust colour; altogether it is an exceedingly poor picture.

3. Filtaûs on horseback.

4. In a wooden framework on a gold ground are two figures, Anba Shanûdah and Anba Rûais. Underneath lies a bolster of relics in a locker.

5. An angel badly daubed.

On the south wall of the choir are five large pictures:

1. Virgin and Child, both crowned. Mary's crown is held by two flying angels; she is giving a rose to the Child, who is reaching forth his right hand to receive it; his left is holding a golden orb.

2 and 3. Coptic saints.

4. A tall majestic figure of the angel Gabriel; he is standing on a relic bolster; in his left hand he is wielding a spear, in his right he holds a lily drooping, and grasps a medallion with a bust figure of Christ. His face wears a look of heavy wrath.

5. The Resurrection.

Against the choir-screen rest two loose pictures —(1) Paul the ascetic with his two lions in the wilderness: this is the founder of Dair Bolos in the eastern desert. (2) The Virgin with cross and palm, set round with twenty little figures bearing the same emblems.

Upon the haikal-screen, about 5 ft. from the

ground, is fastened a small wooden crewet-holder. For the icons stand the usual series of seven paintings : in the centre the Virgin throned and crowned by angels ; on either side three pairs of apostles, who all carry a cross in the right and a gospel in the left hand, and wear glories. Their faces are all of the same type, but two have grey beards, the rest black.

In the haikal both on the north and south side are doorways into the adjoining chapels, the former through a screen, the latter through a partition wall.

The haikal itself is apsidal and contains a tribune : but the side chapels are square. On the highest of the marble steps in the apse are nine loose pictures of no great merit, and in the central niche is a fresco of Christ in attitude of benediction. The high altar is covered by a plain deal canopy resting on four white marble columns : upon it lie vestments, candlesticks, altar-casket, and censers. In one corner of the sanctuary a graceful wooden stand holds a basin and plain earthenware pitcher, for the priest to wash his hands at the celebration of the ḳorbân.

In the south aisle-chapel one sees on the altar the same tumbled disarray. Torn books, dirty vestments, a bronze cross, altar-casket, and a very pretty wooden cross 8½ inches high inlaid with mother-of-pearl. The central design upon the cross is a small engraved figure of Christ crucified : on either side is a medallion—one containing a pair of arms crossed, the other containing a cross with smaller crosses between the branches ⧉ : above and below also are medallions chased with flowers. This is the nearest resemblance to a crucifix I have seen in any church.

In the niche are pitchers of clay and wickerwork bottles; a few flasks of wine, some loose leaves, and some old plain altar-caskets.

In the north aisle-chapel are two very curious pieces of church furniture—a chrismatory and a cresset-stone. The chrismatory is a round block of wood drilled with three large holes for the three kinds of oil for anointing : it has a lid revolving on a central pivot but not opening, only drilled with a single hole[1]. The cresset-stone is a slab of marble in the form of a semicircle, the chord of which is about 2 ft. 6 in. in length. Three parallel grooves follow the outlines, and in the inner semi-circle there formed are nine cuplike hollows for oil. The central hollow alone is pierced through with a small drain. The spaces between these nine circles are chased with designs of flowers. The stone is lying loose upon the ground, and the doorkeeper only tells one vaguely that it is something extremely ancient, but has no idea of its use : conceivably it may be an altar-slab.

The altar here is covered with a mass of old Coptic books—psalms and liturgies—piled together and crusted with dust. In the niche are broken ostrich eggs, and a large heap of leaves and fragments of books in the last stage of decay but showing traces of fine illumination. I saw no sign of any Greek, Latin, or Syriac manuscript, either in this or in any other church near Cairo, though I have always been alive to the chances of discovery.

---

[1] An illustration is given in the chapter on eucharistic vessels.

The Chapel of Mâri Girgis.

Passing out of the porchway past the well and up
a flight of steps, one reaches a series of flat roofs at
different levels, among which the high pointed roof
and the brick dome of Anba Shanûdah rise conspicuous. Along half the southern wall of the main
building, and forming a sort of triforium to it, is the

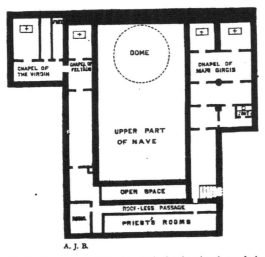

A. J. B.

Fig. 9.—Upper story of Anba Shanûdah, showing chapels attached.

chapel of Mâri Girgis. Its form is nearly square,
but a large pier, a column, and an arrangement of
screens divide it into six compartments—two western
chambers, one of which serves as a baptistery and
contains a pretty domed front panelled off by woodwork; a section for men running all across; then a
choir; and two haikals with altars. The iconostases
are beautiful pieces of wood and ivory work: the
doors especially are magnificent, blazoned with stars
and crosses and flowers of ivory.

The choir and nave screens are low open rails with tall uprights joined by horizontal spars: but the baptistery is fenced off by a splendid panel of mushrablah work. Inside this baptistery there is a recess in the wall, like a blind window-bay, at the back of which are nine extremely rude and ancient monochrome frescoes of saints with glories. The enormous size of the head in proportion to the body, the large starting eyeballs, and quaint pouting lips, are enough to prove the antiquity of these figures. The little chamber screened off from the rest of the baptistery to hide the font conceals also part of the frescoes. It has two little windows with slides and an arched doorway; a little lamp is hanging in front. The font is overshadowed by a tiny dome.

Mâri Girgîs is flat-roofed, and lighted by square gratings or skylights. Owls and bats enter freely, and find their way through the side windows into Anba Shanûdah below. The view from the roof of the chapel is exceedingly fine; to the east one sees long ranges of low rubbish hills backed by the white Mukaṭṭam mountains which trend away toward the lofty mosque and minarets of the citadel of Cairo: to the west one looks across what seems a forest of tamarisks and palms, between which now and then tall white sails are moving, while boats and river are alike unseen: and beyond the Nile rise the Pyramids of Gîzah in that distant blue aerial mist of excessive brightness, which is the charm of an Egyptian landscape.

Passing now round the west end of the main roof, one reaches a tiny courtyard—still on the first floor —whence opens a door. Under a low pointed arch of ancient brickwork one enters a chapel that runs the whole length of Anba Shanûdah, forming the north triforium, and is called *The Chapel of Filtaûs*, i.e. Philotheos,—perhaps the patriarch of that name, who was elected near the end of the tenth century. It is a long and narrow building divided into four sections by screens.

The women's section is bare and empty: from it four large oblong windows, half-blocked with fragments of lattice-work and coloured planks—relics of the old flat painted roof of the chapel—look down into Anba Shanûdah. Between this and the men's section is a railing 4 ft. high, with tall uprights joined at the top. Cross-beams are laid from this screen to that of the choir, which is of the same type, and on them curiously is placed a pulpit.

The choir has no ornaments but a few rotten pictures: and above the haikal-screen or iconostasis, which is ivory-inlaid, is a series of wretched daubs.

The haikal is domed, and the corner pendentives are of unusual size and boldness.

The church of Anba Shanûdah then as a whole is two-domed,—the third dome having probably been removed when the chapel of Mâri Girgis was built.

A door leading out of the choir of Filtaûs gives access to a small *Shrine of the Virgin*, which, like many of the upper chapels, is a mere fowl-house at present. It is a small nearly square room with four divisions. In one division there is a poor triptych with a date showing an age of about a century; and facing it, nailed at the back of the screen, is a tablet of wood with an Arabic inscription in extremely rude and ancient characters very much resembling Cufic.

It is as follows, in three lines :—

يا رب اغفر خطايا عبيدك و نيح

نفوسهم الذين هذا من

اجلهم و عوض من له تعب في الملاكوت

i. e. O Lord, forgive the sins of thy servants, and give rest to their souls, those for whose sake (is) this (church): and reward in the kingdom him who has taken these pains.

This inscription is said to be dedicatory of the chapel—800 years old. The words of the last line 'reward, &c.' are those ordinarily employed, the formula of dedication of any object. On pictures, crosses, screens, the formula occurs with scarcely any variation. The word نيح naîah in the first line would seem to imply that the church was built by a patriarch. For even at the present day the word 'tanaîah' is used when a patriarch or bishop is dead. The Copts say, 'Al baṭrak tanaîah'—'the patriarch has entered into his rest,' not 'is dead.'

HISTORICAL NOTE ON THE CHURCH OF
ANBA SHANÛDAH.

Shanûdah (Arabic), Shanuti (Coptic), or Sanutius (Latin) is a common name in Coptic history[1]. Of

---

[1] There is a learned dissertation on the origin of the name by A. Georgius in his Fragmentum Evangelii S. Johannis, p. cliv seq.

the two patriarchs who bore it, the first, who was elected in 859 A.D., was as distinguished for his singular virtues, as his namesake, elected 170 years later, was for his notorious vices. It is the former who is said to have established the Coptic way of writing the sacred letters still in vogue[1]. But the church of Anba Shanûdah takes its name from neither of these patriarchs, but from a famous anchorite of the fifth century, who rose to high dignity in the church, and went as a bishop to the Council of Ephesus. A brief notice of his life will be found among the legends.

The date of the church cannot be fixed accurately, but it is without doubt earlier than Abu-'s-Sifain and may be assigned to the seventh or eighth century. The first mention of it occurs in a story quoted by Renaudot[2]. About the year 740 A.D., in the days of the turbulent Khail, one Kassim son of 'Abaïdullah came on horseback to Anba Shanûdah accompanied by his favourite mistress. The chief priest forbade them to enter, saying that no woman had ever ventured in without drawing the wrath of God on her head forthwith[3]. They persisted : but no sooner had they set foot within the church than the woman was stricken dead on the spot, and Kassim was seized with a devil, from which he never more was quite delivered. He gave 300 dinars to the church ;

(Rome, 1789, 4to.). He shows that the name means 'herald of God,' i.e. prophet.

[1] Malan's History of the Copts, p. 84.

[2] Hist. Pat. Alex., p. 203.

[3] The absence of provision for women to worship in the church lends a curious air of probability to the main facts of this story.

but some time after, hearing of a sumptuous ebony coffer inlaid with ivory, wherein the books of service were kept, he coveted it, and came with thirty men to carry it away. But finding they with all their force were unable to move it from its place, he departed and gave 300 more dinars to the church in token of repentance.

Thirty years later there is an incidental mention of the church in Al Maḳrîzi, where he states that Sitt Mariam, near Anba Shanûdah, was pulled down[1]: and early in the eleventh century the wild fanatic Al Ḥâkim Bî'amr Illâhi 'allowed the call to prayer from the church of Senuda in Misr[2],' which may mean either that he spared it, or, as seems more consistent with the context, that he turned it into a mosque.

The chapel of Filtaûs and the Shrine of the Virgin were probably built by the patriarch Philotheos about the year 990 A. D.; and it is worth notice that the triforium is entirely occupied by Filtaûs, and therefore was not designed to accommodate women at the services in the main building below. Al Maḳrîzi is very curt in his history of Philotheos: 'He lived 24 years and died: but he was a glutton[3].' Still he may have built chapels.

CHURCH OF AL 'AḌRA, CALLED BID-DAMSHÎRÎAH[4],
OR SITT MARIAM, IN DAIR ABU-'S-SIFAIN.

The church of Al 'Aḍra or Sitt Mariam, the Virgin or Lady Mary, is reached by the first turning to the

---

[1] History of the Copts, p. 80.   [2] Id. p. 90.   [3] Id. p. 88.

[4] العذرا بالدمشيريه. This is the official title, but the meaning of *Ad-Damshîrîah* is now quite unknown. The church is popularly

left after passing through the doorway of the dair. It has been recently repaired and has a newish look: but it has not lost all its interest.

Crossing a courtyard one arrives at the church door, which is on the south side. There is no porch, but a walled passage runs straight into the body of the church, dividing a baptistery, which occupies the south-west corner, from the southern aisle. In this

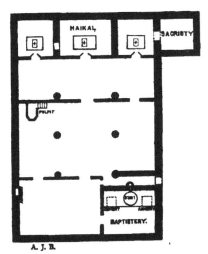

A. J. B.

Fig. 10.—Church of Sitt Mariam.

passage is a stone basin, very like a holy-water stoup, let into the wall: its purpose however is merely to feed the font in the baptistery, with which it communicates by a drain cut through the stone. The water-carrier thus has only to stand in the passage and empty his goatskin into the little basin, as often as required, till the font is filled.

---

called *Sitina Mariam* or *Sitt Mariam,* and I retain the latter here to distinguish it from the many other churches dedicated to *Al 'Adra.*

In structure Sitt Mariam is the most simple, regular, and symmetrical of all the churches. The whole plan is obvious at a glance : there are none of those errant side-chapels and wandering aisles which perplex Mâri Mîna and Abu-'s-Sifain. The division of the building longitudinally into nave and two aisles, and again laterally into narthex, nave and choir, is clear and precise. The main roof covering the nave is wagon-vaulted and very lofty; while that of the north and south aisles and narthex is low and horizontal. The aisles are marked off by six marble columns, three on each side. These columns are, as generally happens, of various sizes and orders, but their arrangement is regular. Above the capital of each pillar is a cubical block technically called a dosseret,—a very unusual arrangement in a Coptic church, and one stated by Texier and Pullan to be a distinctly Byzantine characteristic. These dosserets were originally cased in wood, carved in delicate pendentives, and finely coloured. Few traces of this casing now remain. Next above the dosseret comes a square pillar of masonry continuing the column upwards for 4 ft., the total height being 15 ft. Flat beams are laid across from pillar to pillar, forming a continuous architrave, upon which is built a wall rising to a height of 6 ft. before the spring of the wagon-vaulting begins. From the architrave also run at right angles on three sides, north, south, and west, towards the outer walls, a succession of horizontal beams to support the flat roof of the aisles and of the narthex.

The narthex now serves as a place for the women, but there is a complete triforium or gynaekonitis running all round. The wooden pulpit is in an

unusual place, the north aisle : it is very old, and
adorned with a fine geometrical design in cedar set
with little blocks of ebony.   This aisle also contains
a lattice-work patriarchal chair, the ordinary step-
ladder, and a candelabrum or two.   In the south aisle
are three poor and three ruined pictures.   Over the
choir doorway is a double-faced picture with the
Crucifixion navewards and the Resurrection showing
choirwards : it is recent and worthless, except as
indicating that the traditional place for the crucifixion is still recognised.   In almost all churches it
is found in this position.   It corresponds obviously
with the rood on the rood-screen in the early English
Church.

The sanctuary-screen itself is inlaid with plain
ivory, which forms a number of squares and crosses
upon it.   It is continued north and south by work
of a different and older kind, resembling that of
the pulpit,—fine Arabic mouldings, enclosing centres
of uncarved ebony.

On the north wall is a set of four pictures of
horsemen in a single frame of lattice-work.   On
the south wall are three sixteenth-century paintings, viz. :

1. The Baptism of Christ.
2. Abu Nafr, the eremite ; he is a strange gaunt
   figure, represented as gathering dates from
   a palm tree in the desert.
3. Anba Shanûdah and his pupil Wîsah.

Another sixteenth century painting is a shrine-like
picture of the Virgin and Child on the screen against
the wall which divides the haikal from the north aisle-
chapel ; it bears a date corresponding to 1541 A.D.
The ground is gold.   The Virgin is throned, holding

the Child; her crown is upheld by two flying angels who have blue wings and red robes with scarlet streamers. The Virgin's robe as usual has a hood raised over the head, the outlines coming down and meeting at a point on the breast. The colours are soft, and the decoration of the robes and work of the crown is very delicate; but Mary's face and hands are poorly drawn. Upon the expression of the Child's countenance much more care has been spent; and the artist seems really to have caught a glimpse of ideal beauty.

The iconostasis has on either side a crewet-holder, and above the usual series of twelve apostles with the Virgin for a centrepiece. The apostles stand in pairs under arches, and are painted on a dim gold ground.

There is a smaller series of five unusually interesting pictures over the screen of the south chapel. The priest assured me that there was no date, but by climbing a ladder and peering closely in the dim light, I discovered figures giving the equivalent in the Coptic era of 1478 A.D. The background is curiously divided between two colours; the lower half is a soft olive green, the upper half a clear gold: but in all, except the central picture, the top corners also are marked off with green. The triangular spaces so formed are tricked with a sort of scrollwork in faint yellow. The whole tone is very rich and pleasing.

The central picture is a Virgin and Child. The faces are rude and careless save for a singularly earnest look about the eyes. On each side stands the figure of an apostle, and beyond this an archangel,—St. Peter and Raphael on her right, on the

left St. Paul and Ithuriel. All four figures are
dressed in the same vestments, chasuble, dalmatic,
alb, and stole, but the colours are varied. Raphael
carries a small cross and a staff in one hand, and
a medallion of Christ in the other; he wears a red
nimbus, with a conventional gold design running
round. The wings are blue, with white under-wings.
Ithuriel's figure is much the same, but while holding a cross in his right hand, with his left he holds
a trumpet which he is blowing.

This church is peculiar in having no apse, all
three chapels being rectangular. The triforia are
continued over the north and south sanctuaries;
but there is over the haikal a lofty domed roof
with large pendentives. Over the main altar is a
high canopy resting on horizontal beams fastened
into the walls north and south. The eastern niche
is lined with magnificent Damascus tiles, many of
which are of unusual design, while others resemble
patterns common in all mosques. Unfortunately a
great number of the pieces are mere fragments, and
all are flung together at random without any attempt
at unity. The effect is further marred by the usual
dust and darkness. Above the arch of the niche is
a cross in tilework, which seems to have escaped
restoration; but the tiles are more modern and less
beautiful.

There is an open doorway from the haikal through
the wall to the north chapel, but none to the south;
this latter is entered only from the choir, but adjoining it is a small sacristy.

Among the vestments of the church should be
noticed a very fine cope of silk, embroidered with
flowers in tissue of gold, and fastened by a morse

with a cross in relief. This is used on festivals, and not as an ordinary part of the priest's vestments.

I discovered also, thrown away in a dirty locker and buried in rubbish, two old Arabic glass lamps, one entirely of plain white glass, the other set round with blue bosses and little plaques containing each a lion's head. The latter is of very unusual form; it has a globular body, narrow neck, and wide lip; but below descends in lessening rings to a pear-shaped finial, ending off with a small twisted globe and a boss in deep blue colour[1]. I only know one other lamp of the kind—at the small church of the Virgin next to Mâri Girgis in the Ḳaṣr-ash-Shamm'ah. These lamps have been disused for many years, and only await destruction.

HISTORICAL NOTE ON THE CHURCH OF SITT MARIAM.

The original foundation of this church was at least as early as the eighth century. Indeed the record at that date is a record not of building but of destruction. For Al Maḳrîzi, speaking of the year 770 A.D., says, 'The church of Sitt Mariam anent that of Abu Shanûdah in Maṣr was pulled down[2].' The destruction was perhaps only partial; at any rate the church was rebuilt almost as soon as it had fallen, together with the other churches which had been thrown down, and in its present form doubtless goes back to about the year 800 A.D.

----

[1] An illustration is given in vol. ii.
[2] Malan's History of the Copts, p. 80.

CHAPTER IV.

The Ancient Roman Fortress of Babylon,

NOW CALLED

Ḳaṣr-ash-Shamm'ah (قصر الشمعه).

The Roman Fortress.—The Church of Abu Sargah.—The Church of Al'Aḍra, called Al Mu'allaḳah.—The Church of Ḳadîsah Bur-bârah.—The Churches of Al'Aḍra and Mâri Girgis.

LIKE most other antiquities of Old Cairo, its fine Roman remains have been little noticed, and no plan of them has been published. Yet they are extremely interesting. There is plenty in Egypt to remind one of the period of Greek rule : but the traces of Roman conquest are rare and not striking. One scarcely realises how firmly the power of Rome was planted on the Nile. But the fortress of Babylon with its massive walls and colossal bastions is a type of the solid strength by which Rome won and kept her empire. And beyond its value in the cause of Roman archaeology, this ancient castle has a far wider interest : for it encloses no less than six churches of the Copts, some of which were certainly standing when the wave of Arab invasion dashed idly against their defences. In this fortress, too, the fate of nations centred : for it was here that by their treacherous surrender the Jacobites sealed at once the triumph of Al Islâm and their own doom of perpetual subjection, well content to purchase at the price of their country's freedom a final victory over their religious adversaries the Melkites : it was here that the Greek empire over Egypt fell; and here that the Crescent rose above the Cross.

The wall, as usual with Roman walls, consists of alternate layers of brick and stone, five courses of stone alternating with three courses of brick,— a very common arrangement. The height of a brick layer is nearly 1 ft., and that of a stone layer 3 ft. : taking the two together as 4 ft., one may easily calculate heights without measurement. The mortar is made of sand, lime, pebbles and charcoal; and it is curious to notice that the Arabs of Old Cairo to this day mix their mortar with charcoal in the same manner.

The circuit at present is far from complete, and every year sees some fresh defacement or destruction. Roughly one may say the fortress was quadrilateral : but the northern wall has now almost entirely disappeared. Off the north-east corner a block of masonry stands solitary among the rubbish mounds, representing possibly a small detached fort. The western wall has been severely dealt with the last few years : for the first hundred yards it has been razed almost level with the ground, and the point where it ceases is now concealed behind the new western wall of the cemetery. At this point quite recently traces of a corner bastion were visible showing clearly the junction of the original western with the northern wall. This latter ran across the ground newly enclosed for the cemetery towards the north-east : but even the foundations now lie hidden below the earth. The level of the soil all round the fortress has risen, as I have calculated, at the rate of more than a foot a century since Roman times.

Proceeding southward the wall throws out a sharp shoulder at the dip of the road: this shoulder was pierced with windows and formed an angular bastion. Thence the wall runs at a slightly changed angle for 150 yards to the Greek convent. Halfway comes the Coptic entrance of Kaṣr-ash-Shamm'ah—a door so low that one has to descend into a kind of pit to reach it. The entrance has been cut in early Christian times through the solid Roman masonry, which here is 8 ft. in thickness. A new door has just been made through the wall a little further on as an entrance to the premises of the Greek convent,— the one ancient Melkite church now remaining.

Below the Greek convent the wall disappears under plaster and whitewash and bends inward by a sharp curve for about 10 ft.: after a gap of about 90 ft. crossed by an Arab wall, one finds again the Roman wall bent outwards in a corresponding curve, and thence continuing straight. These two curves were puzzling at first, but by good fortune I found the key to their meaning. A view obtained one day from the roof of Al Mu'allakah revealed a mass of masonry, apparently Roman, lying just behind and adjoining one of the curves: and subsequent research on the spot discovered the remains of a large circular tower of Roman work, to which the wall formed a tangent. Only half the tower remained, showing a sort of vertical section; but there was enough to indicate the plan, which consisted of two concentric circles with the space between them divided into eight equal segments by radiating walls. The approach to the eight chambers was from the central chambers inside the inner circle, but there were no remains of any staircase. On the ground floor in the very centre of the tower I found the Roman sewer, which is still visible without the fortress, and runs nearly all round its eastern side.

Thinking over the matter, I easily conjectured that the corresponding whitewashed curve in the Greek convent wall must belong to a corresponding tower, and that in fact the Greek convent was built on the top of the old tower. This at once accounted for its unusual elevation, and lent colour to its claims to very great antiquity. The first visit set all doubts at rest. Though Arab buildings are clustered thickly round and rise on nearly every side to a great height; and though repairs and additions, plaster and whitewash, have disguised the original building in almost a magical manner; yet having the clue beforehand one could trace all the details of the plan clearly enough, and prove the existence almost in its completeness of a splendid Roman building, unique in construction, though unnoticed by the travellers that have passed inside it for generations.

The modern entrance is on the third story[1]. The aperture of a Roman window has been enlarged, and a flight of stone steps built up to it from outside the tower against the fortress wall which forms a tangent to the tower. Consequently it was from this third

---

[1] Revisiting the scene in January, 1884, I found a vast pile of new buildings in course of construction actually against the tower. The old staircase is gone, and the old exterior wall is now finally and hopelessly concealed. The text is already bygone history.

story that the process of discovery began. Travellers who have visited the Greek convent will remember that after the first staircase, they entered a broad short passage leading into an irregular room, the roof of which is partly upheld by some ancient columns. A little inspection will show that there are really eight columns, though some are nearly buried in Arab walls : that on these eight columns rests a circular wooden architrave to support the ceiling, and that the columns make a ring inside a circular chamber, the original central chamber of the tower. This much being made clear, one may follow round the chamber wall and find it pierced with eight doorways at equal intervals, each doorway leading into another chamber,—one of the segments of the space between the two concentric circles. An eight-spoked cart-wheel with a disproportionately large axletree gives one a very fair idea of the plan. The axletree will then represent the central chamber, the spokes the radiating walls, and the spaces between the spokes the chambers round the central chamber. In the middle of this central room is a so-called well ; but the Arabs say the water is never used, being brackish. The shaft of the well pierces down the very centre of the tower, and I have little doubt that it was never meant for a well at all, but as a sink for sewage : it is of Arab work, but falls directly into the Roman sewer below, and may be a replacement of a similar Roman shaft. Of the surrounding chambers one is a chapel which the priests say is older even than the convent ; a sink-pipe may be noticed in one corner of the stone floor. Another is a sort of hermit's cell, with a rude bed, and some good pictures : one is filled with lumber : and the rest are foul with ages of filth and darkness. All originally had two windows; but except in the chapel, the hermit's cell, and the entrance-way, the windows have been blocked in such a manner that, although outside they are flush with the wall, and under plaster and whitewash the openings are invisible, yet inside, from the greater thickness of the Roman wall, the round-arched headings are clearly shown, and the difference between the ancient and the modern work is obvious.

I have said that there are eight similar chambers round the central one; this is not quite accurate. For one of the segments, the southernmost, is occupied by the old Roman staircase. The visitor entering by the Arab staircase crosses the hall of pillars into a short passage; here is an old carved folding-door, and just beyond it steps mounting up to the convent. These steps leading upwards are part of the old Roman staircase; and by opening the folding-doors one finds the same staircase descending downwards for two stories, with this difference, that below all is in pitch darkness; it is a place of mystery and horror, said to be peopled by devils, and is unknown and unvisited—happily even by the whitewasher.

With some difficulty I persuaded the priests of the convent to light me down with tapers. The staircase proved to be a beautiful piece of work; it is a steep slanting shaft, walled and wagon-vaulted with large courses of finely-worked ashlar, and turning about a rectangular pier by long and short flights alternately. After four flights, completing one turn round the pier, one faces a door 10 ft. high, with flat lintel and void relieving arch. It leads into the central chamber of the first floor, but the original design has been quite altered and disguised by Arab work. Inside the inner Roman circle a third circular wall has been built, corresponding to the ring of columns on the story above. Embedded in it may still be seen two of the eight columns it was designed to replace ; and these are joined by a wooden architrave exactly like that above. Possibly the remaining six columns are completely immured; but no trace of them remains, though there is still visible, flush with the Arab wall, part of a Roman doorway, with lintel of freestone ornamented with dentels. The interior of this Arab circle is piled so thick with dust and rubbish in two of the four chambers into which it is divided, that the level varies 7 or 8 ft. in places, and gives at first the impression of two stories. The well-shaft in the centre is clearly, as it stands, not Roman. Outside, too, there are walls of Arab work joining the Arab circle to the inner Roman wall; one passes from room to room by a doorway just large enough for a man's body. No doubt all these cells were contrived for monastic uses.

The compartments between the Roman circles are also divided by Arab walls, lightened generally by high pointed arches, but forming together a ring; so that altogether round the well-shaft are ranged in four concentric circles two Arab and two Roman walls. The two pillars have each a cross in a circular moulding cut in relief just under the abacus, between the foliage of the Corinthian-like capital; and the crosses were clearly part of the original carving, not an interpolation. It is possible, though unlikely, that the entire capitals may have been changed; otherwise the conclusion would be that the fortress dates from Christian times.   But there is nothing else to detain one ; one is glad to escape from the thick black dust, spiders, centipedes, and other noisome creatures which dwell in this eternal darkness.   Such an experience recalls with vivid meaning the words of Vergil, 'ire per umbras, per loca senta situ . . . noctemque profundam,' and one such experience is enough.   Leaving, then, this story, one continues downwards by the staircase, and after one more complete turn round the pier one reaches the end—a cul-de-sac.   There is, however, a blocked doorway on the north side, which led into the central chamber on the ground floor ; beyond this doorway the staircase issues in a level vaulted recess 7 ft. deep, probably meant for sentinels.   It is paved with heavy slabs, some of which have been torn up, no doubt in search for hidden treasure ; but the natural earth appears beneath.

Returning upwards I noticed that at every landing on the outward or south side of the staircase is a narrow blocked window.   The passage is 12 ft. high, built of nine courses of stone, each 16 in. in depth ; the vaulting consists of seven courses parallel to the line of descent of the passage, not running at right angles across it.   The passage is 4 ft. 2 in. in width ; the pier 7 ft. long, 3 ft. 10 in. broad ; twenty-two steps lead from the ground to the first floor, and the same number from first to second.   The steps average as nearly as possible 8 in. in height.

Directly one reaches the light again one is amused at the look of relief on the priests' faces, and vexed to find nothing but whitewashed surfaces.   The further ascent towards the Greek convent shows the same kind of masonry as far as one can judge ; but it is not easy to pronounce. The best outside view is from a position between the two towers, which can only be obtained by passing through the court of a house; but the goodwife may be moved by politeness and piastres. On this side the Roman work ends suddenly in a level line, which may have been the original top of the tower, though it is continued up much higher by Arab work. Above the second floor, which is marked by a brick-course, five other brick-courses stand clear, with stone-courses above and below, giving a height of 23 ft. This would make the original height of the whole tower roughly about 55 ft. It may here perhaps be mentioned that the Greek church of St. George, now perched like an eagle's nest on the very top of the tower, not only offers a splendid bird's-eye view of old Cairo, but is in itself a most ancient and curious structure. The folding doors of the church contain eight small panels beautifully carved in subjects, but unfortunately smeared thick with layers of paint; they resemble, or at least show the purpose of, the ancient panels in Abu Sargah, which doubtless were similarly enclosed in the framing of a door. The church is hung with ostrich eggs and lamps of silver, and on the walls are some magnificent examples of both Damascus and Rhodian tilework, alone well worth a visit. The church is further interesting as being the only sacred building within these ancient walls which the Melkites have succeeded in retaining. For though called 'the Greek convent,' it belongs not of course to any foreign community, but to the orthodox patriarch of Alexandria. The church was plundered by a mob of Muslims at the time of the war in 1882.

From the same point of view one sees a curious arrangement by which a small but complete semi-circle has been, as it were, scooped away from the outside wall the whole height of the staircase. This semicircle has a diameter of 17 ft., and is designed to relieve the otherwise excessive thickness of the wall, and to facilitate the admission of light through the narrow windows of the staircase.

I have given the foregoing details generally in the order of their discovery. The chief problem remained — to find the original entrance to the tower. The staircase, after leading down to the ground floor, was blocked between the two circles; it seemed impossible that the Romans entered by a staircase from outside, landing on the second floor as visitors enter at present, yet on the ground I had failed to find any sign of a doorway.

The next move was to call on the chief priest, whom I found in a little room at an immense height, even above the convent. Over coffee I drew him to talk about the lower parts of the building, mentioned my visit to the lower regions, and said there were some houses outside, adjoining the tower, which I should very much like to explore. He told me they were ruined, and I could go where I liked, but must take a guide. Gladly accepting, I went down, and after stumbling over broken doors and fallen stones wound through a maze of dark passages among tumbledown hovels, and at last stood before the east side of the tower, and the mystery was ended. Close together—only 8 ft. apart—were two similar doorways 4 ft. 6 in. in width. These both led into the same room or division between two radiating walls : one of these walls is pierced with a door, and the adjoining compartment has three additional doors—two for entrance from without, and one leading inwards into the central chamber. This latter was quite blocked, but the design is now clear. Of the eight divisions on the ground floor one is occupied by the staircase : two eastward of this are open, each by two doorways; the other five divisions, as well as the central chamber, are blocked up in darkness, and apparently have been so for generations. It is not easy to see the need of the four original doorways; but they have their convenience now for the herd of swine, which are the sole tenants of the vacant chambers. The walls of these chambers are of ashlar, but end upwards in brickwork, sixteen courses deep; the brickwork is divided from the stone by timber beams, which show not the slightest sign of age or decay, despite the weight that has been bearing upon them for full fifteen centuries. From the topmost course of this brickwork springs the wagon-vaulting of the roof, which likewise is of very fine brickwork. The courses in the vaulting run at a considerable angle to the line of the wall. The four outer doorways are round-headed; but the inner doorway or passage between the two chambers has an arch of horseshoe form. All the arches are made of brickwork.

Between the two towers there stood, no doubt, originally a gateway and a curtain wall : no vestige of either remains, but the curtain wall must have crossed just behind the modern Arab wall. The place where it joined the northern tower is marked by a lofty narrow pile of native work, doorless, windowless, and apparently purposeless, unless it was meant merely to hide the jagged end of the curtain wall after its destruction.

With a slight change of direction the fortress wall proceeds from the broken tower southwards for about 100 yards, then turns at an obtuse angle to form the southern side of the quadrilateral. There it loops outward into three large straight-sided round-headed bastions, two of which are tolerably well preserved. The first is much damaged, but contains inside a small chamber, with a most beautiful roof of pyramidal brick-vaulting; and the curtain-wall between the first and the second bastion has had the entire facing stripped off for a height of 8 ft., and in some parts is hollowed to a depth of 3 ft., making a sort of cavern where a whole herd of goats find shelter from the heat. The second bastion is split with huge cracks, and shows some Arab patchwork; then comes the well-known gateway of solid ashlar, with a fine triangular pediment still remaining. This pediment is ornamented with dentels, and quite classical in character; under one corner may still be seen the *aëtos*, a small figure of an eagle sculptured in relief. Above the pediment a tablet seems to have been torn away: the relieving arch shows clearly below it, and still lower may be seen the top of the old gateway arch, now only just projecting above the surface of the ground. It is over this gateway, swung as it were between two bastions, with its southern wall resting on the Roman curtain-wall, that the ancient church of Al 'Aḍra is built, hence called Al Mu'allaḳah, or The Hanging Church. Its side-chapels project into and occupy the upper story of the third bastion, which is the most perfect of all; the lower story is filled with tombs of

Coptic dignitaries.   Each floor of the bastion shows seven windows, blocked up in the usual manner.

A little farther on the Roman wall suddenly disappears after turning a corner, and merges in Arab work.   A large rectangular palm-garden, bounded on three sides by Arab walls, here lies close against the fortress.   It was almost certain that the Roman wall formed the fourth side of the garden, but by no means easy to prove it.   There was a heavy wooden door through the lofty wall into the garden, at which I knocked in vain many days.   Sometimes voices would answer, but only to say that the key was lost, or that the master had taken it away with him; mere fictions to hide refusal.   At last one burning day as I passed the door was standing ajar.   I ran up and planted myself in the doorway, hastily changing my ṭarbûsh for an English hat, lest I should be taken for an official.   An infant seeing me shrieked, ' Oh, mother, quick! here's a Frank! quick!' and the mother came forth from the palms to guard the child, drawing her veil over her mouth.   I said, ' I am very thirsty, will you be so kind as to give me a drink of water, O lady?'

' Be so kind, did you say?'   She seemed unaccustomed to so much civility.

' Yes; will you be so kind?   The sun is fiery and the world is hot to-day, and I have come a long journey and am thirsty.   Our Lord lengthen your life.'

' Good; I will go and ask my husband.'   The husband it seems was asleep, but soon came and invited me in.   I called my friend, and we entered and went to the well, which lies in the middle of the garden, and sends forth under the palms a clear cold stream of beautiful water.

There we drank and were refreshed. Then I said to the gardener, 'This is such a beautiful garden, that Paradise itself cannot be fairer; may we eat as well as drink here? we have our noonday meal without.' He readily agreed, and we lunched under the welcome shade of the palm-trees. Afterwards, as we were smoking with our host, I professed astonishment and admiration at the unusual size of the garden. He was flattered, and said there was none like it. 'What do you suppose is the length?' I asked. 'Quite seventy or eighty yards,' he said. 'Not more than that? why, I am sure it is at least one hundred. Will you let me measure?' 'Certainly.' 'Very well; we will measure that wall over there'—which I had from the first moment identified as the Roman wall I was in search of. So we measured and proved it to be more than one hundred yards in length; discovered traces of another bastion; and departed well content with the success of our little stratagem. Something of the kind was rendered necessary by the inveterate suspicion which the natives entertain of strangers coming with strange instruments—uncanny machines which 'devour' their houses, as they put it. And my court uniform had given rise to the rumour that I was an official sent by the divan or government.

At the far end of the palm-garden projects a bastion, the ruined walls of which have been built up with Arab brickwork and crowned with a circlet of pots, like those at Mâri Mîna. This bastion, however, is better viewed from inside the dair, and is reached by a visit to the Jewish synagogue, behind which it stands. The interior is filled with fallen bricks and stones, but it is possible to get measurements. The greatest length is 33 ft. 6 in., width 25 ft.; there are only five windows to each floor, not seven as in the southern bastion. In the first and second story the windows are 4 ft. 6 in. wide, in the third 2 ft. 3 in.; the height of the middle floor windows is 10 ft., and those above 5 ft.; the lower or original ground floor windows are now too deeply buried for vertical measurement. The brick-courses are in all cases bent round the head of the windows forming a circular arch.

This Jewish synagogue is worth a visit. It was originally a Coptic church dedicated to St. Michael, and was sold to the Jews by his namesake Michael, fifty-sixth patriarch, towards the end of the ninth century[1]. Eutychius says that St. Michael in Ḳaṣr-ash-Shamm'ah was the last church held by the Melkites about the year 725 A.D., when all other churches throughout the land of Egypt had passed into the hands of the Jacobites. How long it remained with the Melkites is uncertain; but the violent antipathy of the two factions no doubt gave a cause of quarrel and conquest to the Jacobites, long before the time when, according to Makrîzi, it was made over to the Hebrews.

The synagogue is about 65 ft. long and 35 ft. broad, and shows in miniature a Coptic basilica in its simplest and perhaps its earliest form. If the eastern end has suffered some alteration, the nave, side-aisles, and returned aisle with triforium above, are unchanged from the old design, though whitewash has long since defaced the splendid colours once blazoned on the walls. In point of detail there is not much of interest

---

[1] Al Maḳrîzi, Malan's Trans. p. 85.

remaining, except the fine stucco work about the arch of triumph, the tank or well behind the apse, and the carved doors at the end of the south aisle; upon which one may notice gazelles, and that other ancient Christian symbol, a pair of birds with retorted drooping heads, and between them a bunch of grapes—a symbol one may see graven with equal fidelity in the mosque of St. Sophia at Constantinople, the church of St. Eleutherios at Athens, the cathedral of St. Nicholas at Bari in Italy, and on the minster font at Winchester.

One is tempted to linger among the acacia and pomegranate trees in the synagogue garden; but there is little more of the Roman wall to be seen here, and to see the rest one must return outside the dair and work round beyond the palm garden, noticing on the way and following the Roman sewer that skirts it[1]. The sewer, which is the same as that passing under the round towers, disappears just before another bastion, the last on the long eastern wall. Between this and the synagogue bastion are remains of a third clearly visible; so that there were four altogether on the eastern side. Further research is again baffled by a lofty Arab wall starting from the last bastion and enclosing another garden; but following it round, one discovers on the northern side a piece of Roman wall, which a little examination shows to have been the back wall of a bastion. This is the only trace remaining of the

---

[1] This sewer is about 4 ft. deep and 18 in. wide; it is lined with cement and roofed with slabs of limestone. The fact that it skirts the palm gardens shows that the space they now cover was once occupied by Roman buildings.

northern wall of the fortress, but is invaluable as giving the direction of the line which, if produced across the Greek cemetery, exactly strikes the point from which we started, and completes the quadrilateral. In the middle of this back wall is the garden door, which occupies the original doorway of the ground floor of the bastion; for the ground floor chamber in every bastion was roofed with a vaulting of heavy masonry, and entered by an arched doorway from within the fortress. In this garden may be had a fine view of the domes of the smaller church of Al 'Aḍra : remains there also prove the fact that the bastion stood exactly at the north-east corner of the fortress, and that the wall which crossed the garden formed a right angle before it struck the nearest eastern bastion and resumed its original direction.

To sum up. On the north side we have two rounded bastions at the corners, and there were no doubt at least two others between ; on the western side one angular bastion and two huge round towers ; on the south side three rounded bastions, and on the east four. The walls were 8 ft. thick at the base, changing to 5 ft. at the distance of about 15 ft. from the ground, the offset being of course inwards.

Of the foundation of this fortress there is no record remaining, and its date is very difficult to determine. In Rome the date of a building can be fixed by the style of the work ; but the law does not hold in the colonies, where the accidents of place and material confounded all order of succession and overruled canons of taste. It is clear, however, that a town called Babylon existed long before the Roman occupation of Egypt. There are various legends

of its origin.   Strabo [1] says some revolted Babylonians obtained a settlement there from the kings
of Egypt.   The version of Diodorus Siculus [2] tallies
with this: he writes that some captives brought
from Babylon by Sesostris established themselves in
a fortified castle called after their mother city, whence
they made raids on the country round, but were
finally pacified and pardoned.   Josephus [3] relates
that Babylon was built when Cambyses conquered
Egypt, i.e. 525 B.C.: while, according to Eutychius [4],
the founder was a Persian king called Athus, who
built a temple to the sun on the spot where now
stands the church of Tadrus.   The main fact, then,
of the existence of an early Babylonian fortress,
needs no further question: and I think it must
have been this fortress, or at least the site of it,
which the Romans occupied at the time of Strabo's
visit to Egypt.   Murray thinks that the fort mentioned by Strabo is the Kaṣr-ash-Shamm'ah, but
needlessly perplexes the matter with a misquota-
tion, which occurs I believe in every writer who
has touched the subject since La Martinière.
Strabo does *not* say that the position was 'fortified
by nature:' his words are, φρούριον ἐρυμνόν, ἀποστάντων
Βαβυλωνίων τινῶν, &c.   It is true that ἐρυμνὸς is sometimes used to signify natural strength: but primarily
and usually it denotes artificial strength.   So that in
spite of the low-lying situation of Kaṣr-ash-Shamm'ah,
there is no reason why Strabo, had he seen it, should
not have described it as φρούριον ἐρυμνόν.   The theory

---

[1] Strabo, Geog. bk. xvii. chap. i. § 35.
[2] Diod. Sic. Hist. lib. i. chap. lvi. 3.
[3] Josephus, Ant. Jud. 2. 5.
[4] Eutych. ap. Migne, Patrologiae Cursus, vol. 111. p. 967.

that the rubbish mounds now gathered round the castle may 'conceal its once elevated base' is refuted by a survey of the locality, which reveals no striking difference of level: besides, to imagine any such elevated plateau on the spot is to give the Nile-bed an impossible depression. The fortress is so far sunken now, that however much the bed of the Nile may have risen, the level of the two cannot originally have been very different. Strabo goes on to say that this φρούριον was at the moment he saw it (νυνί) the camp of one of the three legions guarding Egypt; and he adds, 'there is a ridge from the camp (στρατόπεδον) to the Nile along which water is brought by machinery worked by one hundred and fifty prisoners,' i.e. probably by an arrangement of water-wheels, such as may be seen at the mediaeval aqueduct of old Cairo.

Now it is perfectly certain that between Kasr-ash-Shamm'ah and the Nile no ridge exists or ever existed; while 200 yards to the south, between the castle and the church of Tadrus, there is both a place 'fortified by nature,' if such be wanted, and a ridge running Nilewards. A large island of rock detached from the Mukattam range stands with steep sides, and near the Dair Bablûn throws out a spur, which is continued towards the river by a ridge of hill. I have no doubt that this is the spot where the Babylonians built the fortress, and where the camp was seen by Strabo. The conjunction of the words in the Greek shows clearly that in the writer's mind there was a logical connexion between the revolt and the castle: he could scarcely have used such language had he been speaking of a revolt made some centuries ago by Babylonians, and a castle

just built by the Romans. Further, there is no other
ridge in the neighbourhood : and had the water gone
up and along this, it would have had to come down
again to reach Kasr-ash-Shamm'ah. Moreover, the
Romans in Kasr-ash-Shamm'ah could easily have
obtained water by digging wells; and I find in the
Arab historian Murtadi that there was actually a
Nilometer built by the Romans inside their fortress.
On the other hand, the Babylonians, if they were on
the rocky ground, where I imagine their stronghold
and the Roman camp in Strabo's time to have been,
could not have pierced the rock, but would have
been forced to convey water by some kind of
aqueduct. Another point worth notice is Strabo's
statement that from Babylon the Pyramids are
clearly visible in the distance. What is the fact
now ? From the hill-top the Pyramids are easily
seen, and the view of the country on all sides is
perhaps unrivalled for splendour and interest in
the world; but from the low ground by Kasr-ash-
Shamm'ah—ground still lower in Strabo's time—the
Pyramids are quite invisible. For these reasons,
then, I think the Kasr-ash-Shamm'ah cannot possibly have existed in Strabo's time.

Moreover, the evidence of dates alone is almost
decisive. Egypt was made a Roman province in
the year 30 B.C.: and Strabo's journey up to the
First Cataract was made in company with his friend
Ælius Gallus, the prefect in the year 25–24 B.C. It
does not seem probable that a fortress of such size,
strength, complexity, and admirable finish could have
been designed and completed in so short an interval :
and, further, had so striking and beautiful a work
existed, I think it impossible that Strabo could have

passed it over with so vague, obscure, and scanty a notice.

It was only since writing the foregoing that I had the opportunity of referring to Pococke.   There I find that he holds the same opinion of the position of the ancient Babylon, placing it on the island of rock which he calls the Gebel Jehusi.   He gives, moreover, a plan of the Roman fortress[1], and of the two round towers : and a sketch of the southern wall with the gateway.   No doubt in his time, c. 1735, much of the fortress was standing that is now quite gone; and it is extremely disappointing that he should not have taken more pains to be accurate. He represents the walls as forming a neat right-angled parallelogram about 1600 ft. long and 300 ft. broad.   The wall-line cuts through the centre of the towers instead of making a tangent : the towers are 180 instead of 60 ft. apart, and another pair of towers is imagined with the same line for symmetry's sake.   I am quite sure from my own examination that no second pair of towers can have existed. He adds that one tower was then 40 ft. high, and the other much higher, having a church above it : so that the now ruined tower was in good preservation when Pococke saw it.   But he tells us that even then the people were carrying away the Roman stone for building.   On the east side he gives no less than twelve bastions, and carries the wall 350 ft. even beyond the fragment of Roman work marked in my plan as detached from the fortress.   It is possible, of course, that the fortress was enlarged in later Roman times northwards, and

---

[1] Description of the East, vol. i. p. 26. pl. ix.

the wall carried along the dotted line for some
distance : in that case the position of the fragment
with reference to the north-east bastion is less
puzzling.   But Pococke unfortunately neither says
how much he saw of the wall nor whence he got his
plan ; and the latter is so very erroneous in places
where it can be challenged, that it is quite untrust-
worthy in others where it cannot.   The plan he gives
of a tower is fairly correct, except that he omits the
staircase and inserts a door between the two windows
of every compartment.   In this, as in the plan of the
fortress, he assumes a symmetry which does not
exist : he makes a very pretty building, but
it is quite original.   He seems to have measured
one wall and one tower—which he calls 'a very
particular sort of building'—and then either
to have drawn the rest from imagination, or at least
to have twisted his facts to fit his fancies.   He
designs his fortress after some ideal architype.
The elevation which he gives of the principal
gateway is no less faulty : it shows the four bastions,
but they are represented as circular.   The gate with
pediment and relieving arch is indicated in such a
way as to imply that the whole was visible when
the sketch was taken[1].   It is worth noting, however,
that he gives a wall running parallel behind the
south wall at a distance of about 35 ft. inside ;
and though the interval is wrong, there doubtless
was some such rear-wall, on which the northern
wall of the Mu'allaḳah rests, as the southern rests
on the Roman gateway.   Besides Pococke's, one

---

[1] It is to be hoped that some day this gateway may be excavated :
indeed the whole fortress would richly repay exploration.

other plan exists, that given in Panckoucke's
' Descriptions de l'Egypte,' compiled by officers of
the French expedition, and published at Paris in
1823.   A more incorrect and worthless plan never
was made.   It gives with great inaccuracy merely
the boundary walls of the whole group of buildings:
and these walls are flatly called Roman!   The sur-
veyor was unable to distinguish between Arab and
Roman work; even the outer wall of the palm-
garden deceives him.   In the whole circuit only
three bastions—those on the south side—are figured;
the round towers are quite ignored.   Pococke's plan
is far better: at least he knew what he was looking
for, and he does not confound styles and epochs
of building which a child might distinguish.

It is easier to put aside a wrong date for the
fortress than to fix the right.   But there are plausible reasons for assigning it to an early epoch.
The fact that on the high rocky ground the supply
of water might be at any moment cut off by a
besieging enemy, was enough in itself to determine
the Romans to choose a lower site where water
could be had for digging: though the remains of a
six foot sewer[1] near Dair Mikhail show that the
Roman town, which sprang up outside the fortress
walls, extended southward beyond the rocky ridge,
and covered the site of the first encampment.
Moreover the ancient canal or Khalîg, which now
runs through Cairo and once reached to the Red

---

[1] I am not aware that this sewer has been noticed before.   The
road now runs over it, and the vaulting is broken through in several
places.   A steep fall in the ground at one side marks clearly the
ancient course of the Nile for some distance, and the sewer ran
under the Roman quay, as was usual.

Sea, is generally identified with the Amnis Trajanus. It joins the Nile at Old Cairo; and the Roman castle is so built as to block the narrow neck of the Nile valley, and to dominate the entrance of the canal. It seems therefore reasonable to suppose that if Trajan had the canal cut, he also erected the fortress; that he wished to command at once the land and water passage between Upper and Lower Egypt and the trade route to Arabia. Here really were the gates of the East: at Ḳaṣr-ash-Shamm'ah he could hold the gate of the Nile and the gate of the Red Sea. If this theory be right the date would be about A. D. 100. The alternative seems to assign the work to Probus 281 A.D., who certainly built many 'temples, bridges, porticoes and palaces in Egypt'[1]. It is true the pediment of the main gateway is late in style, and true also that the cross-carved capitals on the pillars in the round tower cannot be much earlier than the third century. But it is not certain that they belong to the original building, the general features of which suit better the time of Trajan, even were it likely that the Romans should have deferred for three centuries the building of a powerful fortress in so vital a position.

The names of the place are legion. Although there probably was an early Egyptian town called Kerkau at Old Cairo, Gibbon is wrong in speaking of the fortress as a part of 'Memphis or Misrah'[2]. No theory of the size of Memphis can bring the walls down near Maṣr, which is ten miles as the crow flies from the fallen colossus of Rameses. Still Maṣr is the oldest name and the commonest to-day.

---

[1] Gibbon, chap. 12. [2] Chap. 51.

In Roman times, however, there is no doubt that the prevailing title was Babylon. Both in the *Notitia Provinciarum* and the *Itinerarium Antonini* the station is called ' Babylonia' : among the prelates at the Council of Ephesus is recorded a bishop of Babylon[1] : and this name, which has lingered on side by side with its elder, has still a local habitation at Dair Bablûn, two furlongs south of the fortress.

In the Mohammedan invasion of Egypt 638 ᴀ. ᴅ. 'Amr hurled his troops and his engines in vain against the solid walls of Babylon : until after a fruitless siege of seven months the Jacobite Copts within the fortress parleyed with 'Amr, deserted the walls, and joined with the invader in wreaking their vengeance on the Melkite Greeks, their co-defenders. On the spot where 'Amr pitched his leather tent (fustât) a mosque was built, and the Arab town called after the tent Fustât. The mosque, one of the most interesting monuments of Egypt, is still called the mosque of 'Amr; but though Fustât lasted some centuries, when the new Cairo was built, as the town fell wasted by fire and decay, the Arab name sank into oblivion and the old name resumed its place, Masr the ancient as opposed to Masr the victorious. The disdain with which the Arabs looked down from the splendid citadel and towers of Cairo on the forlorn ruins of Masr is expressed in a current Arabic proverb, ' They made mention of Masr to Kahirah, and Bâb al Lûk rose with her rubbish.' Bâb al Lûk or ' The Gate of Folly'—a contemptuous play on the word Babylon—

---

[1] La Martinière, Dictionnaire Géographique et Critique, s.v. Babylon.

is curious as showing that the name in its wider
sense is not quite lost among the natives of to-day.
According to Pococke[1] the Arabs called the fortress
Kaṣr Kieman, which he explains to mean 'Archer's
Castle,' though I cannot find the word in Arabic
dictionaries and never heard it so applied. The
name Kaṣr-ash-Shamm'ah however was given by
the conquerors, and means 'Castle of the Candle'
or 'Beacon Castle.' Murtadi[2] tells a curious legend
of a certain mirror made of all sorts of minerals
which stood on a high turret of brass at old Cairo in
the days of Sesostris. It showed the states of all
regions in Egypt, and reflected all passing events.
The beacon however is rather less mythical; several
authors mention a πυρεῖον, and the Arab Yakûti,
quoted by Golius, speaks of a Kubbat-ad-Dukhân,
i.e. Dome or Temple of Smoke[3]: which is said to
have been a relic of the old Babylonian fire-worship.
Possibly even in Roman times a beacon-fire was
lighted on one of the round towers: for there are
some very puzzling flues in the ruined tower which
may have reference to some purpose of the kind,
but the walls about them are so broken that it is not
easy to guess their meaning. However that may
be, it is neither the name 'Dair-an-Naṣârah' (Convent
of the Nazarenes) nor 'Dair Mâri Girgis' (Convent
of Saint George), but rather Kaṣr-ash-Shamm'ah
that remains in familiar use to-day among Copts
and Muslims alike: though they seem to have no

---

[1] Vol. i. p. 23: no doubt the word should be kîmân كيمان and
means hills or mounds.

[2] Egyptian History, p. 26.

[3] See D'Anville, Mémoires sur l'Egypte, p. 112.

tradition to tell why the fortress was styled 'The Castle of the Candle'[1].

The Church of Abu Sargah (ابو سرجه).

Abu Sargah, or St. Sergius, is the only church to which tourists in search of shows are annually haled by their exceedingly ignorant dragomans; and it thanks for this distinction rather the legend which points to the crypt as the resting-place of the Holy Family on their arrival at Masr, than any artistic or antiquarian attraction supposed to reside in the building[2]. Yet its inherent interest is very great, though possibly second to that of Al Mu'allakah. There is little reason to doubt that the present building dates—unaltered in its main features. though of course fittings and details have been changed—from at least the eighth century, and this date accords with the tradition as related to me by the priest of Al Mu'allakah, though sometimes it is

---

[1] Pococke mentions in a note that the fortress was called in his day 'Casrkeshemeh' (sic), which is doubtless Kasr-ash-Shamm'ah; vol. i. p. 25 n.

[2] The sort of impression produced by the church and its surroundings on the ordinary traveller is painfully illustrated in most story books about Egypt. Even a careful and just observer like George Fleming puts into the mouth of her characters so falsely coloured a description of the scene, that one hesitates whether to term it rather shameful or ridiculous. The dull grey dust of the rubbish mounds is called 'desert sand, looking like a sea of gold': the crypt, 'a hole in the ground in which the Virgin took refuge on her flight into Egypt': and so on *ad nauseam.* See A Nile Novel, vol. i. pp. 163-4 (second edition, London, 1877).

assigned to the sixth century. The truth probably is that the crypt dates from the sixth century at the very latest, and is doubtless considerably earlier, while the main fabric is only about a thousand years old.

Abu Sargah lies nearly in the centre of the Roman fortress: north and west its walls align a narrow street: eastward it touches ground encumbered with ruined houses: and on the south it is pressed close and hidden by later walls of ashlar and domestic buildings. It is built of ordinary small brown Egyptian bricks, varied here and there with bond timbers of palm or tamarisk unmortised and un-connected, or short square pilasters with cap-like projections. The north wall runs unevenly with an offset inwards some 20 ft. from the north-west corner, a buttress farther on, and then a marked deflection as shown in the plan. It is certain that there were two western doorways: of these the southern is still used, though the part of the narthex into which it led has been strangely altered, and now the passage doubles round a small block of buildings into a porch cut out of the south aisle, whence another door opens into the church. From the passage a staircase (N) ascends to the women's galleries: but there can be little doubt that anciently this corner of the narthex was occupied by the bap-tistery. The original central doorway has been long since blocked up, but the blocking is clearly trace-able outside, and a recess (M) in the wall inside also plainly marks the position. Whether there was even a north aisle door is very doubtful. Outside there are no signs of it: inside the floor has been raised more than three feet above the nave-floor: and though

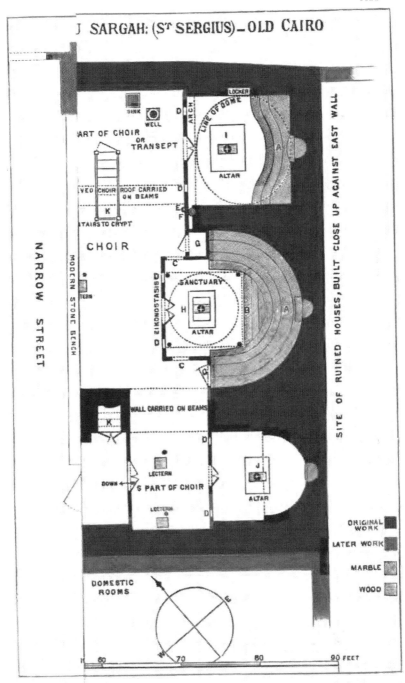

J SARGAH: (Sᵗ SERGIUS) — OLD CAIRO

182b

there is a recess in the wall which might have been saved in blocking a doorway, there is not evidence enough to decide the question.

I think, however, that a comparison of the plan with that of the White Monastery near Sûhâg in Upper Egypt, will settle the fact that the western apsidal chamber in the one case as in the other was either a chapel or a baptistery, and the probabilities are very largely in favour of the former. In the plan of the White Monastery a north aisle door is simply impossible to imagine, and there is definite evidence for the altar in this part of the narthex. Similarly, it is almost indisputable that the apsidal chamber at Abu Sargah was anciently a chapel, and that the original entrance to it was southward from the central part of the narthex, and not westward from the street. It was doubtless this chapel into which the newly-baptised were taken to receive their first communion.

The general shape of the church is, or was, a nearly regular oblong, and its general structure is basilican. It consists of narthex, nave, north and south aisle, choir, and three altars eastward each in its own chapel : of these the central and southern chapels are apsidal, the northern is square-ended. On plan Abu Sargah much resembles a type common among the Syrian churches of the sixth and seventh centuries, such as that of Kalb Lûzah, Tûrmanîn, or Al Barah[1]: but these Syrian churches differ from the Coptic in being built of hewn stone, with windows and wide arches, and above all in their aiming at an *exterior* effect of architectural splendour. The

---

[1] I have not adopted the Count de Vogüé's orthographies.

same plan is found in some Anatolian churches, as at Cassaba in Lycia : also in the church of St. Irene at Constantinople : and in many early churches at Rome, S. Niccolo in Carcere, S. Pietro in Vincoli, Sta. Agnese without the walls, and others : though in some cases the original arrangement has been obscured by later additions or alterations.

Over the aisles and narthex runs a continuous gallery or triforium, which originally served as the place for women at the service. On the north side it stops short at the choir, forming a kind of transept, which however does not project beyond the north aisle on plan. On the south side of the church the triforium is prolonged over the choir and over the south side-chapel. The gallery is flat-roofed : while the nave is covered with a pointed roof with framed principals like that at Abu-'s-Sifain. In the Coptic roofs no metal is used, but the tenons are pinned through by wooden bolts. Outside, the roof of Abu Sargah is plastered over with cement showing the king-posts projecting above the ridge-piece. Over the central part of the choir and over the haikal the roof changes to a wagon-vaulting : it is flat over the north transept, and a lofty dome overshadows the north aisle-chapel. There is a second dome visible from outside above the east end of the south triforium ; though whether a chapel directly over the south aisle-chapel ends the triforium, I cannot say. The churlish priest of Abu Sargah vowed there was none ; but he angrily refused to let me look, and neither soft words nor hard, neither fiat of patriarch nor glitter of money, could conquer his stubborn resistance. One may be sure however that a chapel of the kind once existed, even though now it has been desecrated by domestic usage. For domestic purposes also the large bays or openings from the triforia into the nave have been blocked up with thin walls: but on each side north and south the two bays remain visible, each divided by two small columns: in each bay also three small latticed windows still give a little light to the triforia. The main building is lighted only by a window in the east and in the west gable, and by a single skylight in the nave roof,—the result, of course, being obscurity.

The whole south-western corner of the church has been sadly altered. The south part of the narthex has been cut out of the church, and an entrance porch besides has been thrust into the south aisle. So the modern entrance-way, by the original south aisle door, is blocked in front, but turns to the right, then winds back through another opening in the original south wall to the porch (which serves as guest-room), and so reaches the nave. Over the modern entrance are domestic buildings occupied by the priest's family and communicating with the triforia.

The large Epiphany tank lies boarded over in the narthex: a smaller tank for ablutions and for the Maundy washing of feet, as at Abu'-s-Sifain, is in the women's section, which is divided from the narthex by a lofty lattice screen. Between the women's section and men's section there is the unusual arrangement of a third division, a narrow space co-extensive in width with the nave, but only about 8 ft. broad from east to west; it has four door-ways—one into the south aisle and one into the baptistery in the north aisle, besides those leading into the sections of the nave. Within this narrow space, just beside the western of the four doorways and facing south, stands the chair of the patriarch—the high broad seat of lattice-work on which he sits now upon days of visitation, holding the golden cross and giving benediction to the people as they pass before him.

What remains of the south aisle is railed off from the nave and divided into two parts: it projects further eastward than the nave, running into the choir instead of ending at the choir-screen, where the north aisle ends.   Yet the general arrangement of the north aisle is very irregular.   Part of it, co-extensive in length with the men's section of the nave, is undivided from it by any screen.   West of this part comes a screened baptistery with a round font embedded in masonry: westward still a flight of seven steps leads up to a raised landing before the chapel which occupied the north end of the nar-thex.   Beneath this landing and the chapel floor are said to lie the remains of some ancient patriarch, though there is no record of his name.   The altar is gone from this chapel, which is now used as a mere lumber-room: but the apse remains in the north wall, and where the plaster has not fallen, are traces of some very early and interesting paintings.   The completest figure, which is that nearest the door, represents Christ standing with his right hand up-raised in benediction and held half across the breast: the left hand carries a scroll bearing an inscription in Coptic letters signifying 'Behold the Lamb of God, which taketh away the sins of the world.'   It is worth notice in passing that the Coptic term for 'world' is the Greek κόσμος.   The figure wears a glory but no mitre; an amice covering the head and falling on the shoulders; a fine cope embroidered with a diaper pattern and fastened by a triple-lobed morse; alb, girdle, and perhaps sleeve. The portrait corresponds curiously in type of features with the earliest known likeness of Christ, that depicted on the ceiling in the catacomb of Domitilla at Rome, assigned to the third century[1]: the hair on the face and upper lip is unshorn, but slight; beard rather pointed. The still prominent figure at the other end of the curve is more fully bearded, is vested in an early chasuble, is nimbed, and carries in each hand a cross. Of the figures between which once filled the apse, very faint tokens remain: but enough is left to give the little room great interest, even if it were not the unique instance of a western apsidal chamber in the churches of Cairo.

The twelve monolithic columns round the nave are all, with one exception, of white marble streaked with dusky lines, like common Italian cippolino, which is used for example on the outside of St. Mark's at Venice. The exceptional column (L) is of red Assuân granite, 22 in. in diameter, and seems a later addition replacing a former pillar of white marble. The original columns have what is technically called diminution and entasis; they are about 16 in. in diameter; and their capitals are of a debased Corinthian order familiar in Roman work of the third and fourth centuries. They were doubtless taken from some Roman temple or other building. The bases on which they stand are also classical in character, and stand on square pedestals of the same marble. On each of these eleven ancient pillars is

---

[1] Roma Sotteranea, vol. ii. p. 218.

painted the life-size figure of a saint or apostle, now so begrimed and obscured that in the doubtful light all may easily escape notice, and it requires close attention to make them out when discovered[1]. Near the pulpit, but in the choir, stands a pair of small marble columns with early Saracen capitals and bases formed by inverted Corinthian capitals. Each of these two small columns, and each of the eleven nave columns, is incised with a fine clear dedication cross of the usual Coptic form in an oblong depression. Probably however the original number of crosses was twelve, and they were confined to the nave columns, the others being later.

The columns are joined by a continuous wooden architrave which rests on the abaci, with short flat pieces of timber intervening to distribute the bearing. The whole of this architrave was originally painted in various colours, and traces of coloured arabesque designs are still clearly visible on the soffit. The weight of the upper nave wall which rests on the architrave is relieved by arched openings of the pointed form common in Arab architecture.

The wooden pulpit, standing at the north-east corner of the nave, is mounted only by a moveable ladder. It is of rosewood inlaid with designs in ebony set with ivory edgings. Curiously enough there are no traces of an original stone ambon such as doubtless existed. The pulpit is now used but once a year—on Good Friday.

---

[1] Murray, though noticing the frescoes in the western chamber, is ignorant of these; and I never met a traveller who was aware of their existence. I pointed them out to Mr. Middleton, who mentions them in his paper in the Archæologia.

Abu Sargah is paved with hard siliceous grey lime-stone. The choir floor is two steps higher than the nave floor: a broad stone bench, probably answering to the solea, runs across the nave and north aisle at the foot of the choir-screen, which is of modern lattice-work. In a panel over the central choir door there is written, or rather wrought, in square Cufic-like letters of wood a short text, 'Ya Allah al Khalâs,' i.e. ' O God, Salvation.'   There is also a rude Coptic inscription upon the lintel of the doorway, which closes by double doors.   Over the screen is a row of fifteen small paintings, and higher still nine large ones—all, except the central Redeemer, nearly identical in treatment with those in the corresponding position at Abu-'s-Sifain; and here, as there, the larger series lies between two bands adorned with golden texts in Arabic and Coptic.   The other three pictures in the nave are of no merit artistically: one however, representing Abu Sargah and Abu Râkûs, stands over a locker in which the relics of the two saints are treasured: and another depicting the Flight into Egypt is interesting from the fact that it shows the Holy Family arriving at a Coptic dair.

Before the haikal and the north chapel the choir is of unusual width, but is narrowed southward by the intrusion of the south aisle and by the heavy pier[1] through which one descent is cut from the aisle to the crypt.   The other descent is by an open staircase railed round in the northern part of the

---

[1] On this pier, at a height of about twelve feet from the ground, there is a large stucco cross in relief with small crosses between the branches ; the principal cross is about two feet long and broad, and of Maltese form.

choir (K, K). Near the head of the staircase is a
well surrounded by a stone coping, and close by a
sink—both curiously situated in the very body of the
church. All churches have their own well somewhere
on the premises : in no other case is it found within
the sacred walls. Doubtless tradition attaches a
special sanctity to this, as the well of which the Holy
Family drank.

The haikal-screen projects forward into the choir,
as at Al 'Adra in the Hârat-az-Zuailah. It is of
very ancient and beautiful workmanship ; pentagons
and other shapes of solid ivory, carved in relief with
arabesques, being inlaid and set round with rich
mouldings. Where some of the ivory blocks have
fallen out, the skeleton frame of the screen is
visible, resembling a design in woodwork at the
mosque of Barḳûḳ among the tombs of the khalîfs
(c. 1400 A.D.) : but the resemblance does not decide
the date, which is doubtless very much earlier. The
upper part of the screen contains square panels of
ebony set with large crosses of solid ivory, most
exquisitely chiselled with scrollwork, and panels of
ebony carved through in work of the most delicate
and skilful finish. Above these panels stand the icons.
The screens of the two side-chapels are more recent
and inlaid only with plain ivory : the design however
of the north screen is good, being enriched with
flowers besides crosses and stars. All three screens
are pierced with a small square window (D) on each
side of the door. In the ordinary place, i.e. upon
the screen just before the wall or pier dividing the
haikal from the north chapel, is fastened the wooden
bracket or holder for the crewet (E). Between this
point and the angle formed by the abutment of

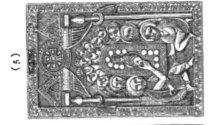

Fig. 11.—Wood Carvings at Abu Sargah (eighth century).

the haikal-screen are some very curious early carvings in relief (F)—panels that were once no doubt framed in the leaves of a door like that of Al Mu'allakah. There are eight panels in all, each 10¼ in. high by 6½ broad : of these, five represent sacred subjects and are probably of the eighth century, contemporary with the foundation of the church; the other three—one containing carvings of gazelles, two merely conventional scrollwork — are rather later. Taking the subjects in order as they stand from left to right, we find—

(1) *The Nativity.* The Child lies swathed in a manger with rays of glory falling from a bow or circle above, in which are carved two faces,—

perhaps meant for the other persons of the Trinity. In the top background an ox on one side of the manger and an ass on the other stand gazing upon it, and behind each animal stands an angel with outspread wings. Below them, and partly concealing them, Mary is seen lying on a couch and Joseph kneeling on one knee. The lower half of the panel is occupied partly by two shepherds, indicated by their crooks and by a lamb, and partly by the magi bringing gifts. Every panel is surrounded by a very beautifully carved border, generally of scrollwork, but all different. In this case crosses are carved at the angles and in the centre of the sides. The Holy Family and the angels all wear plain nimbs.

(2) Perhaps *St. Demetrius.* A bearded equestrian figure clad in richly embroidered raiment: in his right hand he carries a long spear ending upwards in a cross, while the lower end is grasped by a prostrate foe whom he seems to be slaying. In the upper dexter corner an eagle is carved with folded wings. The horseman is turned full face to the spectator: a row of small circles round the brow represents curling hair or possibly a diadem. He wears a fine full glory. The horse has oriental trappings, which might be of any age.

(3) *Mâri Girgis.* This is another equestrian, very similar in treatment to the last: the spear-shaft, however, ends in a loop instead of a point at the bottom : there is no figure, not even a dragon, on the ground : and the eagle, here placed in the sinister top corner, is bending its head very low. The horseman's face is quite beardless, and the hair vaguely indicated.

(4) *Abu-'s-Sifain*, or St. Mercurius. This title, like the last two, is very doubtful. The horseman

is in almost precisely the same attitude as the others, the right hand carrying a long spear, the left reining the steed.   But under the horse's feet a man is seen sitting on the ground and apparently pierced with the spear.   The victim, however, seems unconscious of his wound, and in his right hand is grasping a short rod which rests on a very perplexing little object in the background.   I can only conjecture that it may be an oven, that the figure on the ground is heating a bar of iron, and that he represents some persecutor and torturer of the Christians being slain by their champion.   The horseman is under a sort of trefoil arch : in both spandrels there are indications of curtains : in the sinister spandrel a hand is appearing, as from the clouds, holding out a crown.

(5) *The Last Supper.* This is an extremely interesting carving.   It represents our Lord and the apostles seated round a long table which occupies the centre of the panel.   The shape of the table is remarkable, the near end having square corners, the far end being rounded.   On it are laid twelve small loaves, and in the centre is a large fish on a platter : there is no cup or drinking vessel.   Christ in the lower dexter corner of the panel is grasping the fish. All the figures seem seated on the ground, wear nimbs, and face the spectator.   The whole scene is grouped under an altar-canopy supported on two slender columns with early Arab capitals.   A pair of altar curtains are seen running on rods above, but each is caught up and looped round a pillar, so as to leave a clear view of the scene below.   The canopy is in the form of a circle between two triangles, all with elaborate borders.   The circle encloses

a fine cross, and a smaller cross stands on the apex of each triangle.

The ritual significance of this carving, which is obvious enough, has been commented upon in another part of this work.   It is, I think, the only artistic monument definitely recording the early altar curtains of the Coptic ceremonial; although, as I have pointed out, there is abundance of other evidence to establish their existence.   Possibly even the form of the table may have its own meaning[1].

Over these panels are set three large pictures, neither ancient nor well executed.   One, however, representing Gabriel, deserves remark on account of a strange and puzzling instrument or emblem which the archangel is carrying.   With his left hand he holds a tall three-transomed cross called the cross of the patriarch of Jerusalem : and in the right something which exactly resembles in size and shape an ordinary hand-mirror.   Its straight handle and circular frame are ornamented with the very pattern used by the Arabs, as may be seen in any barber's shop in Cairo to-day.   Very possibly the instrument may be a flabellum or fan instead of a mirror ; but the priest could tell me nothing, and I can give no certain explanation.

Another painting over the locker or aumbry in the pier of the choir pourtrays the archangel Michael holding a Jerusalem cross with his right hand, and lifting in his left a balance.   The stole, marked with crosses and stars, hangs down straight in front, and passes from the centre of the chest over the left shoulder, thence over the right shoulder across the

---

[1] See vol. ii. chap. i.

breast, under the left arm, and round the waist : the end is then thrown over the left wrist—a curious arrangement, because it does not seem to admit of a crossing at the back. The vestment is painted red with frequent vertical lines of gold : the background of the painting is also gold. A picture of St. Stephen on the pier by the south chapel should not be passed over. The saint is vested in a white dalmatic, beautifully embroidered with a repeated pattern of a red rose with stalk and leaves. Only one end of the stole is visible, falling over the left shoulder ; but the stole is crossed also over the breast. The nimb is set round with a dotted border and covered all over with circles and stars of dotwork. The dalmatic opens by a slit down the front in the centre, not at the side, and the opening as well as the collar is edged with a rich orfrey. Both arms are bent at the elbow : the right hand is swinging a covered censer suspended by four chains, which are decked with little bells ; and in the left hand there reposes on a corporal or cloth a splendidly jewelled casket, which is either an incense box, or else a pyx or receptacle for the reserved host. This evidence of the practice of reservation, if such it be, is unique and extremely interesting. The picture, however, is not later than the sixteenth century, when the reservation of the host was not generally practised.

Before the haikal door hangs a magnificent curtain of ancient fabric embroidered with a figure of the Virgin and Child, figures of angels, the Coptic sacred letters, and many texts of Arabic—all wrought in massive thread of silver, and set round with beautiful borders also of silver embroidery, like that used for the vestments at Abu Ḳir wa Yuḥanna. The inter-

pretation of the Coptic sentence across the top of the
curtain is 'Peace to the Sanctuary of God the
Father, Lord of All.' The last word may be easily
identified as the Greek παντοκράτωρ. Besides this
front door there are two side doors (C) to the haikal;
and the usual small slide-windows open one on each
side of the principal entrance.

The haikal itself and the altar (H) are both very
small for the size of the church. The altar is 4 ft.
5½ in. long from north to south, and 3 ft. 3 in. broad:
height, 2 ft. 10¼ in. It stands at a distance of 3 ft.
from the screen, and is overshadowed by a large and
lofty canopy, which rests upon four Saracenic columns.
The spandrels of the canopy are finely painted with
angels carrying lilies or other flowers in their hands.
The two easternmost pillars stand 3 ft. 3½ in., and
the two westernmost 2 ft. 9 in., from the nearest
corner of the altar. The central groove or depression
for the altar-board is 2 ft. by 1 ft. 9½ in., but the
board itself is a more decided oblong, and does not
fit exactly. The side altars (I, J) show no such departure from the ordinary usage.

The four pillars of the canopy are joined together
by four small dark-painted beams on which Coptic
texts are written in white letters; and from the
beams rings are fastened with strings or chains for
hanging lamps or curtains. About the walls of the
apse rises a fine and lofty marble tribune consisting
of seven stages—three short and straight steps (B)
running north and south, and four seats sweeping
round the whole curve of the apse—and in the midst of
the curve is placed the patriarch's throne (A) with a
niche behind it. The outline of the niche is marked
all round by a design of coloured marbles in which

the cross is conspicuous : there is also set about it a square framing, the spandrels of which are inlaid with a fine minute mosaic of coloured marble mixed with mother-of-pearl, such as may be seen in the baptistery of the Little Church at Al Mu'allaḳah, or in far greater richness and profusion at the tomb-mosque of Al Ashraf among the tombs of the khalîfs. In Europe the same style of work is found in the Church of St. Vitale at Ravenna, and at the Cathedral of Parenzo in Istria. The tribune steps and seats are faced with vertical strips of red, black, and white marble. On the top seat a number of bad paintings, two large candlesticks, books, papers and vestments repose in ease and dust untroubled. There is also a picture and a loose wooden cross lying within the niche. The haikal is crowned by a small dome.

A larger and loftier dome covers the north aisle-chapel, the walls of which are square : the spring of the dome is relieved by gated pendentives. Before the eastern wall is a small tribune of three bow-shaped steps and a throne—unusual features in a side-chapel. Beyond a number of books well cased in dust upon the altar, and some loose leaves flung into a rush basket beside it, there is nothing here to notice.

The arrangement of the south aisle-chapel, which is still in frequent use for service, is quite different. It contains a broad apse with a niche, before which burns a perpetual lamp, but no tribune. The apse wall curves into a low semidome above ; but the rest of the chapel is flat-roofed, having, it will be remembered, the triforium overhead. The walls are covered with a low wainscot of deal : in the north wall is an aumbry. An old and disused patriarchal chair is kept within the chapel.

A low dark vaulted passage, blocked in the middle by a partition wall, runs round the haikal underneath the tribune steps[1], but is entered from without by a door (G) on either side of the abutting screen. On the north side there is nothing to discover; but entering the passage on the south, one finds at the far end, by help of candlelight, a recess containing a fine old Arabic lamp of plain white glass, with handles on the shoulder. It is of the same shape as the magnificent enamelled specimens of the thirteenth century, such as may be seen at the British Museum and also at South Kensington, and such as were once in common use in the churches and mosques of Egypt. Now a good example is worth at least £500. The lamp at Abu Sargah has neither colour nor enamel: still it seems to be held in honour, for it is only used once a year—on Good Friday. This vaulted passage is also used as the store-place for the sacred vessels of the church. It contains a large wooden coffer, the lid of which I raised and caught a hasty glimpse of a silver chalice, silver hand-cross, and processional cross, and of two silver fans like those at Dair Tadrus; but in a moment the ill-humoured priest flew into an ungovernable passion,

---

[1] This passage bears a curious resemblance to the passage under the very similar tribune at Torcello. There, however, the crypt—for such it is—instead of being blocked in the centre of the curve under the throne, opens out forming a small apsidal chapel with an altar. (See La Messe, vol. ii. pl. cxxx.) Of course it is just possible that the block under the throne at Abu Sargah encloses relics; but the passage cannot have been designed as an oratory, nor have contained an altar.

shut down the lid, and locked the passage-door, venting his fury in storms of Arabic abuse. Whether this passage can ever have been used as a crypt or confessionary, or contained the relics of the church, is doubtful. It is, however, worth remarking that the position of the entrance doors, the arrangement of the passage circling round beneath the sanctuary, even its barrel-vaulting, are so many points of resemblance to crypts such as that of the ancient basilica of the Vatican, the old crypt at Canterbury, or that of the seventh century still standing at Brixworth in Northampton. Still the lowness of the passage—it is scarcely 4 ft. high—may be a conclusive objection against its claim to be a confessionary.

The Crypt.

The crypt of Abu Sargah is a small low subterranean church, lying under the centre of the choir and part of the haikal. Two flights of steps lead down to it, as was mentioned, one from the north choir or transept, one from the south aisle by the large pier. (See K and K on plan.) The floor of the crypt is 8 ft. 9 in. below the level of the choir, or 7 ft. 1 in. below the nave floor. The nave floor is about 5 ft. 6 in. below the ground-level outside the church, and this again is some 7 ft. 6 in. below the average level of the ground outside the Roman fortress. The crypt floor is therefore no less than 21 ft. 1 in., and the floor of Abu Sargah 13 ft. below the modern level of Old Cairo. The greatest length of the crypt is 20 ft., and the breadth 15 ft. It is wagon-vaulted in three spans, and may be said to consist of a nave with north and south aisle. The aisles are divided off by slender columns, nine in

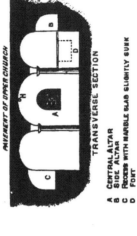

ABU SARGAH.
CRYPT UNDER MAIN CHURCH
DEDICATED TO THE B. V. MARY

PAVEMENT OF UPPER CHURCH

TRANSVERSE SECTION

A   CENTRAL ALTAR
B   SIDE ALTAR
C   RECESS WITH MARBLE SLAB SLIGHTLY SUNK
D   FONT
E E STAIRS TO UPPER CHURCH
F   CIRCULAR SLAB OF MARBLE (OVER VIRGINS WELL)
G   SQUINT BETWEEN NORTH AISLE AND NAVE
H H IRON RINGS FOR HANGING LAMPS

PAVEMENT OF UPPER CHURCH

LONGITUDINAL SECTION

PLAN OF CRYPT

Fig. 12.

number altogether. Two short walls, in the line of these columns, project 6 ft. from the eastern wall of the crypt, and form a sort of haikal, but there is no screen here nor any furniture whatsoever. The columns are about 5 ft. each in height: the capitals are formless, except in one case, where the column has a late classical capital, and a classical capital also used for the base. One shaft near the southern entrance is twisted and fluted, resembling the small columns in the bays of the triforium of the upper church : there is also a pair of similar columns on the ambon at Al Mu'allakah.

In the floor of the central division, just within what may perhaps be called the haikal, there is a circular slab (F) of white marble let into the limestone floor. This is directly underneath the chief altar of the church above, and may perhaps mark the place originally assigned to the well, of which the Holy Family drank when they rested on this spot. Perhaps, however, the most curious feature of the crypt is the structure of three arched recesses, one in the northern, one in the southern, and one in the eastern wall. The last of these (A) is undoubtedly an altar. It is semicircular in plan, with straight walls about 20 inches high and a domical roof—all wrought in finely jointed ashlar work of limestone. Inlet in the bottom of the recess is a slab of white marble containing a beautiful cross, 10½ in. in diameter, sculptured within a roundel. The niche in the south wall (B) is very similar, and likewise contains a slab sculptured with a cross, but of rather different design[1]. It is curious, however, that in neither case is the slab

---

[1] A woodcut of these crosses is given in vol. ii.

placed in the middle of the floor of the niche, nor is
the cross cut in the middle of the slab. The recess
in the north aisle (C) has a slab of nearly the same
dimensions as the other two, but instead of being
flush with the flooring of the niche it is depressed to
the depth of an inch with a raised border on all sides.
It is thus in the form of an oblong tray. The
meaning of this form has not yet been satisfactorily
explained. The Copts say that it represents the
manger, while the eastern niche represents Mary's
resting-place, and the southern niche that of Joseph.
They do not, however, state why the manger followed
the Holy Family into Egypt. The story is obviously
a confusion of the resting-place in Egypt with the
place of the nativity, and is in fact a confession of
ignorance. I am inclined to think that all three
recesses contain genuine altars. The difficulty, of
course, lies in this, that there are no other examples
of altars thus undetached; and the position north
and south is almost unique : but the whole structure
of the crypt and its interest are so exceptional,
that altars may have been erected in this unusual
position each to commemorate some special point in
the ancient legend, of which now all has vanished
but the broad outline. It may be regarded as
certain that the eastern recess was used as an altar ;
and, if so, the close resemblance of the slab in the
southern niche makes it difficult to associate this
with another purpose. Finally, the tray-like slab in
the northern recess has its exact counterpart
on a larger scale in one of the altar-tops at Al
Mu'allaḳah ; and it seems also to have been copied
for the altars of some of the churches in the Natrun
desert.

At the end of the south aisle of the crypt is a baptistery or rather font,—a round stone vessel set in solid masonry near the ground (D). The north aisle has nothing whatever to mark the place where, in an ordinary church, there would be a chapel; but in the wall dividing part of the aisle from the haikal there is a small squint, which however is not splayed towards the eastern altar.

It is quite impossible to fix the date of this crypt; but it is doubtless anterior to the main church by some centuries. It may be taken for granted that a spot said to be hallowed by the presence of our Lord would be walled in, and kept as sacred, from the very beginning of Christianity in Egypt. There was therefore, in all probability, a church upon this spot by the second or third century: the present crypt may be a replacement of the original shrine and may date from the sixth century. It was natural that in after times a larger and more sumptuous edifice should have been erected on the same site, and so arranged that the high altar should cover the omphalos of the earlier building. Moreover, by the eighth century the level of the ground about the little church had risen so high, that the question of pulling it down can hardly have been considered. It was much easier to build above it, and much more in accordance with western tradition, if not with eastern, to make the little church into a confessionary for the larger.

HISTORICAL NOTE ON ABU SARGAH.

WHO the St. Sergius was to whom this church is dedicated is uncertain. Two saints of the name are recorded in the Coptic calendar : one martyred with his father and sister, whose festival is on the thirteenth day of Amshir (7th Feb.), the other a 'follower of Wakas and saddler at the court of King Maximianus,' whose feast falls on the tenth day of Babeh (7th Oct.). Nothing is really known of either martyr. But the name is rather a favourite in Russia, and there is a large monastery with this dedication near Moscow[1].

The history of the church is, as usual, comprised in a handful of scanty gleanings. But it has an early beginning. In the year 859 A.D. the pious Shanûdah was elected patriarch in Abu Sargah— the father who cast the form of the Coptic sacred letters which remains to this day. There also in 977 A.D. Ephraim was elected, and taken thence in chains for his enthronement at Alexandria. Mention has been made elsewhere of the contest for supremacy that arose under Christodulus between Abu Sargah and Al Mu'allakah, ending in the virtual victory of the latter. A hundred years later the claim of the older church was no longer questioned, if Renaudot is right in saying that Gabriel, the LXX patriarch, was elected at Al Mu'allakah although a deacon of Abu Sargah. Al Makrîzi, however, says he

---

[1] Renaudot, Hist. Pat. Alex., p. 301. A curious legend of the pilgrimage of St. Sergius with SS. Theophilus and Hyginus may be found in Lord Lindsay's Christian Art, vol. i. p. clx, translated from Rosweyde's Vitae Patrum.

was deacon of Abu-'s-Sifain, not Abu Sargah[1]. Now-a-days the newly elected primate celebrates first at Al Mu'allakah, and at Abu Sargah afterwards. About the year 1100 A.D. we find Michael excommunicating Sanutius, bishop of Maṣr or Old Cairo, for celebrating on the same day in both churches, just as in the western ritual a priest was forbidden to celebrate twice a day, except on Easter Day and Christmas Day, or when a burial service had to be performed after the ordinary mass[2]. But the successor to Sanutius in the bishopric was escorted to Abu Sargah in a grand procession of clergy carrying burning tapers, thuribles, and gospels[3]. There, after a solemn service, his letters of nomination were read, and he was ordained, but his proclamation took place in the Ḥârat-az-Zuailah of Cairo. A similar procession accompanied by a multitude of priests chaunting from missals attended Macarius from the church of St. Cosmas in Old Cairo[4] to Abu Sargah, where he was formally elected to the chair of St. Mark, c. 1103 A.D. Later we read that a grand funeral service was held in Abu Sargah over the body of the deceased bishop Sanutius, who was afterwards buried in the field of the Abyssinians—a place often mentioned in Coptic history, but quite unknown to the Copts of to-day: it seems, however, to have been near the Fûm al Khalîg.

So the brief story ends, giving us a glimpse of liturgical splendour hard to imagine after looking on the cold and slovenly service in the dim neglected building of to-day.

---

[1] Malan, Hist. Copt., p. 93.   [2] Rock, vol. iii. part 2. p. 166.
[3] Renaudot, Hist. Pat. Alex., p. 492.
[4] There is no trace or tradition of this church left. It seems to have been on the island of Roḍa.

The Cathedral Church of Al 'Adra,

COMMONLY CALLED

Al Mu'allaḳah (العنرا الشهيرة المعلقة),

or The Hanging Church.

PASS along the northern wall of Abu Sargah towards the Jewish Synagogue; thence to the right
down a quaint, narrow, shadowed street with a few
high lattice windows; again to the right where the
street is roofed over in places with palm-beams;
finally, from the street a narrow passage between
blind walls leads to a staircase doorway beside which
lies topsy-turvy a very large and fine Corinthian
capital. This is the doorway of Al Mu'allakah—
the most ancient of the churches in Ḳaṣr-ash-Sham-
m'ah.

As was mentioned before, the church derives its
common name from the fact of its suspension between
two Roman bastions, and the ascent is made by a
staircase built close by one of these bastions, the central one of the three on the southern side of the
fortress. Towards the top of the stairs may be seen
on both sides Roman brickwork, the spring of a
'bridge' as the priests call it, i.e. an arched vaulting
which supported a floor in some building near the
bastion. At the landing the way divides—that on
the left leading to sets of half-ruined cells and chambers, in the first of which one may notice a cross
carved in the capital of a column: that on the right

leading through a lattice-screen to a school, and
through a door opposite the screen to a small oblong
courtyard fronting the western side of the church.
This courtyard is open and surrounded by lofty
walls lightened above by large pointed arches.   The
pavement encloses in the middle a bed of soil, in
which two fine palm-trees are growing in a kind of
large stone flowerpots.   There is something bold
and original in planting date-palms at this height
above ground; but it is a pretty idea to place them
before the entrance of 'the church in the air.' Palm-
leaves are largely used in the church festivals at
Easter, and delicate baskets woven of palm are used
to carry the eulogiae, or blessed bread, and are given
as gifts among neighbours and friends at that season.
There is also a Coptic legend that at the flight into
Egypt the fruit of the palm was the first food of
which the Virgin partook, and that the little dent in
the back of the datestone (not the cleft) was first
caused by the Virgin's tooth.   Another version tells
that the mark is the Arabic exclamation 'Ya,' 'Oh,'
there printed, because on tasting the date the Virgin
cried out, 'Oh, God! this is good.' But it requires
a powerful imagination to detect any resemblance
between the mark and the Arabic يا.

Besides the palms, one may notice another eastern
plant, the aloe, tufts of which hang above the doorway at the foot and at the top of the staircase.   It
is thought to have a magic virtue against the power
of the evil eye[1]—a superstition common to Copts
and Muslims alike.

---

[1] A native once told me, with the utmost possible seriousness,
that a glance of the evil eye can slay a camel.   See on this subject
Lane's Modern Egyptians, vol. i. p. 70, &c.

Close by the courtyard door in the wall is a
pretty, though recent, drinking-fountain, which must
not be mistaken for a stoup; for the only regular
use of holy water in the Coptic Church is at the
end of the Sunday mass, when the bishop sprinkles
the people; there are no vessels of stone to retain
it permanently.

Al Mu'allaḳah is a triapsal church of the basilican
order; but it has this unique peculiarity among the
churches of the two Cairos, that it is entirely domeless. It therefore approximates more closely to
the pure type of basilican architecture than any
of the other churches into the structure of which
some Byzantine element enters. The apses are
very shallow; the curve in all three cases falls
within the eastern walls instead of sweeping round
the altar in such a manner that the chord of the
arc would fall to westward of the altar. But this
arrangement is obviously a structural necessity;
for the architect was building, it must be remembered, not on the ground, but in the air, and could
get no solid foundations for regular apses. Perhaps
the same fact may explain the absence of domes,
which require to rest on walls or piers of great
strength and thickness.

The church has at present a sort of exterior
narthex or porch consisting of two stories, of which
the upper is supported on pillars. The back wall
is of stone, elaborately worked with a debased style
of arcading, and painted to resemble in parts sectile
work of coloured marbles. Above the central arch,
but at such a height as to be quite undecipher-
able, lies let into the wall the cedar beam mentioned by Murray as forming the lintel of an inner

doorway[1]. The priest states that the scene represents the triumphal entry into Jerusalem; but this is questionable. The beam has been moved from its original position in the course of a restoration, still unfinished, which has gone far to mar the interest of the church. It is said that the shape and details of the former building have been exactly reproduced; but the statement must be taken for what it is worth. The shell of the building remains unaltered, except perhaps at the western end; the exterior porch is, I believe, an innovation, and the four doors opening from it are an entire departure from the original design. Inside a fresh west gallery has been built; a number of beautiful old carved screens have been huddled and hammered together into a long wooden wall; the altars and altar-canopies have been thrown down, and will be replaced by new Greek designs from Alexandria; new glass, tasteless and staring in colour, has been put in the eastern windows in lieu of the old; in fact English restorers could not have made more havoc. Worst of all, perhaps, is the loss of the cedar door-leaves sculptured in panels, as described by Murray. When, after searching everywhere, I asked the priest about them, he could only reply, 'Ma fish'—there is no such thing. 'But,' I persisted, 'I have read books written in English by people who have seen the doors; what has become

---

[1] The inscription was copied by Mr. Greville Chester, and is given in his short 'Notes on the Ancient Christian Churches of Musr el Ateekah.' For the translation and date (284 A.D.), he there refers to 'Archaeologia Cambrensis,' series 4, vol. iii. p. 152.

of them ?' 'The church was falling down in 1879,
and doubtless they were destroyed.' 'What? only
a year ago? in 1879?' 'No,' he said, changing his
tone; 'I mean seven years ago.' 'Or seventy-seven,'
I thought; but it was idle arguing, since obviously
the doors had been either stolen, or sold by the
priest[1].

The porch of the church is used as a mandârah or
guest-room, the place of gossip and coffee. Against
each of the three walls is a wooden bench worth
noticing for its antique design. Four doors open
into the church, one north and south and two east
of the porch. But only the south door is generally
used[2]; it leads into a small chamber from which

---

[1] The latter seemed on all grounds most likely, and I have since
ascertained it for a fact. The price given to the priest was £100;
the doors adorned the buyer's house in Paris for some time,
and were ultimately resold to the British Museum,—their fittest
destination if they could not remain in their place at Al Mu'allaḳah:
but of course they are comparatively uninteresting, and quite lost in
their present position. I have no desire to palliate the priest's con-
duct. The rudeness and cupidity of the man, the mean shifts he
found for evading the patriarch's orders and refusing admission
or information, have not prejudiced me in his favour; but in justice
let it be remembered that the miserable pay of the Coptic priest-
hood—averaging £2 monthly—makes it very hard for them to
resist the offers they may receive from wealthy curiosity-hunters.

[2] See plan. I may here perhaps explain how it happens that
M. Rohault de Fleury gives this same plan of Al Mu'allaḳah, which
he calls Sitt Miriam, and I claim as my own. It is figured in La
Messe, vol. ii. pl. ccli, together with St. Sergius, and both plans are
labelled 'd'après M. Middleton.' The truth is that the plan of Abu
Sargah is entirely the work of Mr. Middleton; though I was present when Mr. Middleton made the plan, I cannot claim any share
in it whatever. On the other hand my friend was not even in
Egypt when I made the plan of Al Mu'allaḳah, which I did without

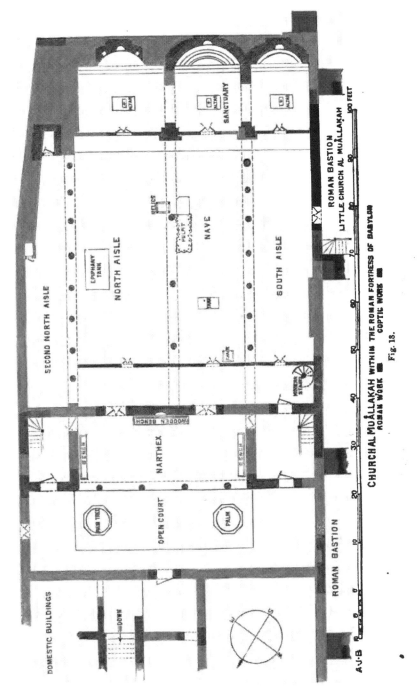

CHURCH AL MUÂLLAKAH WITHIN THE ROMAN FORTRESS OF BABYLON

ROMAN WORK ▦   COPTIC WORK ▦

Fig. 18.

a staircase ascends to the western gallery, which is reserved for women. This gallery projects eight or ten feet into the church, and under it lies the wooden wall of patched screenwork before mentioned. Some of these screens are of very unusual pattern, and very beautiful. One is unique; above and below are narrow panels of carved cedar and ebony alternately, chased with rich scrollwork and interwoven with Cufic inscriptions; the framework also is of cedar, wrought into unusual starlike devices, and the intervals are filled with thin plates of ivory, through which, when the screen was in its original position, the light of the lamps behind fell with a soft rose-coloured glow, extremely pleasing. There is an almost magical effect peculiar to this screen; for the design seems to change in a kaleidoscopic manner, according as the spectator varies his distance from it. Something of this effect is preserved in the illustration here given. There are many other examples of fine early carving and inlaying in this wooden wall, but the motley mixing of styles and epochs makes the result of the whole harsh and tasteless.

---

any assistance. On my return to England I found that Mr. Middleton had drawn out fair the beautiful plan of Abu Sargah, which he generously placed at my disposal. He also very kindly offered to draw out fair from the rough my plan of Al Mu'allakah, and my plans of other churches, K. Burbârah, Abu-'s-Sifain, Mâri Mîna, &c. In communicating his own plan of Abu Sargah to M. de Fleury, he inadvertently included with it the fair drawing of Al Mu'allakah. The latter I believe had never before been published, and I may claim it as mine, if the claim is worth making. I may add that the 'Baptistère' inserted by M. de Fleury is a purely imaginary description—an antiquarian's fiction resting on analogy, not on evidence.

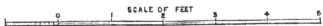

SCALE OF FEET

0   1   2   3   4   5

Fig. 14.—Cedar and ivory Screen at Al Mu'allaḳah. (Perhaps eleventh century.)

All the old transverse screens have been torn down, except that of the haikal; the result is a much greater unity of appearance in the church. The division into nave and aisles is clear and un-broken by cross-screens; resembling rather that of a Greek church, or the English arrangement of church and chancel; and this is doubtless a rever-sion of the original arrangement at Al Mu'allakah.

But there is one very curious, not to say unique, feature to be noticed, the entire absence of the choir. Before restoration no doubt a place for the choir was marked off by screens; now there is no sign of any choir having belonged to the original arrange-ment of the church. In front of all three eastern chapels is a continuous narrow platform or solea; but from this point the floor of the whole church is of uniform level; whereas elsewhere the choir is almost invariably raised at least one step above the nave. The omission is very remarkable, but probably the solea served the purpose of the choir. It is at least broad enough to hold the lecterns and a number of singers.

The south aisle is parted from the nave by a row of eight columns, joined by a continuous wooden architrave, which is lightened by small pointed relieving arches as at Anba Shanûdah. Between the nave and the north aisle are only three columns spanned by wide pointed arches without architrave; but there is beyond a third or outer aisle, divided off by an arrangement of columns symmetrical with that between nave and south aisle. The north wall runs at an angle with this line of columns, with an offset inwards; the outer aisle thus narrows eastward to a width of only 7 ft. and ends with a small sacristy, the door of which the priest declined to open. The southern wall of the main building is also relieved by small arches, and a doorway in it leads into the 'little church,' as it is called, of which more anon. The nave and the main aisles end eastward each in its own chapel; and they are roofed separately in three spans with lofty wagon-vaulting of timber; while the outer aisle has a low flat roof forming a floor for a small gallery above, a sort of triforium, continuous with the western gallery, whence the women look down through lattice windows on the church below.

Al Mu'allakah may then be styled a double-aisled church, and as such is extremely remarkable in having no transepts. So rare is this peculiarity that Mr. G. Gilbert Scott says boldly, 'There is no example known of a double-aisled basilica without transepts [1].' But another very distinct instance is supplied by a Coptic church, viz. that of Al 'Adra in the Hârat-az-Zuailah at Cairo, where there are two double aisles and no transept. It is difficult to see why, in point of architectural fitness, double aisles should necessitate transepts, and the Coptic examples tell against Mr. Scott's assumption that the church of St. Felix at Nola *must* have been transeptal.

The columns are all of white marble except one which is of black basalt. On four are consecration crosses exactly like those at Abu Sargah: a fifth has a group of four crosses of slightly different and perhaps more recent design. These are all southward of the nave. On another shaft near the north-west corner of the nave is a cruciform depression

---

[1] History of English Church Architecture, p. 63, note nn.

dotted with nail-marks : here originally a silver dedication cross was fastened, which measured seven
inches each way. The pillars have all been moved
in restoration, and the crosses face all ways ; so that
their present position proves nothing. But not only
is the shape in this case remarkable, but I know of
no other instance of a metal cross attached to a pillar
in a Coptic church ; though evidence of the same
practice is found in English churches. The dedication crosses outside Salisbury Cathedral were of
metal : inside Chichester Cathedral are two incisions
with nail-holes over them, showing that a metal cross
was hung before the incision : and in Westminster
Abbey the crosses painted in the south aisle of the
Lady Chapel have a central hole plugged with wood,
into which a spike from the metal cross was fastened,
while a similar plug below held a small metal taper-
stand for use at the feast of the Virgin. The figures
of apostles or saints, which doubtless here as at
Abu Sargah were painted on every pillar, have all
vanished under the scrubbing and polishing which
I am told they received during the restoration : there
remains, however, one interesting though damaged
painting of an early patriarch, and here and there a
few traces of colour. The design on the pall of the
patriarch closely resembles on a smaller scale a
design upon the sides of the mumbâr or pulpit in
the mosque of Sultan Hassan at Cairo, built in 1356
A.D.: but I think the Coptic fresco some centuries
earlier, notwithstanding.

There is a large Epiphany tank in the north aisle—
an unusual place—and a smaller tank for the Mandatum in the nave. At the west end of the nave
is the patriarch's chair of old lattice-work, and on it

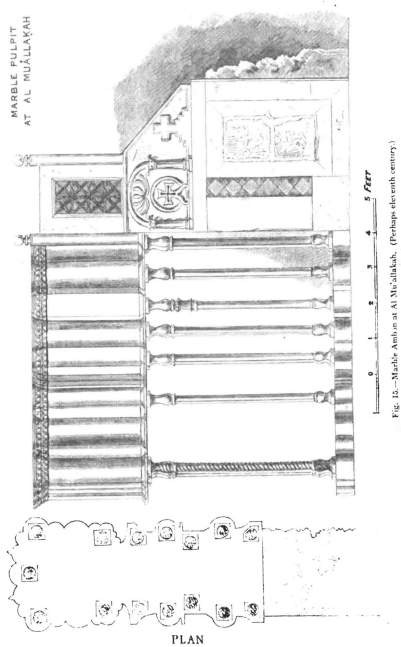

MARBLE PULPIT
AT AL MUÁLLAKAH

PLAN

5 FEET

Fig. 15.—Marble Ambon at Al Mu'allakah. (Perhaps eleventh century.)

a shabby tin almsbox.   Further east is the ancient
ambon, a most original and beautiful piece of work,
of which I give a woodcut.   It stands on fifteen
exceedingly delicate Saracenic columns arranged in
seven pairs with a leader.   The two columns of
each pair are identical, but no two pairs are alike.
They stand on a slab of white marble carved with
wavy outline, and this rests on a base raised nine
inches from the floor and faced with vertical strips
of coloured marble.   The body of the ambon is
faced in the same way, but has a coping of white
marble carved with most exquisitely minute and
graceful pendentives.   Under the floor of the balcony
are six crosses in circles finely sculptured and filled
with rich designs: the two larger are 13 in., the
others 8 in. in diameter.   Of the twelve steps which
formed the staircase only the upper four are now
left : but on the marble sides of the staircase remain
two crosses cut in relief, one a low broad resurrection cross, the other between pillars joined by an
arch—a common early design that may be seen, for
instance, on a stone taken from the ancient church
of St. John at Ephesus now built into the Greek
chapel which stands on the original site.   Though
this ambon is distinctly Arab in character and possibly not older than the twelfth century, yet it is
perhaps the most interesting thing left in the church
so far untouched by the restorers.   I need scarcely
add that they talk of pulling it down[1].   This ambon

---

[1] According to Mr. Greville Chester 'a certain patriarch named
Abraham lies buried under this pulpit.'   A patriarch is certainly
buried behind the ambon at Abu-'s-Sifain, but I can find no 'Abraham' in the list of Coptic patriarchs.   Al Makrîzi mentions one
'Afraham,' or Ephraim, a very pious man, poisoned by a clerk

follows the rule invariable with Coptic ambons of extending lengthwise from east to west and not across the church from north to south.

Near the steps of the ambon, but standing rather in the north aisle and facing east, is a curious old reliquary—a sort of large wooden coffer on four legs with a front of lattice-work and a square doorless opening veiled by a curtain. It contains four bundles or bolsters of relics, covered in silk brocaded with silver as usual: the bones enclosed are those of Mâri Girgis, Tadrus, Baskhârûn, and Abu Ishâk. Round the opening and at the sides of the reliquary hang pictures of these saints and of angels. As a rule such bolsters of relics are placed in a locker in the wall under the principal pictures in the several churches: this moveable reliquary is unique in the churches of the two Cairos.

The paintings here are not very interesting or ancient. On the south wall are (1) Abu Nafr with his palm and fountain, (2) a patriarch, (3) an angel, and (4) a rather curious throned Virgin. She is seated before an iconostasis with the usual three chapels: in front of each chapel a lamp of the old Arabic sort is hung by a pulley: above in the background the roof of the church is represented by twenty-nine little domes with crosses. Round this scene are painted separately thirty-four saints each carrying cross and palm-branch. The date of this picture is 1777 A.D. (5) Another modern picture

---

whose sins he rebuked. This was about 980 A.D., and if the tradition points to this Ephraim, the pulpit may be as old as 1000 A.D. But it is very questionable whether the thickness of the floor of the church is sufficient to allow of any burial beneath it.

shows Virgin and Child surrounded by ten little scenes—curious but not fine work.

The sanctuary-screens at Al Mu'allakah are very remarkable for their beauty. That of the northern chapel resembles a screen at Abu-'s-Sifain, having a design of squares with crosses at all the angles. But the details vary. The body of the crosses is alternately ivory and ebony: the ivory body is framed in ebony bordered again with ivory: and the ebony body is framed in ivory bordered again by ebony. The squares are ebony bordered with ivory and enclose ivory octagons, which again enclose ivory crosses set in ebony. But description of such work is dangerous: it can convey little idea of the clearness and splendour, while it retains all the complexity, of the original.

The piers at either side of the central or haikal screen are cased in deal, carved and set with a star-and-tongue pattern in flat ivory. This is modern; but the haikal-screen itself is very old, and though it has suffered some repairing, it remains a marvel of art. The frame is ebony and rosewood, exquisitely chased and set with beautiful designs in worked ebony. The pattern is chiefly what I have called star-and-tongue,—a central many-branched star in a ring of tongue-shaped plaques divided off by elaborate mouldings. Above this screen, and above the two side-screens also, is a delicate boarding set with panels of chased ivory and very fine through-carvings of ebony. Similar work of equal skill and beauty may be seen at Abu Sargah and Abu-'s-Sifain.

The southern screen shows a cruciform pattern: each cross is filled with carved ebony in an ivory border, and between the crosses runs a sort of key pattern. On top of this screen is a series of small scene pictures, old but not specially good: those above the northern screen are of the same type, but recent. The seven large pictures which stand on the central iconostasis are set in a single frame; and on the frame are Coptic and Arabic gold writings in relief. In the midst is Christ throned, in the attitude of benediction, instead of the more usual Virgin Mary; on the dexter side the Virgin; the other figures are two angels and three apostles. Each picture is about 4 ft. high.

Al Mu'allakah is triapsal, but all the three apses vary slightly in span. The central haikal has a tribune with three straight and three curved steps besides the topmost bench: the other chapels have a different arrangement. The haikal is divided from the side chapels by wide openings with lofty pointed arches which had originally, no doubt, a wooden casing splendidly gilt and painted. This painted woodwork still remains on the soffit of the similar arches over the tribune and in the southern chapel. Of the three altars not a stone was left standing at my last visit in 1884; they were pulled down, one might say out of sheer mischief, four or five years previously; and are to be replaced, if the priest is right, by slabs on pillars—the latest Greek fashion from Alexandria. But leaning against the wall in the northern chapel were two curious ancient altar-slabs of white marble, which belonged most likely to the north and south chapel altars, while that of the haikal was of the ordinary type. Of these tops one is horse-shoe shaped, the chord and the greatest diameter of the curve being each 3 ft. 9 in. The interior surface

is depressed about 2 in., leaving a narrow fillet or
border all round, except that in the middle of the
chord a channel is cut through the border, of a depth
corresponding to that of the depression. The design
very much resembles that of the altar-top in the
chapel of Mâri Buktor, Abu-'s-Sifain. The other
is perhaps unique in these Cairo churches : it is a
rectangular slab 3 ft. 11 in. by 3 ft., hollowed like the
last to the depth of 2 in. all over, with a narrow
border left standing round. The centre of the slab
is pierced through with a hole. Further remarks
on these slabs will be found in the chapter on
the Coptic altar.

The north apse has two straight steps, and
above these two more following the curve. In the
wall is a niche and on each side of the niche an
aumbry.

There is a niche without aumbries in the eastern
wall of the haikal, and a good many pictures lie
scattered about on the steps in both chapels: but
none are worth notice except a double picture, the
Virgin and St. Gabriel, in a frame carved with
Coptic letters in relief. The work is early but not
very skilful. There is however another picture of
Mary with Christ, which is earlier and certainly
better : while another subject, Michael slaying Satan,
is treated in a most powerful and masterly manner.
Here the prostrate fiend, the angel's flying drapery,
the back-swung sword just balanced for the blow,
and the look of heroic strength and anger in the
face, prove that the painter had very great imaginative sympathy as well as power over form and
colour—unusual qualities in Coptic art. The date
of the painting is the sixteenth century, and the

style is scarcely inferior to the Annunciation and the Christ on the altar-casket at Abu-'s-Sifain.

The apse wall in the south aisle-chapel was faced to a height of 10 ft. with coloured marble arranged in very beautiful patterns. The upper part of this work remains, although lower down the lost facing is replaced by plaster painted in imitation. The niche is splendidly inlaid with opus Alexandrinum, which contains a fine cross inwrought in the design. There should be noticed in this chapel a very singular and beautiful recess for relics, set in the south wall at a height of 11 ft. from the ground. A space about 4 ft. high and 9 ft. long is enclosed by an exquisitely carved marble border, within which is a triple arcading worked with very delicate pendentives. The central arch rises over a sort of wooden locker : the side arches are filled with some wonderfully fine open-work carving in marble—a grill almost as fine as the ebony through-carving on the iconostasis. Above is a space filled with Arabic writing, tracery, and crosses,—the whole forming as rich and skilful a piece of chisel-work as can be found in Egypt. Walled up behind the grills are doubtless relics of saints, and some less sacred were also kept in the locker.

The three altars were recently canopied with baldakyns, two of which I saw dismounted from their columns and thrown one above the other in the western aisle-chapel. They were very old, and had been finely painted with figures ; but time and neglect had ruined them. It is uncertain whether they will be replaced or will disappear entirely.

The wagon-vaulting of the nave and two main aisles is continued eastward over the altar, and ends in each case with a gable having a semicircular window of painted glass. Most of the work is new ; but traces of the old remain, particularly in the north chapel, where one or two ancient lights still show clearly enough the original effect. The panes or quarries are extremely small, with a lustre of soft harmonious colours,—a sort of bright mosaic arranged in cypress-tree and other eastern designs. Like designs may be seen in the painted windows of the mosque of Ḳait Bey, among the tombs of the khalífs, or the mosque of Al Ghûrî dated 1500 A.D. in Cairo : and are common in Damascus tiles of the sixteenth century, of which the most magnif.cent display in Egypt and perhaps in the world may be seen in the mosque of Ibrahim ʿAgha near the citadel of Cairo.

THE LITTLE CHURCH.

Opening out by a door in the south wall of Al Muʿallaḳah on the same level is the very ancient and curious 'little church,' fortunately almost untouched by restoration. It occupies the floor of a Roman bastion, but the windows have been blocked up, and a huge central pier of Arab work added to support the floor of a chapel above, and to strengthen various structures crowded within. The little church is used now chiefly for its baptistery; but it is divided into a number of tiny chapels. Of these the northernmost adjoining Al Muʿallaḳah has four regular divisions—haikal, choir, men's section, and women's section. The last is only 3 ft. deep, and capable of containing eight or ten women : but the screen before it is good,—lattice-work with panels above of finely carved cedar.   In the haikal are candlesticks and altar-casket: also a corporal and altar-frontal of very rich embroidery: against the wall reclines a plain bronze processional cross.   The baldakyn is quite rude and unadorned, but it is in replacement of an earlier one; for there are many signs of departed splendour in this chapel besides the altar-vestments.   The eastern window, set as in the large church at the gable-end of a wagon-vaulted roof, is of painted glass, and survives less damaged than the others.   The eastern wall has been adorned with a very fine painting in distemper, of which faint traces are left, indicating a central figure and a group of figures at each side.   The priest could only say that they stood for the twelve apostles; but I counted twenty figures, and there may have been a few more originally, possibly as many as twenty-five.   If I remember rightly all wore the nimbus: but there is no other evidence to decide the subject.   The painting is at some height from the ground, in a wide arched recess: the dimensions are nearly 14 ft. by 3 ft. 6 in.   The Coptic inscription carved round the arch points to an early date.

From the haikal one passes through a screen southward into a tiny narrow room filled with lumber, and by another screen into a second chapel, which has an altar under a baldakyn, and a deep recess eastward,—the bay of a Roman window: a short Arab wall parts this chapel from the very beautiful little baptistery.   In the Arab wall is fixed a stone basin standing out 16 in. and measuring 2 ft. across: it communicates by a drain with the font in the baptistery, and may possibly have been

used as a piscina : though I think from its size it
was rather meant for filling the font, like the basin
in the church of Sitt Mariam.   For while the position corresponds to that of the piscina in western
churches, it is difficult to believe that the rinsings of
the priest's hands flowed into the font, more especially as they would have to be removed thence,
because the font has no drain to carry them
away.   The question however is open : though the
long disuse of the chapel renders the priest's
evidence of little value.   In the Ecgbert Pontifical
is a rubric ordering the 'water in which the corporals have been washed' to be turned 'into the
baptistery[1]'.

The baptistery itself consists of two tiny chambers : the outer is reserved for women and screened
off from the inner, which occupies a window recess
in the Roman wall.   The recess, originally less than
5 ft. square, has been very slightly enlarged : a second
small recess, about 3 ft. deep, has been hollowed in
the heart of the wall, and a font has been placed low
within it, and secured at the back with mortar.   The
font is a deep round basin with out-curved rim and
fluted sides, hewn of white marble, but unpolished—
a very pretty piece of sculpture.   The arch above
the basin is covered with mosaic of coloured marbles,
and the walls are overlaid with vertical strips of
marble in many colours.   A shallow recess opposite the font, and another beside it, are also decked
with the richest and finest mother-of-pearl and marble
mosaic, the main design being a sort of conventional
lotus pattern, singular and pleasing.   This baptistery

---

[1] P. 15.

is still used, but it can only be seen by the light of candles : for there is no window.

The gospel-stand belonging to the baptistery is ancient, and departs from the usual design in having at each corner a floriated cross of metal, fixed on wooden stems rising about 18 in. above the board. It lies among a heap of church lumber,—window-frames, broken screens, strips of marble, doors, lattice-work, panels, &c. The rest of the space within the curve of the bastion is vacant, but formerly was divided by many screens into irregular compartments.

The central pier has been mentioned as upholding the floor of a chapel above. This floor however lies only to the south side of the pier, so that it roofs that part alone of the little church which lies in the actual curve of the bastion, and not the first chapel described as adjoining the Mu'allakah. The wagon-vault roofing of the first chapel is very lofty : whereas the ceiling over the second chapel and over the baptistery is but half the height, and this ceiling is the floor of an upper room called the chapel of St. Mark. The ascent is made by a staircase at the west end of the first chapel.

The women's section at the west end of St. Mark's is divided into three parts : on the south is a tiny oratory railed off by lattice-work : on the north side is a door opening into a flying gallery or bridge, which crosses the little church and enables worshippers to look down on the choir and haikal. From this bridge the best view is to be had of the painted window. The sanctuary-screen in St. Mark's is of ancient ebony and ivory resembling the principal screen in Al Mu'allakah, but not carved with the same delicacy. The altar has an unusual feature : instead of the ordinary wooden board a kind of circular marble tray 2 in. deep with raised border is let into the masonry, so that the top of the border is flush with the altar-top. The latter is oblong, 3 ft. 11 in. by 3 ft. 3 in. : the tray is 3 ft. in diameter.

In the small sacristy northward of the haikal are various relics of church furniture, but nothing of interest or value, except the fragments of a plain colourless Arabic lamp,—fragments which seem to have been cherished for some years.

It is probable that this little church is either the original Al Mu'allakah or part of it, and has remained with only trifling alteration of detail unchanged from the day of its dedication. It may therefore lay claim to the surpassing interest of being one of the oldest places of Christian worship in the world.

Historical Note on Al Mu'allakah.

The church of Al Mu'allakah competes with Abu Sargah for the honour of being reckoned the earliest of the surviving churches in Maṣr : but it is certain that both Christian and Arab writers alike make mention of the Hanging Church long before Abu Sargah ; and the former, if not of remoter antiquity, is at least of more ancient importance. The recent restoration of Al Mu'allakah has done much to silence internal evidence : still if one may hazard a date, perhaps the present fabric of the larger church may be assigned to the sixth century, and the smaller to the third or fourth of the Christian era. This estimate however neither clashes with the probability of there having been an earlier building in place of the main church, nor denies the fact that some of the decoration in the little church is very considerably later. The first great epoch of church-building in Egypt as elsewhere was the reign of Constantine : but there is no doubt that even in the second century churches sprang up in many parts of the country. The fine condition in which the two bastions of the Roman fortress and the gateway upholding Al Mu'allakah remain,—the clear level line where the Roman work ends and the native work above begins,—this shows at least that the first church was fitted on to the Roman wall at a time when the parapet was uninjured, i.e. before the ruin or dismantling consequent on the Arab siege in the seventh century. The history of the siege, the betrayal of the fortress by Maḳûḳar and the Jacobite Copts, the toleration they received in return from the Muslim, and the vengeance they wreaked on their Melkite co-defenders, are too well known to need recounting here : but the facts furnish the reason why the Jacobite churches were saved from destruction at the Mohammedan conquest.

But there are two other points on which I think great stress may be laid, as determining a very early date for the first structure. These are—the occurrence of the cross sculptured on the classical capitals of some of the columns, and the testimony of Arab legends. Both here and in the pillars on the first floor of the round tower, crosses set in roundels and carved in relief are so worked into the foliage of the capitals, that they cannot be other than part of the original design.   Like columns are found in the earliest Syrian churches, and may be attributed to the third or fourth century with some confidence. To the third century also belongs, it will be remembered, the carved beam already mentioned as lying over the principal doorway.   The date given to it (284 A.D.) is the first year of Diocletian, (not the third as Mr. Chester's pamphlet says,) which is the starting-point of the Coptic era, though the great persecution was nearly twenty years later.   Of course it does not follow that the beam is in any way dedicatory of the church to which it belonged, or determines its foundation.   When the inscription was carved, the church may have been many years in existence; but the coincidence of the two pieces of evidence— the crosses on the capitals and the Greek inscription— might be taken, even if no further testimony could be derived from other sources, as proving that some church existed on the spot at least as early as the third century.

The evidence however of Arab legends corroborates this conclusion.   Passing over the wild but not worthless myth[1], which tells that Al Mu'allakah was built by one Bursa, son of Nebuchadnezzar, who was born of a 'captive Coptess' and returned with his mother to Egypt, it is worth while to give at length another tradition related by Murtadi[2], who quotes it from Abu Nafr :—

'Abu Nafr of the west (God's mercy on him), in the book of the Histories of Egypt, (which God continue prosperous and well-cultivated,) says that on the castle gate at Maṣr, in the time of the Romans

---

[1] Murtadi, p. 174.   [2] p. 254.

before the Musulmans conquered Egypt, there was
near the gate of the Church of Mu'allaḳah called the
Gate of Grace an Idol of Brass in the form of a
Camel, with the Figure of a man riding on him, having
an Arabian Turbant on his Head, and his Bow over
his Shoulder and shoes on his Feet. The Romans
and the Coptites, when any one injured or unjustly
persecuted another, came to that statue, and standing
before it he who suffered the injury said to him who
did it, "Give me what belongs to me, otherwise I
will make my complaint to that Cavalier who will
oblige thee to do me right by fair means or by foul."
By that Cavalier they meant Mohammed (God's
peace and mercy be with him), for it is written among
them in the laws of Moses and the Gospel where
the countenance and posture of Mahomet is thus
described: "He shall ride on a Camel and have
Shoes on: he shall carry the Arabian Bow and have
a Turbant on his Head:" God's peace and mercy be
with him. When Gamrou ('Amr) came to Egypt,—
he and the Musulmans (God's peace be with them,)—
the Romans perceiving they would certainly be sub-
dued, hid that Statue underground that it might not
serve the Musulmans for an argument against them
in the dispute. "I have heard" (says the son of
Lahigus), "that that Statue had continued in that
place several thousands of years, and that they know
not who had made it: God knows how it stands."'
A safe verdict.

This Abu Nafr was one of the companions of the
prophet, took part in the siege of the fortress, and
became one of the founders of the famous mosque
of 'Amr at Old Cairo, which remains to this day—
the earliest mosque in Egypt. His story refers

probably to some sphinx or other figure of ancient
Egyptian work, which had been placed at the portal
of the church : the dress and equipment are no doubt
purely fanciful.   But I think that without either
wresting or straining the sense of the legend one
may fairly gather, that at the time of the siege the
church had been already so long built as to date in
the rude imagination of an Arab from time immemorial.

For nearly two hundred and fifty years after the
taking of Kasr-ash-Shamm'ah I can find no further
notice of Al Mu'allakah.   The next mention of the
church is quite incidental, where Al Makrízi states[1]
that in the days of the Sultan Ahmad Ibn Túlún the
patriarch Khail 'sold to the Jews the church adjoining Al Mu'allakah,' i.e. the church of St. Michael,
still used as a Jewish synagogue.   This was about
the year 880 A.D.   Túlún was the builder of the
superb mosque bearing his name and now standing
in ruins near the citadel of Cairo.   About the year
1000 A.D. the wild fanatic and persecutor, called
Al Hâkim bi'amr Illâhi, is said[2] to have 'built a
wall round the church of Al Mu'allakah'—whatever that means.   Perhaps the precincts within the
Roman wall were enclosed, and the church turned
into a mosque, like Anba Shanúdah.   It is quite
certain that the same khalif sanctioned an indiscri-
minate persecution of the Christians and plunder of
their churches.   'All the gold and silver vessels in
them were plundered, their endowments were for-
feited; and those endowments were splendid and
bestowed on wonderful edifices,' says the Arab his-

---

[1] History of the Copts, p. 85.   [2] Id. p. 90.

torian : and he specially mentions that in the Mu'al-lakah was found 'a very great, endless quantity of gold fabrics and silken vestments[1]'.

It may be noted as a curious fact in this and in many other cases that there was no destruction of the fabric, whether it was shielded by the indolence or by the superstition of the Muslims. In 1049 A.D. we find the church and the monastic buildings in good repair, and the services unbroken in order, if diminished in splendour. It was in this year that the well-known Christodulus was chosen patriarch, and signalized his election by reviving an ancient usage. The proclamation of the new patriarch, after his return from the Natrun monasteries, as well as his election, had lately, but wrongly, been made at Abu Sargah, 'quod ea ecclesia esset Catholica seu Cathedralis[2]'. Christodulus, however, got the consent of a council of twenty-four bishops, beside the bishop of Old Cairo, and was proclaimed in Al Mu'allakah where he duly celebrated. The priest of Abu Sargah, angry at this infringement of his prerogative, refused to mention the patriarch's name in the diptychs at the holy eucharist : whereat Christodulus was so concerned, that he was fain to make peace by celebrating also in Abu Sargah. Nevertheless he wholly usurped and retained the churches of Al Mu'allakah and Al 'Adra in Hârat-ar-Rûm of Cairo[3], driving out their bishops :

---

[1] History of the Copts, pp. 91 and 90.

[2] Renaudot, Hist. Pat. Alex., p. 424.

[3] Al Makrîzi is clearly wrong in saying that Christodulus 'made' this church, and that of St. Mercurius or Abu-'s-Sifain. (History of the Copts, p. 92.)

and after thirty years he 'died in the Mu'allakah,' i.e. in the episcopal or patriarchal residence attached to it. There too died in 1102 A.D. the iniquitous patriarch Michael; who having given his solemn bond in writing that he would, if elected, restore to their bishops these two churches which Christodulus had usurped, no sooner felt himself secure upon the throne than he laughed in the faces of the bishops, denied flatly all knowledge of his promise, and threatened to excommunicate any who dare produce one of the duly signed and sealed copies of the document. This story, given in Renaudot, seems to show distinctly that Al Mu'allakah was the episcopal church of the see of Maṣr or Babylon: nowhere is a bishop of Abu Sargah mentioned.

The successor of Michael, named Macarius, after the customary journey to Alexandria for installation and visit to the monasteries of the western desert, returned to Old Cairo to celebrate in Al Mu'allakah: and the pre-eminence asserted or re-asserted by Christodulus seems ever after to have been quietly acknowledged. Certainly patriarchs were consecrated there all through the twelfth century. Early in the thirteenth the patriarch Johannes died there, but was buried outside: thither the dishonest and unscrupulous David, called Cyril, the LXXV patriarch, came in a grand procession with crosses and gospels, tapers, thuribles, and music, preceded by priests and deacons and followed by a great multitude of Christians and Muslims: in 1251 A.D. Athanasius was consecrated there: the church was plundered about 1259, when a chalice of wonderful workmanship was found buried under the altar, i.e.

hidden in the altar-cavity; and again in 1280 A.D. under the Mameluke sultan Al Ashraf Khalîl, founder of the beautiful mosques which bear his name, and of the Khan Khalîli in Cairo, still the finest bazaar in the world. Some twenty years later the same relentless enemy of the Nazarenes closed all the churches of Cairo, and Al Mu'allakah remained shut for nearly two years.

There the history ends abruptly, and the imagination has to leap over a gulf of nearly six centuries to find the ancient and venerable fabric in danger of suffering to-day, at the hands of its friends, worse ruin than it has received in the shocks of war and the clash of creeds during perhaps sixteen hundred years of existence[1].

The Church of Burbârah, or St. Barbara.

St. Barbara to whom this church is dedicated was, according to the Coptic calendar, 'the daughter of a great man in the land of the East,' and suffered martyrdom under Maximinus[2]. The church is a large and lofty building of the eighth or ninth century, and must have been of great importance: but I can find

---

[1] I revisited the church early in 1884, and am bound to admit that as a whole, and with the exceptions noted at the beginning of this chapter, the restoration has been carried out with more care and truthfulness than seemed possible when I wrote the above paragraph.

[2] Malan, Notes on the Calendar, p. 61.

no direct mention of it in Al Maḳrîzi or other authors. It lies on the eastern side of Ḳaṣr-ash-Shamm'ah close to the Roman wall, and is entered from the street of the Jewish synagogue.

Its monastic character is proved by the strange entanglement of domestic and ecclesiastical buildings around it. The dwelling-rooms have been little altered, but the church obviously has suffered a good deal, and is still undergoing a mischievous restoration. Here, as at Al Mu'allaḳah, all the screens

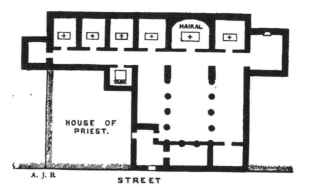

Fig. 16.--Plan of the Church of St. Barbara.

in the body of the church have been taken down, and probably will not be replaced : while the ancient and most interesting stone ambon has entirely disappeared.

Though the plan of the main church was originally of the orthodox kind, with nave and two aisles, haikal and aisle-chapels, and a triforium over the aisles and narthex, yet this plan has its peculiar modifications, which include two transepts of singular shape and extent. Part of the north aisle and all the narthex have been walled off and secularised, the

former making a sort of passage leading either to
the church or the dwelling-rooms, while the narthex
serves now as the mandârah, where coffee is drunk,
and tobacco is smoked none the less because the
fumes may wander through arched openings into the
church.   The mandârah is of the same width as the
nave, and the wall dividing the two encloses two
columns that formerly stood clear.   Ten other
columns, five on each side of the nave, made the
complete number twelve as at Abu Sargah, and
were doubtless painted with figures of apostles or
prophets, symbolizing the teaching on which the
Church of Christ rests.   But of the whole twelve
only half now are disengaged, the rest being more
or less lost in walls or piers.   They are as usual
joined by a finely painted and carved wooden architrave, and the masonry above is lightened by small
arched openings.

The triforium or women's gallery at present shows
five oblong bay openings, two north, two south, and
one west.   Each of the bays north and south is
divided by a single column, while the western bay
has two clear columns.   Others stand engaged, so
that the columns of the triforium correspond in
number and position though not in size with those
upholding it.   This arrangement seems to indicate
that the entire gallery originally was open, as in
many western basilicas, and that the interior wall
with its bays is merely a later addition.

The transepts are carried out north and south
beyond the aisles,—southward into a plain square
chapel now reft of altar and all ornaments, and retaining only a small niche in the eastern wall to
mark its former purpose :—northward into a dark

corridor about 45 ft. in length, ranged along which
are three little chapels (or rather two chapels and a
baptistery), with a continuous iconostasis. Each of
these three divisions is entered by its own double
door through the screen. They are now mere rubbish holes, where a few books and many pictures lie
rotting and decaying in deepening dust and unbroken
darkness. The baptistery lies northernmost of the
three, and the priest affirms with some show of
reason that this corridor is much older than the rest
of the church. Indeed it may be regarded as absolutely certain that the three divisions represent the
haikal and aisle-chapels of some smaller earlier
building. Opposite the more southern of the
corridor chapels, the corridor is widened out
and the additional space encloses a large Epiphany tank.

A very curious hiding-place for the sacred vessels
exists at the north end of the corridor. A door
flush with the wall opens revealing another door
inside the wall, and when the latter is thrown back
the floor of a secret chamber is seen 3 ft. above the
level of the threshold, whence it rises without steps.
This chamber, like the chapels, is unillumined by a
ray of light, and at present is a mere storehouse for
pots and cauldrons and vessels, used to prepare the
viands which the priest sets before his friends and
neighbours at the yearly festival of dedication. A
more likely place for hidden treasure it is not easy
to imagine : but though a light was flashed in
every nook and corner, it discovered neither silver
nor gold, nor anything more precious than the wares
of an Arab scullion.

Returning now to the main building through the

open screen that marks off the corridor, one may notice that the haikal proper and the two aisle-chapels are under lofty semidomes.   But the eastern wall of the haikal has the unusual form of a seven-sided apse below changing roofwards to a semicircle. The haikal-screen is ancient and good, though somewhat battered : and in each spandrel of the doorway inlaid with ivory is a remarkable design of a rude winged figure climbing among and holding a creeping plant.   These figures can scarcely be meant for angels, or for mere grotesques : for that strange love of mingling the solemn and the ludicrous, the sublime and the grotesque, which seems a permanent trait in the English character, has no counterpart among the Copts ; though early Byzantine churches abound in quaint ridiculous carvings and impossible figures.   There is nothing in Coptic churches like our ape-headed corbels, gurgoyles, frescoes of devils, and the monstrous beasts common in mediæval churches, where a sacred subject is treated in a jesting manner : as for instance in the church of Stanley St. Leonards, Gloucestershire, where the fall of man is represented by a splay-footed, fish-mouthed, frog-eyed, melancholy quadruped, holding in one hand an apple, and with the other pulling the tail of a heavily-moustached ape or cat, whose pursed lips and fixed averted eyes convey most amusingly the idea of shocked virtue.

In the haikal I saw three fine processional crosses of silver, each cross hung with six small bells, and on the staff a banner.   The two candlesticks on the altar are fine pieces of brass-work : there is also a small oval wooden incense-box now used as a crewet

(5 in. high and 4 in. across) beautifully carved with foliated scrollwork and Arabic letters in high relief. The lid unfortunately is missing.

The screen before the south aisle-chapel is new: the chapel is square, but in the east wall is a wide niche, in the north wall a large aumbry 3 ft. across and 2 ft. deep. A score of small pictures lie rotting under the orthodox quantity of dust.

Against the screen of the north aisle-chapel hangs a picture of St. Barbara and her daughter Juliana. With a palm branch in her left hand, the saint is pointing to a model of a church which she holds in her right. The church is a six-domed Byzantine-looking building with a turret and cross-capped spire—probably a purely conventional symbol, as there is no trace of tower or spire in any Coptic church near Cairo at present. A silver plate, like a crescent, nailed round St. Barbara's head represents a nimbus. Before the picture is a stand for a bolster of relics, and a curious three-branched pricket candlestick of iron, somewhat resembling that at Abu-'s-Sifain. The interior of the chapel is wainscoted, and over the altar is a plain baldakyn. A curious little portable tower-shaped shrine (2 ft. 3 in. high and 9 in. square) shows in front a very fine deep-shadowed painting of John the Baptist, who carries a scroll with the legend ' Repent: for the kingdom of heaven is at hand.' Before the picture is a little beam or bracket for tapers. The altar is littered all over with more or less ancient books of ritual that have been flung and tumbled together. Scattered among them or tossed in heaps on the ground at random lie candles, altar-caskets, old pictures, candlesticks, incense, ostrich-eggs, and silver censers in even unusual profusion and disorder, under layers of dust immemorial.

The triforium is not usually shown to strangers, for a reason unanswerable in the logic of eastern life—that the priest's harlm (i.e. wife and children) use it habitually, though they live and sleep in adjoining chambers. But at my request the priest very kindly sent a messenger to clear out the ladies: and that done led me through a courtyard and up a dark rickety staircase on to a flat roof, that lies over the chapels of the north transept. Here in bygone times had clearly stood another chapel or chapels, of which now only the eastern and northern wall remain, and a few small columns and loose fragments of screens and church furniture. The triforium is entered by a door on the north side. It forms a continuous gallery running round three sides of the church, stopping of course at the transepts.

Originally there must have been several chapels in and about the triforium; but the only one now standing is at the east end of the north triforium, and is called the *Chapel of Mâri Girgis.* It is railed off by a screen, within which lies an extremely fine and interesting iconostasis, though the icons have long disappeared. The panelling is about 7 ft. high, and is continued upwards to the roof by later latticework. The wood seems to be cedar, but the peculiarity of the work is the entire absence of geometrical patterns. The whole screen is divided by broad borders into small panels, which are beautifully carved in relief with figures and arabesques. The double doors have each four vertical panels : each spandrel has a figure on horseback enclosed in a circular moulding : above the doorway in a small square is a symbol not uncommon in western Christendom but very rare in these Coptic churches—two peacocks standing face to face on opposite edges of a flower-vase.

The other carvings represent chiefly animals. Gazelles are frequently pourtrayed, one being torn by an eagle, another devoured by a leopard or lion, a third having its eyes plucked out by a vulture or roc. Hares and camels are well rendered in other panels, and there are two figures of four-legged winged griffins. Two curious little life-pictures deserve special notice : they represent two men in flowing drapery sitting cross-legged in eastern fashion on the ground, each waited upon by two standing slaves or ministers. The existence of this screen is quite unknown even to the few travellers or residents who have ever visited any church besides Abu Sargah : and I could not hear that any one had ever before been admitted to the triforium[1]. But the extraordinary interest of these carvings alone will well repay the trouble of a visit—a trouble the politeness of the priest will probably lighten. At

---

[1] Since I wrote the above, the screen has had a narrow escape of being removed and carried away to England. When it became clear that the priest could not be prevailed upon to sell it, he was threatened with the displeasure of the British Government (!) : and, the threat failing, an effort was made to frighten the patriarch into yielding up the screen. Fortunately all endeavours proved unsuccessful. They were known, however, all over Cairo, and produced a great deal of natural ill-feeling among the Copts. I protest in the strongest manner possible against such attempts to rob the Coptic churches of their few remaining treasures : more particularly when the object in question has a structural importance, and loses its chief interest in being removed from its original position. In such a case museums may be gainers ; but the cause of art and archaeology suffers.

the same time it is to be hoped that some action
will be taken to prevent the use of this and other
parts of sacred buildings for domestic purposes.

No doubt the triforia were meant for the women
originally, and communication was often made
direct with the women's apartments in the buildings attached to the churches, as for instance
was the case also at St. Cross, near Winchester.
It is easy to understand, moreover, how when provision was made in the body of the church for the
presence of women, and the galleries were no longer
needed for the purpose of worship, they were grad-
ually turned to profane uses.   But this is not only
a departure from primitive custom and a desecration,
but it places one of the most interesting parts of
these ancient buildings at the mercy of ignorant and
reckless people, and leaves visitors dependent on
the temper of a priest, who may be courteous and
obliging as at Ḳ. Burbârah, or may be morose and
bearish as the priest at Abu Sargah, who flatly and
effectually refuses permission of entrance.

What treasures have been destroyed or still remain in such inaccessible places, may be conjectured
from the fact that in the one church of Ḳ. Burbârah
I discovered besides the beautiful screen some very
remarkable wall-paintings on plaster.   These are
chiefly on the south wall of the south triforium, and
formed the decoration of a chapel corresponding to
Mâri Girgis, but now quite abolished.   The paintings
are difficult to decipher, owing to the fact that at
least three layers of plaster may be distinguished,
each coloured with a different design at a different
period.   In some places too one coating has fallen:
in others two if not three are gone, while various

attempts at restoration or repainting have left the
work in helpless confusion. But as far as I could
judge, the earliest painting was a conventional pattern of roundels enclosing crosses and the sacred
letters. This design shows clearest on a pilaster of
the north wall of the south triforium. Another
design clearly distinguishable, though it seems to
have been painted over the first, is a series of large
figures of apostles or prophets under a continuous
painted arcading. One figure is still in fair condition
though the head is gone, and probably represents
the Redeemer : the left hand carries a scroll. There
are traces of ten other figures.

The second layer is covered with a large bold
design showing crosses with circles both on the
branches and in the angles between the branches.

On the third layer human figures are again
painted : of these the best preserved and most remarkable are two equestrians, probably Mâri Girgis
and Abu-'s-Sifain, drawn with great spirit and well
coloured. They lie to the westward end of the
triforium. But the face of the wall is not, and apparently never has been, quite level; so that the
various layers run one into another, as successive
coatings of plaster have been carelessly laid on an
uneven surface. Thus where a slight curve or splay
has been filled up level, leaving a figure half-con-
cealed and half-exposed, sometimes a new design
has been painted over the junction, sometimes the
original figure has been restored. The result is a
mass of scattered details extremely puzzling. Under
the chief remaining figures are Coptic writings—
very fragmentary, but no doubt worth deciphering.

But it is evident that the whole of the south triforium was covered with mural paintings : there are also traces of paintings on the piers in the north and west divisions. These latter are the parts now most in domestic use, and I feel sure that traces of like work could be found under the plentiful whitewash of the main walls, and that the triforia all round were once blazoned with figures, rivalling in their own degree the triforia of St. Mark's at Venice[1].

I made great exertions to obtain a photograph of the carved screen. It was quite invisible through the camera at a distance of even ten feet owing to the darkness : but by an arrangement of mirrors we brought the sunlight from out-of-doors and flashed it round a number of corners. Thus the photographer was able to play it over the screen, and he spoke of the experiment as likely to prove a great triumph. There is no reason it should not answer again : but he misjudged the time, and the picture showed the panels clearly enough, but only a dim blurred outline of the carvings. It was my last opportunity and a vexing failure.

The following measurements of the church were all I could take, but they will serve to give some idea of its size :—

Length of mandârah or original narthex
(E. and W.) . . . . 11 ft. 6 in.

---

[1] I deeply regret to say that at my last visit in January, 1884, I found that these interesting frescoes had been almost entirely destroyed. All the heads had been deliberately cut out of the wall, and now blank circular holes in the plaster alone show their position. Besides this, every available fragment of the smallest interest has been removed, and nothing whatever is left but a few incoherent patches of colour. There is reason to believe that this is the work of an Englishman.

Wall between mandârah and nave   . 2 ft. 6 in.
Length of nave.   .   .   . 56 ft. 9 in.
Length of haikal (from outside screen
    to centre of apse) .   .   :.   12 ft.
Width of nave .   .   . . .   . 25 ft.
Width of church (nave and two aisles) . 46 ft. 6 in.

Thus the total length is 82 ft. 9 in., the width excluding the transepts 46 ft. 6 in.

The graveyard belonging to K. Burbârah lies behind the church and is bounded eastward by the Roman wall. It contains some extremely curious and interesting tombs, which date undoubtedly from a very early epoch, whether or not the priest is right in ascribing to them an age of 1500 years. The majority are pits, square or conical, hollowed out beneath the earth and lined with brick. One or two of these are open; but the bodies have either vanished or are hidden under the bricks and rubbish that has fallen in with the roof upon them. But one floor of the Roman bastion at the angle of the wall here remains uninjured, and this is the only place where a clear idea can be formed of the original design of the lowest story in these bastions. The entrance had been blocked up at some remote period in such a way that the windowless chamber within was completely sealed. But shortly before my visit in the spring of 1881 some of the masonry had fallen from the archway, and the light that streamed in through the opening revealed as horrifying a sight as any that can well be imagined. The chamber proved to be a mere vault about 6 ft. by 10, walled and roofed with Roman tiles, and in it piled one over another in hideous disorder lay a score of human bodies. Some of them were in coffins: from

others the wood had fallen or decayed. Some were
lying face upwards, some on their side: some straight,
some doubled up with arms bent behind the head,
or limbs twisted and distorted in various ghastly
fashions. All had their faces muffled up and their
forms shrouded, save where fleshless bones protruded
from beneath their decaying drapery; one head was
resting on a sort of velvet cushion; and all lay with
their feet towards the east. It seemed as if some
of the bodies had become mummies, not skeletons,
as withered flesh here and there was showing, a result quite possible in an excessively dry climate,
especially as in an air-tight chamber of the kind the
temperature would scarcely alter winter or summer.
Close by, aligning the Roman wall, is a row of modern
sepulchral vaults above ground, each with an arched
doorway westward, blocked by a single doorstone
which is lifted away by an iron ring. This arrangement is that of the traditional early eastern tombs,
and in looking upon it one feels the old words 'roll
away the stone from the door' quickened with a
vivid meaning.

The Churches of Mâri Girgis and Al 'Adra.[1]

Of the two remaining churches which complete
the list of those lying within the walls of Kaṣr-ash-
Shamm'ah, there is little to be said. They are
situated close together, nearly adjoining the modern

---

[1] The latter is curiously called العذرا الشهيرة بقصرية الريحان or
the Virgin of the Pot of Basil. The reason of the name is quite
lost by the Copts of to-day.

cemetery. The entrance to the precincts of Al'Aḍra is through a low narrow arched doorway, such as belonged once to nearly all the churches. The priest is an extremely fine and venerable old man, with snowy patriarchal beard; and, like the priest at Ḳ. Burbârah, he is conspicuous for having refused bakshîsh; for he excused himself with the graceful remark that visitors came as his guests. Such an idea is quite out of fashion with the Copts generally. The church is a small, dark, nearly square building, with the usual features. Hanging before the iconostasis is a small ancient Arabic or Venetian glass lamp, the stem built of rings tapering downwards, the body encrusted with medallions. It resembles one of the lamps noted at Sitt Mariam, Dair Abu-'s-Sifain. But unless there are any curious vessels in the treasury or sacristy—a fact I was unable to ascertain—there is nothing else of interest in this church, which is said to have suffered some rebuilding. The ancient Epiphany tank, however, which lies south of the main building, remains unaltered.

Mâri Girgis also may be shortly dismissed. The original mandârah, which is first entered from the street, was a magnificent piece of work, and still retains tracery and carvings of great beauty. The high pointed arches, painted woodwork, and delicate arabesques remind one very much of the Arab domestic architecture of the best period, such as still may be seen in a few old houses in Cairo, the finest of which is owned by the courtly and genial Shaikh Aḥmad as Ṣadât. But all that remains now is a neglected ruin. The church, which stands a little way beyond, is a most disheartening structure. The old church was destroyed by fire, and has been replaced by a half-gaudy, half-sordid, altogether pitiful building, in which all that bad taste and unskilful workmanship could do has been done to produce the nearest imitation of a third-rate Greek model. Northwards of this new church are the ruins of an old one; but I cannot say whether they mark the site of the original Mâri Girgis, or of some chapel attached to it. Traces are still distinguishable of a nave, two aisles and triforia; the lines of the eastern wall may also be followed, and one or two columns are standing with the cross sculptured on their capitals.

According to Eutychius the church of Mâri Girgis was built about the year 684 A.D., by one Athanasius, a wealthy scribe, who also founded the church of Abu Kîr 'within Kaṣr-ash-Shamm'ah.' This description of Abu Kîr is not accurate, for there is now no church of that name within the walls, but it lies so close to the Roman fortress that the misstatement is not very serious. The fortress may however have contained a church called Abu Kîr, though every vestige of it has now vanished.

CHAPTER V.

The Minor Churches of Old Cairo.

The Churches of Dair Bablûn.—The Churches of Dair Tadrus.

MOUNDS of rubbish piled to the south of Kaṣr-ash-Shamm'ah, and the natural ridge, spoken of by Strabo, on part of which is now settled a Muslim village, completely close the view and screen off a little group of very old and curious Coptic churches. The shortest way to reach them is through the village; but it is far better to climb a windmill-hill a little to the left, whence a bird's-eye view may be had of the Roman fortress on the one side, and of these churches on the other. The churches lie within two dairs, which will be seen standing close together in singular isolation, like a pair of time-worn towers, built in a barren hollow between high mounds. The nearer is called Dair Bablûn, the other Dair Tadrus; each is girt by its own belt of lofty wall, built of grey brick, and covered in places with plaster; but Bablûn throws out northward a low fence-wall, which forms an enclosure before the entrance. Tadrus is at once distinguished by three palm-trees, that lift their tufts well above the dair. By keeping still on the high ground, but moving a little southward, and back from the churches, a rocky point may be reached whence opens a view for range and magnificence almost unrivalled in the world. Eastward the white Mukattam hills spread till they touch the citadel of Cairo, and seem to vanish away in the Delta beyond. At their feet stand the ancient tombs of the Mamelukes, looking very sombre and sad in contrast with the minarets of the shining city, but har-

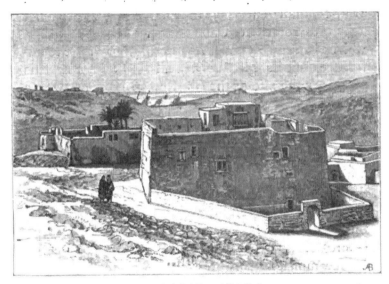

Fig. 17.—Dair Bablûn and Dair Tadrus.

monising with the dark tract of desert that surrounds them and reaches past Babylon. On the west the land is divided by a huge sweep of the Nile from above Bûlâk and the palaces of Cairo to below Bidrashîn and the palm-forests of Sakkâra. The pyramids of Gizah and the whole group of the Sakkâra pyramids may be seen together; and nothing can be finer than the latter, as they rise severed from the river by thick masses of palm, and stand high on the horizon, which seems and is the beginning of infinite unknown solitudes. This side the Nile, bounded by a great arc of the stream on the one hand, and by yellow cliffs on the other, lies a broad plain covered with corn and clover in the greatest richness, and dotted with shady villages. The nearest of these villages, conspicuous for its ring-wall and white dome showing within between palms and acacias, is the Coptic Dair Mikhaïl[1] enclosing the church of St. Michael.

But to return to Dair Bablûn. This little dair, which is scarcely one hundred yards in circumference, but is girt by a wall 30 ft. high, stands very near the site of the pre-Roman Babylon, whose name it preserves, though the site was subsequently covered by the Roman town that sprang up round the fortress. The Roman sewer, running along the edge of the plain near Dair Mikhaïl, has been already mentioned as marking the ancient bank of the river and the extent of the town in a southward direction. The dair is occupied entirely by the *Church of Al'Aḍra*, which is called in full 'the Church of the Virgin by Bablûn of the Steps[2],' and by the few monastic cells or dwelling chambers attached to it. Three or four women live there now, and sometimes are obliging enough to let one enter the door; but the key of the church is kept by the priest who lives at Cairo, and comes over only on Saturday evening and early Sunday morning for service. It is therefore extremely difficult even to get into the

---

[1] Called in full الملاك مغايل or the Angel Michael.

[2] ببابلون الدرج : the Copts do not know the origin or meaning of this title.

church, much more to study it. The plan nearly approaches a square, and it consists of narthex, nave, and two aisles, haikal and two aisle-chapels, while above the narthex and aisles are triforia. The aisles are nearly of the same breadth as the nave, from which they are divided by an alternate arrangement of pier and pillar supporting the triforia above. The choir runs the whole breadth of the church, but the nave, or men's section, is shut off by screens from the aisles as well as from the narthex and the choir. There are no transepts, but the architrave, either side of the nave, is carried across the choir on a pillar, and runs into the wall which divides the haikal from the side-chapels. The south aisle is probably meant to be reserved for women. The baptistery lies at the south-west corner of the church in the narthex; the font being, as usual, against the east wall, which divides the baptistery from the south aisle. Near the entrance in the narthex a large basin of stone rests on the ground; it seems to have been used anciently as a font, but has now no purpose. The nave is a step higher than the narthex, and the choir than the nave: there are rows of pictures over the choir-screen and the haikal-screen; the former are quite devoid of merit, and the latter have no special interest. Of the two pillars standing in the choir to uphold the architrave one is plain, the other, or northern, is fluted and twisted. All round the choir are various inferior pictures.

The lectern here is very fine and of unusual design, being panelled with fine Arab lattice-work. The standard candlestick too departs from the common pattern; and the silver censer, generally hanging from its plate, has little bells upon the chains, as depicted in the painting of St. Stephen at Abu Sargah and elsewhere. Over the high altar in the haikal is a canopy painted inside with a figure of Christ in the attitude of benediction. The sanctuary is walled off on each side from the aisle-chapels, but a thoroughfare is open to the south aisle-chapel against the eastern wall. The walls all round the haikal are decorated with fine mural paintings : on the north side is the figure of Gabriel between two panels, each containing the six-winged seraphim ; on the south is a corresponding device with Michael in the centre. The eastern wall is apsidal, and in the niche is a fresco of our Lord seated, the right hand uplifted in benediction, the left holding a gospel. By the head of the niche are also two evangelists, one at each side upon the wall. These paintings are all very ancient, and, though partially damaged, retain enough colour and spirit to make them singularly interesting.

The altar in the north aisle-chapel is not only stripped of its vestments as usual, but part of the plaster coating has fallen away, revealing a mixed structure of brick and stone. The eastern wall is faintly curved, containing a central niche and two aumbries, like the corresponding chapel at Al Mu'allakah. There is here the ordinary litter of sacred books and ornaments, dismounted eggs, rubbish and lumber generally ; but nothing noteworthy.

The chapel south of the haikal is curious, and perhaps has no title to be called a chapel, for it contains at present no altar. It is, however, difficult to believe that this little church should furnish a solitary exception to what seems otherwise a universal custom. Moreover, the likelihood of its having been designed for a sacristy or a dia-konikon, as in Greek churches, is disproved by the fact that a separate little storeroom for sacred vessels and vestments actually exists on the south side of this chapel, entered by a door from it, and divided by a party-wall On the other hand, the choirward screen is of a kind quite unparalleled in this position; for being made of lattice-work, or mushrabíah, it is of course transparent; and though a chapel screen may have slide windows to open on occasion, it is never allowed to be transparent. Another point to notice is that there are no icons, as there should be before every chapel, and that the screen is little more than 5 ft. high. But the truth doubt-less is that the altar was removed at some distant time for convenience sake, and the original screen was then replaced by the present low lattice-work.

There is nothing specially remarkable that I could discover in the furniture of this church, except a small textus-case of silver repoussé, which has the peculiarity of opening at one side, instead of being closely sealed up for ever, and a small but very finely chased processional cross of bronze.

Both the north and the south triforium are occu-pied by a chapel, dedicated respectively to Mâri Girgis or St. George, and Al Malâk Mikhaîl or the angel Michael, but they contain nothing of interest beyond an altar-casket in the latter, on one panel of which is painted the Last Supper. The painting, however, is of very average merit.

It should be mentioned that the nave of Al 'Aḍra is covered in with a wagon-vaulting of stone. For

the following measurements I am indebted to the
Rev. Greville Chester :—

	ft.	in.
Length from west wall to haikal-screen	38	6
Length from haikal-screen to centre of apse	14	9
Total length	53	3
Total breadth, including two aisles .	52	0
Breadth of central apse . . .	14	10
Depth of niche	2	0

DAIR TADRUS.

THE little dair lying close to Bablûn contains two
dim and ancient churches, remarkable not so much
for any peculiarity of structure as for the extraordinary number and richness of the vessels or vestments belonging to the service. These churches
are named Abu Kîr wa Yuḥanna, and Tadrus,—
the former lying to the right and the latter to the
left of the narrow courtyard into which the door
of the circuit-wall gives entrance. This courtyard
divides the dair into two halves, one of which is
covered by each church together with its own monastic buildings. Provision seems to have been
made in each case for about twelve residents : and
from the cell-like character of the rooms, it seems
more likely that they were meant to hold a body of
monks, than merely to shelter a tiny colony of refu-
gees rendered houseless by the decay or destruction
of their homesteads. Yet one may imagine, with
fair show of reason, that the three churches were
once part of a larger village or town, that they were

in fact built before the ancient Maṣr was split up
and scattered into isolated strongholds, as at present:
and that when the houses in the vicinity were wrecked,
a ring-wall was thrown round the churches to defend
them from the results of the consequent exposure.
These walls have been plastered and patched again
and again, as windows and doors have been renewed
or altered: but substantially they are unchanged
from a very remote antiquity. It requires some
courage to guess at the date of an Arab wall of
brick; but the period may lie between the tenth
and the twelfth century: and the churches may
belong to the seventh or eighth.

The Church of Abu Ḳîr[1] *wa Yuḥanna* is dedicated to two martyrs, Abu Ḳîr and Yuḥanna, or SS.
Cyrus and John of the town of Damanhûr in Lower
Egypt. Their festival is on the fourth day of the
month Abîb, i.e. about the 20th of June.

The doorway leading from the courtyard already
mentioned towards the church is a low narrow
postern with an arched head: it is closed by an
extremely thick and massive wooden door, and is a
rare example of a type once common in ancient
churches. Fortunately however the type is preserved
in indestructible material: for the mosque of Zainum
al 'Abidîn, which lies among the rubbish mounds
east of Mâri Mîna, and is built upon the site of a
very early Christian church, still contains an extremely fine doorway and door of black basalt, once
the entrance to the church. One jamb was originally
a separate piece, while the other jamb and the round

---

[1] Vulgarly but wrongly pronounced Abu'eer: the ق is not
sounded in the base Arabic of the modern Egyptians. The Arabic
is ‎ابو قير ويوحبا.

arch were formed of a single stone—like a ⌐ reversed.
A crack now divides them, but the door, still uninjured, is a ponderous rectangular slab—8 in. thick—
which swings on its own pivots. The massive size
and strength of the stones incline one strongly to
suspect that they may have belonged to some ancient
Egyptian treasury or tomb, before they were used
for a church: in any case the work is extremely
old, and the design was regularly copied for Christian buildings. It is the common form of entrance
to the monasteries in the Libyan desert now. In
the middle of the door a cavity is cut to receive a
lock which must have exactly resembled the wooden
lock in common use among the Arabs to-day, and
such as still remains upon the door at Abu Kîr wa
Yuḥanna. There the lock consists of a heavy square
beam, the under face of which is cut into large
notches or teeth : when the beam is shot home some
of these teeth fall upon and fit into corresponding
teeth in a socket in the wall. The key is a small
rod of iron with a loose joint near the middle and a
flange, but no wards. It has no bow : but the swinging handle makes a lever to turn the key: every
turn lifts the beam and frees a single tooth, till the
beam comes out of the socket and the door opens.

A short passage leads into a second small courtyard whence steps ascend to the dwelling chambers,
and a door opens at the south-west corner of the
church. The building is quite shapeless, though by
a stretch of language a nave and two aisles may
perhaps be distinguished : it contains, however, the
usual haikal and two side-chapels with a continuous
iconostasis, in front of which is a choir : but the little
space remaining westward of the choir-screen is so

irregular in shape, the walls run at such odd angles, that no name will cover its usage. Its position answers to that of the narthex generally, but probably in the rare event of women coming here to worship they would be placed in this section and the men would stand within the choir. At the farthest point westward in a gloomy corner is a door opening into a narrow sacristy, in which are stored some extremely valuable and interesting ornaments.

The altar in the haikal is dedicated of course to the patron saints of the church, St. Cyrus and St. John. The wall-niche contains a distemper painting of Christ in glory on a gold ground. The north side-chapel is dedicated to Al 'Adra, and the south to Mâri Girgis. Neither the icons nor any other of the pictures in this church have any merit or attraction. Relics of the two martyrs are preserved, in silk brocade cases, in a small shrine named after them, on the south side of the church.

Before the sanctuary-screen hangs a small bronze corona, and another larger one reposes disused in the chapel of Al 'Adra. Near the first one is also suspended a metal lamp which I take to be a traditional copy of a Venetian design in glass. It has a wide flat rim, with a globe below, then descends with sharply tapering hoops to a point. On the globe are three heads, or rather bust figures, from which slender rods are fastened by rings. A single cross-piece meets and joins the rods above, and from the centre of this the lamp is suspended by a chain. The pattern curiously resembles the glass lamps described at Al 'Adra, Dair Abu-'s-Sifain, and Al 'Adra in the Roman fortress: and, what is more curious, the very model of it may be seen in brass

or silver at St. Mark's and other churches in Venice.
Besides several altar candlesticks of bronze, brazen
cymbals, and silver thuribles both plain and parcel
gilt, the church also possesses a plain silver chalice
and paten with its asterisk or dome (ķubbah) of
silver, and silver spoon, also belonging to the service
of the altar.   There are also two fine processional
crosses of silver with silver sockets, two small hand-
crosses of silver, and two silver fans or flabella,—
circular discs, each with two figures of six-winged
seraphim in repoussé work, a cross above, and a
beautiful design round the border.   Here also is that
' marvellous faire booke,' the magnificent textus-case
of silver given in the engraving (vol. ii). It is 15 in.
long, 13 in. broad, and 3 in. deep.   It is covered all
over with repoussé silver: the front and the back
are nearly similar in design, and round the sides is
a conventional pattern.   The large plates of silver
overlap the sides, and are rivetted down upon them.
The copy of the gospel is first enclosed in a silken
wrapper: then cased all over with cedar or ebony,
which in turn is completely overlaid with plates of
silver.   The rivet-heads fastening down the silver form
a graceful border about all the edges, and are taste-
fully scattered besides over the whole design.   Inside the rivet-border runs a narrow band of dotted
work: a like band cuts off a space top and bottom
to enclose a raised inscription in Coptic—'The
beginning of the Gospel of Jesus Christ the Son
of God.'   Farther inward an oblong is marked off
by another dotted band, and the interval is filled by
very beautiful interlacing arabesques with a cross at
the four angles.   Touching the dotted band inside
comes a flat band with raised edges set with rivets;

and from the enclosed space two vertical lines divide
off a square, leaving side compartments, which are
worked over with fine feathery scrolls. In the midst
of the square stands out a fine large cross with pear-
shaped branches starting from a central boss : and
all the remaining surface is richly decked with
flowers closely resembling the Rhodian or the Persian cornflower. The five crosses and the flat border
round the central cross are delicately gilt. Altogether it is a sumptuous and really glorious work of
art—one of the finest treasures of all in the Coptic
churches. It dates probably from the sixteenth or
late fifteenth century[1].

---

[1] The trouble it cost to get the photograph of this gospel-case
taken will not be soon forgotten. A letter from the patriarch was
not easy to get : a photographer was hard to find : and the priest
almost impossible to catch except at impossible times, late Saturday
evening and early Sunday morning. But having with untold exer-
tion brought the priest, the photographer, and the letter face to face
at the church door, only two or three days before my departure
from Cairo, I nearly found all my labour in vain. The priest read
the letter bidding him show me all honour, and allow me to draw
in the church : but said the letter only referred to the walls not to
the vessels or ornaments! Logic was lost labour and threats wasted
breath : even bakshîsh seemed powerless. He seemed really afraid
that the book would be stolen ; and seeing this, I promised, on the
word of an Englishman, not to touch it, and only to require it outside the church five minutes, adding, 'I am tired of asking : now
answer me once for all—speech single and speech straightforward—
will you bring out the book or will you not?' In a moment he
relented, locked the dair door, and laid the book on the bench.
I was in alarm lest he should snatch it away before the photographer could finish ; but a magic change had passed on his mood ;
and he afterwards very kindly allowed the stole and the sleeves to be
photographed also. All were unfortunately so badly taken, that only
the exceptional skill of the friends who copied them for me could
have produced anything like the beautiful drawings given in vol. ii.

Scarcely inferior in interest to the textus-case are
the splendid ancient vestments belonging to this
little church. Besides some finely embroidered stoles
and dalmatics, now sadly worn and tattered with age
and neglect, there is a very fine paṭrashîl, with a pair
of armlets to match, and a girdle with silver clasps.

The paṭrashîl, answering to the Greek ἐπιτραχήλιον,
is about 6 ft. long and 8 in. wide: the upper part
is pierced with a hole for the head. It is made of
crimson silk-velvet, most richly embroidered with
figures and designs in thick thread of silver. On
the top under a double line is a dedicatory inscription in Arabic, enclosing two crosses: a double border
runs all down the front on each side worked with
a pretty olive or other leaf-pattern: two twisted
lines also run down the centre, and the whole space
is divided into twelve little compartments each containing the figure of an apostle, with his name in a
little band of Arabic writing above his head. Each
figure is clothed in a kind of hooded cope, bears his
hands crossed upon the breast, the right hand clasping a cross: the dalmatic under the cope shows three
crosses between diagonal lines. The embroidery of
these figures is so closely wrought that they look as
if made of solid metal without its stiffness. The
same is true of the Arabic writing and the borders,
which like the figures are finely gilt. The whole is
so massive with weight of inworked silver, that it
must be as uncomfortable to wear as it is beautiful
to look upon. The paṭrashîl is merely the ordinary
stole, as it hung in front over both shoulders, brought
together under the chin, and sewn down the whole
length: and the absence of any border at the bottom
may be a reminiscence of this origin.

The armlets are also of crimson silk-velvet, lined with silk, and richly adorned with silver embroidery. They reach as far as the elbow, where they widen slightly as compared with the wrist, and correspond to the Greek ἐπιμανίκια. Round each wrist is a double band filled with a sort of crossbar design: the space between the two bands is covered with Arabic writing. Then comes the main part of the sleeve, which is worked all over with beautiful arabesques and stars enclosing floriated crosses, in the midst of which, on the right sleeve, is a figure of the Virgin Mary holding the child Christ, and on the other the angel Michael holding sword and balance: both these figures are done in fine needle-work embroidery of choice colours. Next a wide band between two lines is filled with alternate crosses and stars, both very intricately worked: this is followed by another band of Arabic writing, and finally the elbow-opening is trimmed with a border like those about the wrist. Lengthwise also, from wrist to elbow, there runs a narrow band, crossing all the others. All the devices on these armlets, and the nimbs on the figures, are wrought in thread of silver.

The girdle is made of the same stuff as the patra-shîl and armlets, but is quite plain, without any embroidery or other embellishment. The clasps however are of massive silver: when closed they show as a single plate of curved metal 7 in. long and 2 in. broad, the angles rounded and the ends slightly pointed. The joint is covered by a large gilt shield-like boss, decked with smaller bosses in rings, and divided by lines of raised dotwork. At either side is another large boss worked over with enamel and set with an enamelled outline of wavy form: and all along the edges of the clasp there runs a border of the same dark-coloured enamel.

These are all the treasures that the writer saw in the church : but there may be others to discover. On all alike the dedicatory inscription is the same; it runs thus :—

A perpetual comely gift to the houses of the glorious martyrs Abu Ḳîr and Yuḥanna between the hills. Reward, O Lord, him that hath taken these pains.

Some of the engraving is very rude, and clearly done by an illiterate person, who writes for instance بيعت for بيوت. The expression 'between the hills' (بين الكمان) is a curious variation from the fixed formula. There can be no doubt however that it is the ancient title and description of the church, and denoted its position in the remotest times as accurately as it does to-day. The hills therefore are not mere rubbish-mounds of mediæval date, as they might seem to be, but are part and parcel of the high ground occupied by the Babylonian fortress and by the Roman camp, as seen and recorded by Strabo.

The solitude of the two churches in Dair Tadrus is worse than that of Al 'Aḍra in Dair Bablûn : for while the priests of all three churches live at a distance, and come only for evensong on Saturday and matins on Sunday, in Dair Tadrus there is not a single inhabitant—not even a woman as at Bablûn— but only a forlorn and friendless cat, locked within the monastery walls for six days, and left foodless till the seventh.

The Church of Prince Tadrus the Oriental[1] is

---

¹ الامير نادرس المشرقى.

consecrated to a martyr of that name, and 'prince,'
as he is called in the dedicatory inscriptions. His
legend will be found in its place. Tadrus, or Tâdrus,
is the Arabic form of Theodorus.

This church has the usual three chapels at the
east end, each with its own niche: in the northern
side-chapel is also an aumbry, where lay an ancient
marble capital of Roman form, and a plain bronze
censer. Before the niche in the haikal there hangs
a very beautiful little lamp of silver. The body of
the church consists of nave and two aisles, the aisles
being divided off on each side by two piers, between
which stand close together a pair of slender columns.
North of the choir is a shallow recess or shrine
fenced off by lattice-work, and adorned with pictures
of no merit. In the south aisle is a cupboard or
bookcase containing a great quantity of books, a few
of which are both ancient and in fine condition. The
roof of the building is irregular, but comprises four
domes, one of which over the centre of the church
shows four crosses in relief upon the plaster, which
possibly may be consecration crosses, though they
are quite out of reach.

But like Abu Ḳîr wa Yuḥanna, the church of
Amîr Tadrus is more remarkable for the number
and beauty of its ancient ornaments, than for anything strange or striking in its architecture. Besides
the bronze censer mentioned above, and the little
lamp of pierced silver-work hanging by chains of
silver before the haikal niche, in the haikal may (or
might) be seen two very fine censers of solid silver,
engraved with scroll-work, and hung by silver chains
with little bells upon them: a silver cross: two plain
white shamlahs, 16 ft. 9 in. long and 1 ft. 3 in. broad,

of linen, embroidered near the ends with two large crosses in red and yellow needlework with the sacred letters between the four branches, α above, and ω below it. The centre of one cross is 2 ft. 6 in. from the end, and of the other 3 ft. 4 in., and a thin stripe of red is drawn across each end of the shamlah nearly 4 in. from the hem. Here also are two dalmatics, embroidered in front with a figure of the Virgin and Child throned, and two flying angels holding her crown : on either side the throne a blue cross outlined in black, and underneath it a figure of the Amîr Tadrus on horseback slaying a dragon : below in a wide curve runs an inscription in red, and a date 1217 Coptic, or 1501 A.D. Round each sleeve is a yellow border edged with black, and decked with an olive-branch pattern : above the border is a row of three crosses, and above that a star between two crosses—all in various colours : and above the star is the figure of an angel holding a Latin cross. In the middle of the back is a yellow cross edged with black. All this work is embroidered in fine silk.

In the south aisle-chapel are an ancient paṭrashîl and pair of sleeves to match : they are of yellow-brown colour richly brocaded, but not worked with silver. There lie on the altar two fine large gospel-cases, one of silver covered with repoussé ornament of crosses, flowers, scrolls, Coptic and Arabic writing : the other made of plain copper is altogether of ruder workmanship, but bears some figures of angels, and a title in the two languages. When used at baptism the silver gospel is set upright upon the gospel-board—a wooden frame that closes by hinges in the middle : round the edge of the frame are prickets for candles. Four fans or flabella of fine silver with wooden handles, half cased in silver, are among the best treasures of this church : they resemble those of Abu Ḳîr wa Yuḥanna mentioned above, but their original use seems forgotten, and now they are employed merely to decorate the gospel-board. The wooden handles are hollowed to receive a pricket, so that the four fans stand upright round the gospel at solemn service : sometimes tapers are even fastened on to the fans at top, by forcible compressment of the wax upon the silver !

In the niche of this chapel was a fine fifteenth or sixteenth century picture divided into four panels— the Virgin, St. Peter, and two equestrians—identical in form and treatment with a painting to be seen in one of the cells opening out of the eight-pillared room of the Roman round tower, and belonging to the Greek convent.

But the treasury of Tadrus, where the great mass of precious things is stored, is a low dark room entered from the south-west corner of the church : and though it is by no means rich enough to compare with the treasuries of Priam or Atreus, or like the treasury of St. Mark's at Venice to tempt a second Stammato, yet the nature of the scene, if not the value of the possessions in ward, gives a visit here a sharper flavour of oriental romance even than life in ' grand Alcairo' ordinarily furnishes. The strange site of the lonely convent in its desert valley, the high walls and dim passage, the massive doors that close with ponderous locks and bolts behind one, the silence and gloom of the ancient church, would quicken the dullest imagination : and visions of hoarded wealth come thick, when one is led by the venerable grey-bearded priest to the secret chamber, where by the scanty taper-light that flickers about the walls one sees a bronze corona or two, some ostrich-eggs and many old lamps scattered about, and close together two deep and roomy coffers. One of these contains nothing but ancient books of ritual, chiefly torn to pieces or eaten through and through by worms: a pair or two of cymbals and a score of tapers are flung in with them. But from the next coffer, when the lid is lifted, comes a great flash of silver. Here are half-a-dozen beautiful hanging lamps of silver in a peculiar kind of pierced work: the shapes as well as the sizes vary a little but are very graceful, and the piercing gives a pleasing lightness and delicacy to the design. There is also a plain silver chalice, silver paten and dome: several silver spoons and small silver crosses: three or four silver censers and several silver-gilt diadems, one of which is figured in the engraving (vol. ii). These diadems are used at the marriage service. I have never seen them at any other church, though Mr. Chester mentions two at the church of Anba Shanû-dah. The raised Arabic inscription upon them means in English 'Glory to God in the highest and on earth peace:' there is nothing said about 'men of good pleasure.' The words incised at either end are merely the usual 'Reward, O Lord,' of dedication. Besides these silver ornaments there was a fine chalice of plain white Venetian glass, with gilt decorations; some old Coptic and Arabic books in a fair state but devoid of illuminations; and one or two silver-embroidered corporals, and some brazen cymbals.

The priest of this church rides over on his donkey

from Dair Abu-'s-Sifain on Saturday evening: he passes the night in the church—not in a devout vigil, but sleeping wrapped in his rug on the floor under the central dome.

The Church of St. Michael has been mentioned as lying in the rich plain that touches southward the Old Cairo desert. The dair is not half-a-mile from Dair Tadrus, but is scarcely worth a visit except for the beauty of its situation. The present church is quite modern, though the foundation apparently is ancient enough. But neither in the structure nor in the furniture of the church is there much worth special notice. The one unusual feature it possesses is a Jesse-tree, painted in distemper on the flat inside of the chancel-arch above the iconostasis. The work however is new, and in idea seems more Greek than Coptic. Against the western wall, in a kind of shrine covered with a wire grating, rests a large painting of the angel Michael, which is held in high veneration by all the Copts of Cairo. Great belief is placed in his powers of intercession, and his influence is thought specially potent in controlling the rise of the Nile: so that many prayers and vows are offered up to him, and his shrine is adorned—or disfigured—with gold-embroidered kerchiefs, silk bands, and various cloths and clouts of humbler stuff, that are tied on the bars by pious pilgrims in deprecation of wrath threatened or in remembrance of prayers granted. Outside the church two small bells are hung—one at an open window half way up the wall, the other in a sort of lantern above.

The last of the minor churches called *Al 'Adra bil 'Adawîah* at Ṭûra, like that of St. Michael, is un-interesting, because it has been entirely rebuilt. It lies three miles south of the latter across the plain in a little dair perched upon the bank of the river. Everything in it is modern, down to the curious but ugly little textus-case of silver embossed with cherub-heads and a figure of the Virgin and Child. Yet the lintel of the outer door is formed by a slab carved with hieroglyphics. But even though wanting in antiquarian interest this church is well worth a visit : the ride along the river-bank is extremely picturesque, as well as the situation of the dair. And there is always the hope and chance of finding some ancient treasure that has passed unnoticed before, or that has been lost or forgotten by the Copts themselves, but rediscovered and brought again into usage.

CHAPTER VI.

The Churches in Cairo.

The Churches in the Ḥârat-az-Zuailah.—The Churches in the Ḥârat-ar-Râm.—The Chapel of St. Stephen.

NOT very far from the Rond-point of the Mûski in Cairo is an ancient Christian dair, a block of buildings containing the churches of Al 'Aḍra with the adjoining chapel of Abu-'s-Sifain, and, above, the church of Mâri Girgis, besides a small nunnery of some eighteen nuns with their lady superior. It is curious that the churches in the heart of Cairo should alone have retained their monastic uses,—though the buildings were meant, no doubt, for monks and not for nuns—while from the more remote and solitary churches of Old Cairo the friars or brethren have completely vanished.

The upper church in the Ḥârat-az-Zuailah, dedicated to St. George, is very small, and though fairly old it possesses no special points of interest. It is a squarish, characterless building with three domed chapels, choir, men's section, and women's section; the aisles are divided from the nave by classical columns, and in the middle of the eastern division a space is railed off and set with benches, to serve as a sort of porch to the church. There priests and guests sit chatting and smoking, regardless of the fact that the fumes wander through and over the screens into the sacred building.   There are lamps of silver and glass hanging before the haikal, but no ornaments of great value; the chief interest of the church seems to lie in the reputed healing power of its relics.   I have seen women sitting crosslegged about the floor on the old oriental carpet, with which it is strewn, gossiping together and taking it by turns to nurse the little silk-covered bolster of relics with simple faith in its miraculous virtues.   Outside the church there is also a shrine of the Virgin, a chamber about 20 ft. by 12, one end of which is screened off.   It may have contained an altar in former times, but no traces of one remain.   Within the screen a shelf some 7 ft. from the ground runs round the walls; on it are ranged many paintings of saints and martyrs, and in the midst a little shrine opens with latticed doors, revealing a picture of the Virgin Mary.   Candles are lit before the picture on the days of solemn service for the sick, when the priests stand in the doorway of the screen, reading or chaunting to the wild music of bells and cymbals. In the church, too, may be seen at times the ceremony of laying-on of hands upon sick people, i. e. such as are able to come to the church.   This takes place on Sunday morning, after the celebration of the eucharist.

It is more difficult perhaps, but far better worth while, to pay a visit to the lower church, called

The Church of Al 'Adra.

This is without question the earliest church in the city of Cairo; and it differs from the church

above and those in the Ḥârat-ar-Rûm in its basilican structure. In many points it reminds one of
Al Mu'allaḳah; in others it is peculiar. It lies
about 14 ft. below the present average level of
the neighbourhood—proof enough of its great antiquity. Its length is about 60 ft.

The entrance is curiously placed at the eastern
end. This is not likely to have been the original

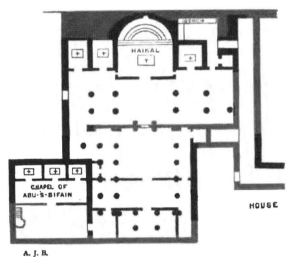

A. J. B.

Fig. 18.—Plan of Al 'Adra.

arrangement; but the growth of the soil at the
west end doubtless choked up the doors there many
generations ago. There are signs of a later entrance
in the middle of the south aisle, though this also
has been blocked up. Round the body of the church
—choir and nave together—there are twelve ancient
columns, six on each side. Nine more columns stand
in the narthex, which is divided into four small sections by screens. There are ten other columns in
the aisles, placed, for the most part, in rather a

random fashion, and four against the choir-screen.
The nave contains a women's section as well as
one for men, and the choir opens out at either side,
embracing the width of the aisles. There is no
transept, however, for the painted architrave, which
rests upon the nave pillars, is carried across the
choir, and runs into the wall dividing the haikal
from the side-chapels. The triforia therefore extend
over the choir, which in common with the nave is
covered with a wooden wagon-vaulted roof. The
south aisle is very narrow; northward are two
aisles, the outer one of which is barely 3 ft. wide in
the western half of the church, but about midway
opens out, and at the eastern end becomes wide
enough to terminate in a chapel of ordinary dimensions. It is possible that there may have been a
corresponding outer aisle on the south side also;
for on the south side of the haikal, though only one
aisle-chapel remains, the choir is wide enough for
two, and the present entrance has clearly been cut
through a second chapel from which the altar has
been removed; but, as only half the area of the
chapel was required for the passage, the remaining
half has been railed off and made into a shrine.
The church, then, originally had four chapels, besides
the haikal, three of which are still uninjured. The
capitals of the pillars are chiefly debased Corinthian;
two of Byzantine form have crosses sculptured among
the foliage; there are besides one Doric and three
Saracenic capitals. The choir-screen runs into a pier
of masonry on either side, and is continued northward
into a third pier. The doorway of the choir stands
between two pairs of octagonal Saracenic columns,
each of which has two well-cut consecration crosses,

one eastward and one westward. They resemble
roughly the crosses at Abu Sargah, but are larger,
measuring 6½ in. by 3½. Beyond these four there
seem to be no other dedication crosses; and the
fact that they occur on Saracenic pillars is interesting, as possibly determining a date for the recon-
secration of the church in the tenth century, when
Cairo was founded. The pillars with crosses in
relief among the foliage point clearly to a much
earlier date for the main edifice, which cannot be
later than the sixth or seventh century.

The pulpit in the nave is an imitation of an older
one, the marble mosaics being imitated in painted
woodwork. It remains without staircase other than a
moveable ladder. There is a little shrine railed in
between two columns in the north outer aisle; and
another rather larger in a recess 6 ft. by 4 off the
south aisle. In the latter, called the Shrine of the
Virgin, the pictures are fenced by a wire grating
hung with shreds, in remembrance of prayers or
vows, as at Dair Mikhall. The principal painting
represents Mary with the Child in the branches of
a Jesse-tree, which is surrounded by a number of
saints, each in a separate little panel. The face,
unfortunately, is burnt by candles that have been
carelessly held before it; still the painting is interesting from its style and treatment, as well as from its
antiquity. A lamp hangs in front of it burning
perpetually.

The pictures on the iconostasis are also ancient,
but much decayed; above them towers conspicuously
a large cross or *rood*—the only instance I have seen
of a true rood on the haikal-screen of a Coptic church
in Cairo. At either side of the foot of the cross an

eagle is carved in conflict with a strange human-headed dragon; on the curved neck of each eagle a panel is supported, painted with the usual figures of Mary and John. The work has a very modern look, but the priests declare it to be ancient; it may, therefore, be a copy or restoration of a rood coeval with the church. On the frames, or rather mountings, of three pictures in the choir is some fair carving of roses, crosses, and small curious birds.

The haikal-screen projects, like those at Al Mu'allakah and Abu Sargah, into the choir about three feet beyond the line of the chapel-screens, and has two side-doors as well as the central door. The screen is old, inlaid in uncarved ivory with the design repeated of a star in a double ring divided by mouldings. The design on the screen of the south aisle-chapel is a unique kind of cross-in-square pattern. Over the haikal is a lofty dome rising above the wagon-vaulting of the nave, and ornamented with gated pendentives, i.e. pendentives retaining a delicate 'gate' or pierced panel of stone before the hollows. On three sides of the dome are coloured windows of Byzantine form—two round-arched lights with circular light over the mullion between them.

The haikal apse is remarkable for a very fine and clear-cut tribune rising in six marble steps, of which the lower three are straight, the upper three curved parallel to the wall, which is covered with mosaic of coloured marble in large panels. The patriarch's throne and the niche are in the centre; above the niche is a good design of old Damascus tilework. The rest of the haikal wall, north and south, is covered with inferior tiles of the eighteenth or nineteenth century.   Intó the north wall there is inlet a curious tablet, or rather fragment of white stone, which shows a border of dolphins enclosing three sets of figures between strapwork—a pair of human-headed harpies, a centaur, and two human forms.   The last are broken across, and it is not clear what they were meant for.   The work is early Byzantine ; whatever place the slab was destined for, it has been removed from its original position, and is set topsy-turvy in the wall.

A door in the north-west corner of Al 'Adra opens into the adjoining chapel, or rather   .

Church of Abu-'s-Sifain the Lesser,

which contains a pulpit of rosewood, carved in panels showing sunflowers, with starlike ivory centres, springing from vases.   Here too may be seen in actual usage a moveable ladder for mounting the pulpit, such as must have been employed at Mâri Mîna, Abu Sargah, and elsewhere.   Neither the haikal nor the side-chapels are in any way remarkable, though in the former may be seen some seventeenth century yellow tiles, and a small square altar-frontal, finely embroidered with a figure of the Virgin and various crosses.   But if the church be visited in Lent, the curious wooden winepress belonging to Abu-'s-Sifain the Greater in Old Cairo may here be seen in working; for it is brought here every year, and wine for all the churches is made within this building.

One may note that the arrangement of this outer chapel singularly resembles that of the chapel of SS. Servulus and Justus, adjoining the basilica of Trieste, except that here it opens out from the north-west instead of the south-east corner of the main building. The plan of the Trieste basilica is given in Lenoir's 'Architecture Monastique,' and may be compared with that in the text.

The Churches in the Ḥârat-ar-Rûm of Cairo..

In the Ḥârat-ar-Rûm or Greek quarter of Cairo city is a Coptic dair called Dair Tadrus, containing a nunnery in which twelve nuns reside, and the two churches of Al 'Aḍra, or the Virgin, and Mâri Girgis, or St. George. They are best reached by the narrow lane branching off from the Sukkarîah at the Sibîl of Muḥammad 'Ali. The old gate of the quarter may be seen in its place, though the soil which has risen about it now prevents it from closing. The churches are near the end of the lane ; from which there are two entrances, one by a passage through the ancient patriarchal residence, where the flat stone roofing near the doorway is adorned with fine Arab tracery ; the other from a little by-lane farther on. Some steps have in either case to be descended, and some dark places to be traversed before

The Church of Al 'Aḍra

is reached. The first thing at once that strikes one is the roof, which consists of twelve domes—one over each of the three eastern chapels, and nine over the rest of the church—in all four rows of three domes each. Six piers, of which two are within the haikal-screen, uphold the domes, and are connected by

round arches. The plainness of the architecture
is unredeemed by any ornament, even the common
Arab pendentives being absent from all the domes
except that above the haikal. The haikal dome is
pierced with a small stained window, and the others
have a few small round holes glazed. These with a
small grating or two give the only entrance to day-
light. The same union of temple and fortress strikes
one here as in the churches of Old Cairo: the same
necessities of defence have shaped the shell of the
building. The church is very small—perhaps 50 ft.
by 40—but the division of nave and aisles is plain
enough. A sort of narthex too, exists, and over it
a screened gallery for women. The choir is not
marked off from the nave—a most unusual omission
—though its position is denoted by two plain lecterns
standing on a Persian carpet. In the nave, on a
beam crossing between two piers, is a large rood,—
a cruciform picture of the crucifixion: on the cross,
Christ is hanging dead; at the foot is a skull and
bones, below which the entombment is figured. The
branches have trefoil ends, each containing an angel.
Near the foot of the cross on each side, carved in
wood, an eagle is strangling a serpent; each eagle
bears on its head a tablet painted with the figure of
an angel. The work possesses no merit.

The under-part of the altar-canopy is embellished
with a painting, resembling that at Abu-'s-Sifain: and
though the haikal-screen is rather plain and modern-
looking, the doorway is finer; a row of seven silver
lamps hanging before the screen shed their lustre
upon it, and a single lamp hangs before each of the
side-chapels. The choir is slightly lengthened out
at each end, forming in each case a shrine adorned

with pictures. That to the south contains paintings of

1. *Takla Himanût al Habishi,* an Abyssinian saint,
as the title denotes. He is an aged man robed as
patriarch, and bearing in his left hand the Coptic
patriarchal staff : in his other hand he carries a cross
and a rosary.

2. *St. Marina* trampling upon Satan.

3. A fine tablet 3 ft. by 2 ft. 6 in. painted in nine
panels—the Virgin and Child in the centre, and sacred
scenes all around. This seems an unusually skilful
piece of work, both for the modelling of the figures
and the management of the colours, but it lies in so
deep shadow, not to say darkness, that judgment is
difficult. The Virgin is holding Christ on her right
arm, and lowering her face to meet his, which is up-
raised. The tablet is set in a niche : it is ill preserved.

4. An angel on a gold ground, and with it

5. A triptych, with a pair of angels in the centre
panel, between two single angels at the sides. All
are rudely-drawn full-face figures on a gold ground.
Most if not all the other paintings are recent and
artistically worthless. One treating of the Annunciation is curious perhaps for its arrangement: the
angel holding a lily is advancing from the sinister
instead of the dexter side, and in common with Mary
wears a very hurried, frightened look.

The baptistery, some 24 ft. long by 12 wide,
opening out of the church by a door at the north-
west corner, has a flat roof of palm-thatch upheld by
two pairs of slender columns. Upon the font, which
is screened off at the eastern end, lies an old iron
cross, a bronze cross, and a book of service. The
gospel-board is of good design.

The church itself possesses a gospel finely cased in silver, embossed with flowers and letters, and a good silver cross for benediction.

The Church of Mâri Girgis, with a small nunnery adjoining, in the Ḥârat-ar-Rûm, is built one story above the ground, close to but not directly over Al 'Aḍra, which in size and general structure it greatly resembles. The twelve-domed roofing is the same, and the piers supporting the domes are joined together by round arches. The west end or narthex is raised about 4 ft. above the level of the nave and aisles : it serves at once for a baptistery, and for the women's section at the ordinary services. The font is railed off at the north end, and the whole screened by lattice-work from the body of the church.

Next comes the men's section, divided by an open 5 ft. railing from the choir : it contains a plain pulpit. In the choir are two lecterns, a standard candlestick of bronze, and a three-branched iron candlestick like that at Abu-'s-Sifain and Ḳadîsah Burbârah. Before the haikal hang two silver lamps, several glass lamps, and some ostrich-eggs. Each of the three chapels has its own screen inlaid with plain ivory or bone in different designs. There is nothing remarkable in either of the side chapels, though the niche of the haikal contains a fine gold-ground painting of Christ in glory, crowned. North of the north aisle chapel lies a sacristy, which I was unable to enter.

The church is not rich in pictures : scarcely any are worth notice save one of Anba Shanûdah in patriarchal robes; and one of Sitt Dimiânah, who is reclining on a divan, and is girt round with forty dim little figures. But the church derives peculiar sanctity from the possession of the relics of the great

and famous prince and martyr Tadrus. These relics
are treasured in the *shrine of Tadrus*, which opens
by a pretty door in a large panel of fine Arab lattice-
work set flush in the south wall of the choir. The
shrine is a little vaulted chamber, a recess $3\frac{1}{2}$ ft. deep,
and 6 ft. wide. Fronting the door an arched niche
of elaborate woodwork with seven little pillars on
each side encloses a picture of Tadrus—a mounted
cavalier encountering a dolphin-headed dragon and
rescuing a youth whom the dragon was about
devouring: on an eminence in the background
stands a fair maiden lifting her hands in encouragement of the hero. The horse of course is a
ridiculous-looking animal, but the Arab trappings,
saddlecloth, stirrups, and the rest, as well as the
drapery of the figure, are well rendered and well
coloured. There is also something very pleasing in
the frank open smile, the confident, determined face
of Tadrus : the woman's face too is singularly sweet.
Before the picture a lamp or candle is generally burning, and the silk-covered case of relics reposes in the
niche. This shrine is held in the greatest veneration,
not only by the Copts but by the Muslims also, and
the virtues of the relics in casting out devils were
publicly and solemnly put to the proof on Wednesday
in every week, when Coptic and Muslim women
resorted in great numbers. Strange stories are told
of the cures wrought upon believers of both nations;
stranger still of scandals and immoralities to which
the ceremony gave occasion: till in the year 1873
the practice was abolished by the then patriarch[1]. But those possessed with evil spirits can still

---

[1] See Murray's Egypt, sixth edition, vol. i. p. 189.

proceed to the church of Lady Dimiânah between the rivers Balkâs and Nabru, in the north of the Delta. There, once a year, a great festival is held in the church, and while the possessed are being exorcised, a shadow-play of departing devils exhibited on the interior of a large dome confirms the belief of the superstitious: and the contrivances by which it is produced are so cunningly hidden as to completely puzzle those who have no faith in miracle-working.

Even the priests of Mâri Girgis seem scarcely to have abandoned their powers or their claims. On one of my visits to the church, when I wished to enter the haikal, I was not allowed to pass the threshhold until the priest had given me a solemn censing, and signed my forehead with the sign of the cross. So the evil spirits were exorcised.

HISTORICAL NOTES ON THE CHURCHES IN CAIRO.

Though very little is known about the history of the church in Hârat-az-Zuailah or Hârat-ar-Rûm, yet there is enough direct mention to establish their claim to a great antiquity. The former is a patriarchal church, the latter episcopal. Soon after 1100 A.D. the bishop of Masr who succeeded Sanutius was proclaimed in the Hârat-az-Zuailah, though elected and ordained at Abu Sargah[1]. With this church, too, the notorious Cyril, LXXV patriarch, was closely associated. It was here that a council of bishops met to protest against his barefaced simony and extortion about 1250 A.D., and Cyril resided in the

---

[1] Renaudot, Hist. Pat. Alex., p. 492.

monastic building between his first and second imprisonments[1], when probably he devised his canons.

The usurpation of the episcopal church of Al 'Aḍra in the Ḥârat-ar-Rûm by Christodulus, c. 1050 A.D., has been mentioned in another context, where it was shewn how Michael forty years later violated his solemn vow to restore the church to its bishop : but beyond these meagre allusions history seems silent.

THE CHAPEL OF ST. STEPHEN BY THE CATHEDRAL.

The Coptic cathedral, built in the present century, is so ugly and void of interest that it is not worth a visit, except to those who care to see how the Copts of to-day depart from their own traditions and adopt forms and practices of the Greek Church. It contains, however, a superb ancient lectern most richly inlaid with crosses and other designs of chased ivory. This lectern once belonged to Al Mu'allakah. But adjoining the cathedral is the much older chapel of St. Stephen, with choir and haikal, and a baptistery lying to the north. On the south side of the haikal a raised platform of plain stonework is said to cover the remains of a patriarch. Before the haikal door hung recently a curtain most beautifully embroidered, with a figure of the Virgin and Child and of two angels set in separate panels. The work was very old; and therefore, although it was well preserved, it has been removed and replaced by a new curtain of green silk with a red

---

[1] Renaudot, Hist. Pat. Alex., p. 582.

cross sewn upon it. The old embroidery, as a Copt
told me, will probably be used to make a pinafore
for a child: at present it is merely flung aside in
a corner. The usual altar vessels—paten, chalice,
and dome of silver, wooden altar-casket, and corporals—may be seen here more easily than at some of
the larger churches, both because the chapel is more
accessible, and because the vessels are less jealously
hidden from travellers. One of the corporals is remarkable in being fitted with little bells—one at each
corner and one in the centre : it is of red silk, having
a square of green silk in the midst embroidered with
a cross. The baptistery has a place as usual railed
òff for women : the font lies eastwards, and in a
niche just above it stands a very beautiful little
painting of Christ's baptism. Above the four principal figures—our Lord, St. John, and two angels—
the dove is descending in a golden circle, round
which is an outer circle of cherub-heads : from the
inner circle a widening beam of golden light is falling
upon the head of Christ. The ground of the picture
is of very singular tone—a pale faded green colour,
extremely pleasing. The deep golden aureoles of
the four figures are set with real jewels—rubies and
emeralds.

CHAPTER VII.

The Monasteries of the Natrun Valley in the Libyan Desert.

*Dair Abu Makâr.—Dair Anba Bishôi.—Dair-as-Sûriâni.—
Dair al Baramûs.*

ALL the ancient churches of the two Cairos have now been passed in review; and if I have lingered too long among them, it is because they are almost daily losing something from wilful destruction or destructive renovation. Moreover, even where the churches are spared, they are fast falling out of harmony with their surroundings; as in place of the old Arab houses and gardens vast and unsightly cubes of modern buildings are arising. Hence every detail seems worth recording, in the fear that soon it may have no other record left. The same is true in a far less degree of the monasteries in the Natrun valley, to which we are now coming. There at least are no new houses building: but the monasteries seem to stand in eternal harmony with the eternal solitudes around them. Yet fourteen centuries cannot have passed over these ancient abodes with quite so light a touch as over their changeless sands. Here and there the ruins of shattered convents lie about the desert, marking sites of which the very name is long forgotten: the churches within the convents bear the marks of various styles, and date from different epochs: most of them have long been under the shadow of decay, and lately one has suffered severely under sentence of restoration. But the traditions of the place remain unbroken, and fadeless as the scene that enshrines them. The life too, in its outer guise at least, is scarcely altered since the dawn of monasticism; though the high ideals of the early recluses are long since levelled with the dust, though their heroic enthusiasms have sunk down to a dull stagnation, though the lamp of their knowledge is extinguished, and the pulse of their devotion is still.

The monasteries lie to the north-west of Cairo, three days' journey in the Libyan desert. Of the fifty mentioned by Gibbon only four now remain inhabited: most of the others have vanished and left no vestige behind[1]. Vansleb[2] mentions seven as having formerly existed, namely Macarius, John the Little, Anba Bishôi, Timothy, Anba Mûsa, Anba Kaima, and Sûriâni, of which, he adds, only Bishôi and Sûriâni now survive:—an obvious error, for besides Macarius there is still left one other called Al Baramûs, which lies nearest to the Natrun lakes. The locality is variously termed the desert of Scete, desert of Schiet, desert of Nitria, and Wâdi Naṭrûn or Natrun valley: it seems however that the name Scete applies more properly to the southerly part of

---

[1] Gibbon probably derived his information from Rufinus, who speaks of fifty 'tabernacula,' adding that some of these had many tenants, others but few, while some held solitary recluses. It is clear therefore that single cells or caves were included in the term. See Rosweyde, Vitae Patrum, p. 364.

[2] Voyage fait en Egypte, p. 227.

the valley, and Nitria to the northerly part. Thus
Dair Abu Maḳâr is spoken of as being in the desert
of Scete, while the region about Al Baramûs takes
its name from the ancient town of Nitria, which dated
at least from Roman times. The salt lakes in the
valley furnish abundance of nitre, whence their name:
the nitre has been worked for full two thousand
years: and a small colony of fellahîn at the present
day is settled on the western borders of the lakes to
collect both nitre and salt for the Egyptian government[1]. There is reason to think that from Roman
to mediæval times glass-works existed almost con-
tinuously at Nitria. Such at least is the tradition,
which is confirmed both by the evidence of travellers[2],
and by the fragments discovered on the site of the
town. And even within the last generation the
monasteries were rich in those famous—but now
almost fabulous—enamelled glass lamps of Arab
workmanship. In Coptic the town was known, as
ϫⲁⲡⲓϩⲟⲥⲉⲙ, and the district as ⲡⲙⲉⲙ ⲡⲓϩⲟⲥⲉⲙ.

The monasteries of the eastern desert by the Red
Sea coast, which are called after the first anchorites
St. Anthony and St. Paul, are said to have been
founded by those worthies, and therefore to be
anterior in date to the convents of the Wâdi Naṭrûn. But this statement, if pressed, can mean no

---

[1] The best account of this settlement is to be found in Sir
Gardner Wilkinson's 'Modern Egypt and Thebes' (London, 1843).
The author mentions also the Coptic monasteries, but on these his
remarks are singularly slight and barren. He scarcely notices one
single detail of architecture or ritual. See vol. i. pp. 382–398.

[2] Thus Le Sieur Granger, who travelled in Egypt in 1730,
mentions 'trois verreries abandonnées' between the lakes and
St. Macarius. See 'Relation du Voyage fait en Egypte' (Paris,
1745), p. 179.

more than that the one region was occupied by
hermits some time before the other.   For it is very
improbable that SS. Anthony and Paul were the
founders of any monastery at all, in the ordinary
meaning of the term.   They doubtless chose some
lonely spot, which speedily was haunted by other
recluses : but, there can be no question that both in
the eastern and in the western desert the first recluses
were solitary hermits living apart in scattered cells
or caves, and not united in any cœnobitic rule of
life, much less congregated within the walls of any
monastic building.   Moreover St. Anthony was not
born till the middle of the third century, whereas
the Nitrian valley is said to have been frequented
by the Therapeutæ even in the days of St. Mark;
and it seems certain that St. Frontonius withdrew
there with a company of seventy brethren in the
second century, and St. Ammon, who founded a
hermit settlement there, was rather earlier than St.
Anthony.   The monasteries of the Natrun desert
may therefore claim to rest on a site hallowed by
the history of eighteen centuries of Christian worship, although none of the surviving religious houses
date their first foundation earlier than the third or
fourth century.   When to this historic interest is
added the romantic picturesqueness of their situation,
the boundless waste of barren sand that severs
them from the world, the changeless sunshine that
brightens their desolation, their loneliness broken
only by sudden troops of marauding Beduin, the
yearly convoy of friendly camels, or the rare advent
of pilgrim or wayfarer; and when one remembers
the true fairy-tales of the hidden treasures of the
monks,—not gold, but books worth their weight in

rubies : then one may feel some astonishment, perhaps, that the charm of the Natrun valley should have worked with so feeble a spell, as not to draw one traveller in ten thousand of those who visit Egypt.

No doubt, however, the route is tedious and even dangerous. When first I wished to make the journey in the spring of 1881, the khedive ordered careful enquiries to be made by the authorities; and the result was a prohibition. It was reported that the Beduins were in a restive and hostile mood owing to some recent fighting with Egyptian soldiers, and would be certain to rob and turn back any travellers they might encounter in the desert, though on the whole the chances were against their caring particularly for unnecessary murder[1]. I was on the point of leaving Egypt, as it seemed for ever, and the disappointment was bitter: yet to go would have been fruitless folly. But in the winter of 1883–4 I was enabled to revisit Egypt[2], and a journey to the Wâdi Naṭrûn fell within the compass of my mission. This time the khedive, with his usual ready knowledge of the country, pronounced the route secure; and with customary kindness sent a telegram to the mudîr of the province, whence our party was to start across the desert, ordering all arrangements to be made for our safety and honour. We

---

[1] Some idea of the perils of the journey one hundred years ago may be formed from Sonnini's account. He was robbed, and only saved from a second ambuscade by a sudden change of route which foiled the plot of the Beduins for his destruction. See Voyage dans la Haute et Basse Égypte, vol. ii. p. 179 seq.

[2] As an envoy of the Association for the Furtherance of Christianity in Egypt, to whom my thanks are due for this opportunity.

were, however, recommended to wear the ṭarbûsh or
fez, as the sight of western hats is somewhat irri-
tating to the children of the wilderness.   The Coptic
patriarch furnished us with letters both to the priest
at Trîs, which, although a Muslim village, contains
a small Coptic colony and two churches, and also to
the superiors of the four monasteries in the desert.
So we started on the morning after Christmas day,
not unaccompanied by predictions of disaster.

We reached Wardân by train, and there the mudîr's
representative, summoned by the telegram of the
khedive, met us : but, instead of waiting for us to
alight, he came into the carriage to deliver his mes-
sage.   We received his obeisance, and bade him be
seated.   At the same time the envoy of the priest
at Trîs entered the carriage, and we had a long and
leisurely conversation drawn out with copious compliments, for which of course the train politely waited.
The mudîr offered us horses and camels and guides,
placing in fact his province at our disposal : but
when we heard that the Copts had already been
warned of our coming and had made every prepara-
tion for our journey, it only remained to thank the
mudîr for his kindness.   We found, however, that
the natives were widely impressed with the ceremony
which surrounded our arrival.   An hour's ride in
hard rain brought us to Trîs, where the kindly priest
Ibrahim welcomed us to the guest-room, specially
reserved for the patriarch's use on the rare occasion
of his visit to the desert convents.   According to
ancient custom, as recorded for instance by Rufinus[1],

---

[1] See Rosweyde's Vitae Patrum, pp. 348, 349, etc.   For a still
earlier reference to the custom, the earliest in eastern literature, see
Genesis xviii. 4.

our host offered water to wash our feet : but we were really more grateful for a large brazier of burning coals which was set in the middle of the room, and replenished, as the fire sank, with logs of wood. The heat and the smoke together soon dried us : and as the rain without continued, and quickly drenched our tents, we were very thankful that night to sleep with ·a roof above our heads.

Next day rose clear, but with a strong gale blowing from the west. The shape and relief of the desert hills were blurred by a ceaseless storm of sand, in the teeth of which lay our line of march. It was soon decided that advance against such a wind was impossible : our guides said that the driving sand would strike like shot upon our faces, and that the camels would refuse to move. So as it blew with unabated fury till sundown, we were forced to remain another day, which we spent partly in revolver prac- tice and partly in talking theology with our Coptic hosts. We saw the little domed churches which lie one at each side of the village : but they offered nothing of interest. The dair within which we were staying contained, beside the priest's house, a school for little children, whom we saw through an open door sitting on the ground in a windowless room, with their tin slates on which they write with reed pens and ink. At our approach they all rose, and thronged to the door to kiss our hands.

The Copts had been living in daily terror of death at the time of Arabi's rebellion. At Trîs the story was the same as at Cairo, all agreeing that only the arrival of the English army had saved the Christians from massacre. It was curious to notice that the gratitude of the Copts seemed directed personally to the 'gracious lady Victoria the queen,' whose name and praises they were never tired of repeating. This unfortunately is no longer the case with dwellers in the cities, with whom all gratitude seems cancelled by the usury of suffering added to their lives by English misrule as the price of English deliverance. Here in the country the little colony planted in a hostile village had not yet recovered from the shock of a danger, such as the oldest Copts could not remember, and such as could scarcely be found recorded in the wildest pages of their troubled history.

With the morning the wind had fallen : but though we rose at dawn, it was quite eight o'clock before we got under weigh. As we were taking leave Ibrahim, whom illness prevented from coming with us as the patriarch had ordered, stood at the door of the dair, and lifting hands and eyes said a prayer for our safety. Then he walked a short distance with us on our way, ere we parted and filed across the plain. An hour's ride brought us to the Beduin village of Bani Salâmah, to which our guides belonged : we exchanged greetings with some of the men, passed on across the canal where our beasts drank deep, as if they foreknew the parched wilderness before them, and mounted the ridge that borders the desert table-land. As the green plains and clustered palms of the Delta fade from the view, the world seems to close behind one, leaving a sense of helpless abandonment and desola-tion :—a sense that soon passes away, as one yields to the silent magic of the desert. The journey lies over a monotonous series of slightly undulating hills : ridge after ridge they rise and fall, and each ridge is precisely like the last; the ground slopes gently away, remains flat for a while, and then curves gently upward again to make another hillock. The distances vary a little, but the view is always bounded by a ridge in front and a ridge behind. After a long and toilsome day, just as the sun was setting, we mounted the last ridge, and saw an immense valley of sand stretching far away below us. The brief purple twilight showed us too in the remote distance a momentary glimpse of Dair Macarius, where we hoped to make our quarters for the night. But the darkness fell, moonless, almost starless, and so deep that we could scarcely see each other. We were still some miles from our monastery, which had vanished again like an evening ghost : our beasts were tired, our guides seemed doubtful of the way, the party could only keep touch by continual shouting, and our camels were far behind, we knew not where. The sensation of being lost in the Sahara at night without food or water is something to have experienced, if only for two hours : nor was the feeling less real at the time, because the after result proved it to have been unnecessary. The descent into the valley was steep : then we stumbled on over loose sand mixed with rushes and Christ-thorn, and we found the way much more difficult than the hard stony surface of the desert during our journey by day. The gloom and silence around us were awful : it was like the valley of the shadow of death. But it ended at last, when a light flashed out in the distance and then burned steadily,—welcome as ever light was to benighted wayfarers in desolate places : for though at first we took it for a star, we soon knew that it was a lantern burning on the convent walls to guide us.

We hastened on, and found the monks waiting in a group outside the dair to receive us : they kissed our

hands with exclamations of thankfulness for our safe
arrival, and led us through the narrow doorway
within the fortress, where we were soon lodged in
the guest-chamber, and lay on rugs upon the floor
to rest and wait for our tents and camels. The
guest-chamber was a bare room with latticed but
unglazed windows: it was on the first floor, and
reached by a flight of steps in the open air without:
some dark cells are annexed to it, but did not look
very tempting. The monks gave us the usual eastern

A. J. B.

Fig. 19.—Dair Macarius from the south-east.

thimbleful of coffee, but it was nearly ten o'clock
before we dined. Next morning the unwonted sound
of a church bell roused us at five o'clock, and with
the dawn we got a view of the monastery, which the
darkness of the night before had rendered impossible.

All the four monasteries here are built roughly on
the same model, although the details vary in arrangement, and a description of our first resting-place,
Dair Macarius, will more or less accurately describe
the others. The monastery is a veritable fortress,
standing about one hundred and fifty yards square,

with blind lofty walls rising sheer out of the sand.
A high arched recess in one wall of the quadrilateral
marks the place of the doorway; this however is
very diminutive, being scarcely four feet high, and is
closed with a massive iron-plated door, behind which
tons of loose stones are piled in times of danger.
The door is further shielded in front by two large
granite millstones, which the monks roll before it,
and are then themselves hauled up to the top of the
wall by a pulley. These precautions now are seldom
taken: but they have sufficed to secure these dairs
in their age-long existence. Their enemies among
the Beduin in bygone times had of course no artillery,
and soon tired of the idle siege: but the tribes which
now most frequent that part of the desert are engaged
largely in carrying bullrushes from the lakes across
the desert to the Delta for the making of mats: and
as they find the Coptic monasteries very convenient
places to replenish their scanty stock of food and
water, they are wise enough to remain on friendly
terms with the monks. The walls within have a
platform running round the whole circuit, with a
parapet: but the defenders seem never to have used
any other weapon but stones. Each monastery has
also, either detached or not, a large keep or tower,
standing four-square, and approached only by a drawbridge. The tower contains the library, storerooms
for the vestments and sacred vessels, cellars for oil
and corn; and many strange holes and hiding-places
for the monks in the last resort, if their citadel should
be taken by the enemy. Besides the well which
supplies the dair with water in ordinary times, there
is sometimes another in the keep.

The four walls of Dair Macarius, or Dair Abu

Maḳâr, as the natives call it, enclose one principal and one or two smaller courtyards, around which stand the cells of the monks, domestic buildings such as the mill-room, the oven[1], the refectory and the like, and the churches.   The mill-room, where they grind their corn, is a square building, roofed with a large dome : the mill-stones are driven by cogs worked by an ox or a donkey, and the flour, though very coarse with the husk unsifted, makes a wholesome bread, when baked as is the fashion in small round cakes. The refectory is a long, narrow, vaulted chamber, with a low stone bench or rather shallow trough running down the middle : the monks sit on either side the bench, while one of their number reads a portion of

---

[1] Tischendorff, who visited these monasteries, is not more satisfactory than Sir G. Wilkinson or other writers.   He tells us a great deal about the nitre, very little about the churches, and that little mostly wrong.   Here, for instance, he speaks of an 'oven behind the sacristy' as being one of the peculiarities of arrangement which struck him most; a remark upon which Neale, with his usual inaccuracy, founds a statement to the effect that 'in some part of the Coptic church, especially in the Desert of Cells' (sic), a small building with an oven is 'attached to the east end of the *sanctuary*:' as if sanctuary and sacristy were the same thing (Eastern Church, Gen. Introd. vol. i. p. 190).   As a matter of fact the place of the sacristy in these churches is quite indeterminate, and so is the place of the oven.   Similarly Tischendorff speaks of a 'grotto chapel' at Dair-as-Sûriâni which certainly does not exist; and calls Anba Bishôi by the odd compound 'St. Ambeschun.'   Of other travellers, Russegger mentions two monasteries called 'Labiat' and 'U-Serian' (!): Andréossi gives the names Amba Bischay and El Baramus : Sicard mentions four, and has the names nearly right. See Travels in the East, by C. Tischendorff, tr. by W. E. Shuckard, London, 1847, pp. 45, 46.

I have been at some pains to ascertain the names of the monasteries correctly; and the names as given in the text may be taken as accurate and final.

scripture all through the meal. Sometimes the old
garners are still used for storing corn; but the
monks do. not scruple to pile their wheat on the
cool paved floor of the nave in their larger churches.
For their oil they have large earthen jars, of the
kind common in all countries: wine they do not
keep, as it cannot be made on the spot nor brought
across the desert; but they make their sacramental
wine, like the rest of the Copts, from dried raisins.
Each dair has a few palm-trees, but not enough
to keep the monks in dates, of which they eat
largely. Their coffee comes with the corn by
convoy from the Delta, and is pounded in an
earthen mortar with a large club-like pestle of
wood to a coarse powder, which does not make a
good drink. At times of festival the corn and oil
and dates and coffee, which form the rude fare of
the monks, are varied with olives and oranges: and
their good cheer is at its height, when a luckless cow
or sheep has been driven across the burning sands
to make them a Christmas dinner.

Round the court at Abu Maḳâr are three churches.
The smallest of these is marked by a detached bell-
tower: it is called the church of Al Shîûkh [1]. Its
greatest length is from north to south, not from east
to west, and may be said to consist of sanctuaries,
choir, and narthex without any nave. The narthex
is divided from the choir by a row of three columns,
one of which has a late classical capital, and the
columns are joined by a screen. Arches spring
in all four directions from the pillars, and the roof

---

[1] الشيوخ as written for me by one of the monks; the word is the
plural of the familiar 'Shaikh,' and means the Elders.

of the church is consequently a groined vaulting
except over the haikal, which has its own dome,
while a second dome is placed over part of the choir
in front of the haikal.   The haikal here, as in most
of the desert churches, has a pointed arch, which
corresponds to the English chancel-arch, but is due
of course to Byzantine influence.   The church contains nothing of interest except a latish picture of
St. Macarius, who is wrongly represented with a
jewelled epigonation.

The church of Abu Maḳâr is much larger and
finer.   Like Al Shîûkh, it must be styled Byzantine
in character, and cannot boast of any nave or of any
very clear plan.   It has three sanctuaries, a continuous choir partially walled off from the rest of the
church westward, and a western end very irregular
in shape.   The chief interest here lies in the central
haikal, which is very remarkable, being no less than
25 ft. broad from south to north and 20 ft. long.   It
is covered in with a splendid dome of fine brickwork,
which recalls the best period of Arab art.   The small
windows in the dome contain remains of fine stucco-
work, set with tiny panes of coloured glass: and
though much of the plaster has fallen, enough
remains to show that the whole inner surface of
the dome was once adorned with fresco paintings.
The ancient doors of the haikal are finely carved
with arabesques in low relief: over the screen rises
a lofty chancel-arch, the soffit of which is cased
with wood, whereon are painted nine medallions enclosing sacred scenes.   The haikal here and without
exception in all the churches of the Natrun valley
is square-ended, a curious reversal of the rule
among the Cairene churches, in which the apse is

almost a universal feature. But the eastern wall
contains the usual central niche, which is covered
with faded frescoes; it contains also one side niche
and two other recesses, which are square-headed:
while the north wall contains no less than five niches.
A tier of three large steps runs along the whole
length of the eastern wall, making a sort of tribune;
but it is doubtful whether it has more than a formal
value. The altar of course is of stone, and of
the usual description: but by a very remarkable
peculiarity, quite unparalleled in the churches of
Maṣr, it stands on a raised platform. This platform
is 10 in. high and 12 ft. 6 in. square. In most of the
desert churches the altar either stands on a similar
detached platform, or is raised one step above the
westernmost part of the haikal: but I have not been
able to find any reason for this marked departure
from the structure of the altar normal in the
churches of the Delta. There are two other peculiarities to notice in regard to these altars in the
desert: first, that they very seldom have any canopy
or baldakyn overshadowing them; secondly, that
they usually, as at Abu Makâr, have two stone
candelabra standing close beside them, one at the
north and one at the south side. The latter
arrangement is doubtless in virtue of the early
canon against the use of lights upon the altar.

The chapel adjoining the haikal on the north,
which is dedicated to St. John, is remarkable in
having a sort of inner choir. The outer screen is as
usual in a line with the haikal-screen, but at a distance
of about eight feet eastward from this outer screen
there stands a second, which serves as the iconostasis. I know no other example of an inner choir

stolen, as it were, from the area of a side chapel in this manner. Of the two screens, that to the westward is the more noteworthy: for it contains a number of small vertical oblong panels carved with exquisite arabesque devices in extraordinarily high relief. Closely as the lines of the design are grouped together, they stand out no less than $1\frac{1}{4}$ in. from the background. Such carving surpasses anything in woodwork in the Cairo churches, and is a real triumph of skilful workmanship. The panels are older than the screen in which they are framed, and are probably not later than the eighth century. The altar here stands on a raised platform, not detached but running across the chapel into the north and south walls. On the east wall are the remains of some frescoed figures, now almost indistinguishable, and there are traces of an interlacing pattern in the recess. Between this chapel and the haikal stands a partition wall, which is pierced towards the westward with a door having an arched heading of carved stonework. Nearly all the plaster has fallen in from the north dome, but the fragments that remain are coloured. Round the lower part of the dome runs a border of conventional design clearly visible by aid of a glass[1].

The choir of the church of Abu Maḳâr, like that of Al Shîûkh, contains a reliquary: the bones of St. Macarius are said to rest in the latter.

---

[1] Mr. Greville Chester, in his 'Notes on the Coptic Dayrs in the Wady Natrûn,' speaks of 'fine Cufic inscriptions in red upon the dome.' This is an error. There is not a letter of Cufic or Arabic in the church, though in the dim light it is easy to mistake the angular character of this design for Cufic writing.

The third church lies on the southern side of the courtyard, and is dedicated to *Abu Iskharûn*[1], or St. Ischyrion, a martyr of Alexandria. It is perhaps rather more basilican in structure than the other churches, but not of a very decided type of architecture. The choir and nave are almost covered by one magnificent dome of brick, the low pitch of which secures a curve of great beauty. A door once leading into the north part of the choir is now blocked: it is square-headed, and above the lintel there is set a large panel of finely wrought mosaic of brickwork. Ornamentation of this kind, no less than the noble span and superblightness of these desert domes, shows that the ancient monastic builders possessed an unrivalled mastery over brickwork, and delighted in producing effects on which western architects would scarcely venture. The shell of these churches is generally built of unhewn limestone, which is found in large quantities in the desert hills: but the bricks, which are small and dark red in colour, must have been carried on camels from the far-off cities of Egypt.

The north chapel of Abu Iskharûn contains at present no altar, but doubtless had one originally. In the haikal there is an unusual feature: against the wall in the north-west corner is placed a sort of small table of stone, which possibly may have been designed as a credence, and close by it an unmistakeable piscina. The latter is formed of an ordinary earthenware jar, or ḳullah as the natives call it, with the bottom broken out, and the mouth set downwards in the wall, in which it is cemented. This is doubt-

---

[1] .ابو أسخرون

less in replacement of a marble piscina, and there is a proper drain to carry off the rinsings. In the south cha el also is a curious fitting—a sort of small marble basin, half engaged in the wall at the north-east corner. The monks told me that it is used in making and consecrating the oleum infirmorum.

We found posted on the wall by the haikal-screen in this church a paper covered with finely written Arabic characters, clearly denoting some sort of festival occasion. It proved to be a form of thanksgiving for the entry of the English army into Cairo in the year 1882.

Quitting Abu Iskharûn and mounting a steep and broken flight of steps, one comes to the drawbridge of the ḳaṣr or tower. The drawbridge now rests across the deep chasm which divides the tower from the staircase, but can be raised by a windlass in case of danger. One lands on the floor of the first story, which contains three separate chapels.

The first of these, dedicated to St. Michael, consists of a single room divided roughly into haikal and nave by screens. In the nave stand five pillars, the shaft of each composed of two small columns set vertically one on top of another. Among them there are two Doric capitals, and five late Corinthian, with crosses carved among the foliage. The Corinthian capitals, and one other of a graceful design not assignable to any classical order, were picked out in colours: touches of red and blue are still discernible. On the south side of the chapel there are some rude but ancient mural paintings, which represent horsemen: they are executed in pale red and yellow shades, and beneath them are Coptic inscriptions. The haikal-screen, which is a fine piece of ivory inlaying, is surmounted by another inscription carved in ivory. The haikal is square-ended and not remarkable, except for a consecration cross, which is incised upon a slender marble shaft placed against the eastern wall, and for a curious collection of relics. No less than sixteen patriarchs are here preserved in plain deal boxes! Eight cases, each containing two bodies, are piled one upon another at the south side of the altar: and so far from being hermetically sealed, they are so loosely put together and so slender in make, that one may clearly see the shrivelled forms of the patriarchs lying like so many mummies in their coffins.

Next comes the chapel of St. Anthony, which possesses no attraction except in three very ancient frescoed figures. Of these the dexter figure wears a decided chasuble of yellow colour: the central figure wears a white chasuble lined with red : while the sinister figure is clad in a cope fastened by a morse. All three wear glories.

The last of the three chapels is dedicated to a saint called in Arabic Sûâh[1], who may possibly be St. Sabas. Like St. Anthony, it contains some frescoes, which are interesting as preserving a record of the vanished chasuble. Here there are nine figures, of which the greater part show a chasuble with rounded front falling a little below the girdle. One figure has also a vestment possibly intended for an epigonation ; but in the present state of the painting one cannot affirm positively what would, if established, be very remarkable testimony.

---

[1] سواح as written by the monks.

A sort of dungeon staircase leads down to the ground floor of the tower, where there are many empty vaults and chambers, and the church of Al 'Adra, which is larger than the chapels on the first floor, and contains three altars arranged in the usual fashion. But the altars are not separated: they all stand on one continuous raised platform, which is 7 ft. distant from the screen. An arch on each side the haikal forms the only division here as at Al Mu'allakah; and another point of coincidence between the two churches is this, that the altar-tops are all of the exceptional kind found at the great church in Cairo. The south altar-top encloses a semicircular slab of marble with a sunken surface and border, but no outlet westward: the top of the haikal altar is a marble slab of oblong form with a similar depression: while on the north altar there rests another semicircular tray of marble, so large that it projects in places five inches beyond the side of the substructure. I thought here to recover the tradition of the usage or ceremony for which these curious altar-tops were designed, and was disappointed to find that the monks of the desert could tell me no more than the priests of Cairo.

The foundation of this monastery is no doubt rightly ascribed to the saint whose name it bears. Rufinus[1] mentions 'two lights of heaven shining there,' both called Macarius. Of these the elder was surnamed the Egyptian; the younger, or the Alexandrian, flourished in the fourth century: and the latter it was who founded the dair, distant twenty-four hours' journey from the Nitrian monasteries, at a

---

[1] Rosweyde, Vitae Patrum, p. 367 seq.

place called Scithium. Rufinus adds that there is
no path or sign by the way to guide the traveller
thither: the monastery has little water, and that
bituminous and very foul of smell: '*sunt ergo ibi
viri valde perfecti.*' In proof of this perfection is told
the well-known story of the grapes given to Macarius,
and handed from monk to monk and at last returned,
all refusing to partake so sinful a luxury. Macarius
himself once killed a mosquito that was biting him,
and in sorrow for the deed retired naked to the
marshes where the largest and most venomous sort
abounded, and suffered six months' torment beneath
their stings: so that, when he returned to his monks,
they could not recognise his swollen face and body,
but knew him only by the sound of his voice. This
legend, it may be noticed, is very remarkable in being
founded on a trait rare in those early times, and
perhaps now rarer still in Egypt—a tender regard for
animal life. He had a power of seeing visions, by
which we are told he once beheld the evil thoughts
of the monks, in the form of little black imps playing
about them in church; and when a bad monk put
out his hand to receive the consecrated bread, one of
these 'Æthiops' placed hot coals in the monk's hand,
and the wafer flew back unaided to the altar. In
short Macarius by his virtues and powers, his fastings,
self-chastisements and abasements, gained a reputa-
tion for saintly austerity which made him the wonder
of his own time, and carried his name all over the
Christian world after his death[1].

---

[1] For further details concerning him see Rosweyde, l. c.; Lord
Lindsay's Christian Art, vol. i. p. cxxxviii seq.; Curzon's Monasteries
of the Levant, pp. 91–2.

Of the subsequent history of the monastery, next to nothing is known. It was repaired and strengthened about the year 880 by Sanutius the patriarch, whose body may be one of the sixteen mummies. About the year 1000 A.D. one Joseph, a deacon of Abu Makâr, complains that this is the only place where Christians 'come to the throne with confidence,' i. e. during the great persecution. Abu-'l-Farâg mentions it in his book of the Christian convents: and Abu-'l-Birkat relates that in his day the Coptic liturgy was·used without Arabic at Dair Macarius, implying that the monks still understood the ancient language of their ritual. Quatremère[1], remarking on this statement, is anxious to know whether it still holds good; but observes that travellers who have visited the place since, are silent: and Sonnini, who testifies to the use of both Coptic and Arabic at Al Baramûs, did not even visit Dair Macarius[2]. Of course there is not a grain of truth in the statement as applied to present day practice; and I very much doubt whether it was true when Abu-'l-Birkat wrote it.

At the time of my visit the number of monks at the convent of Abu Makâr was twenty, of whom twelve were in priest's orders. They are allowed sometimes to visit the patriarch, and even to see friends living in Cairo, by special permission: but they must return to live and to die in the desert.

---

[1] Recherches Critiques et Historiques sur la Langue et la Littérature de l'Egypte; par Etienne Quatremère. Paris, 1808.

[2] It was the sudden abandonment of his proposed visit to Abu Makâr, where an ambush of Beduins awaited him, to which Sonnini owed his life.

Dair Anba Bishôi[1].

At our departure from the kindly shelter of Dair Macarius, the monks escorted us without the walls, and the ḳummuṣ or abbot prayed for our safety, spreading both hands palm-upwards towards the skies. The surface of the valley proved very different from that of the desert before we descended: the hard-set ground covered with dark sheeny pebbles had now given place to stretches of soft loose sand and beds of broken limestone, while tufts of reedy grass and low prickly shrubs relieved the utter deadness of the wilderness. The ride takes only about four hours, and is extremely picturesque; especially as the lakes come into view, and the strangely brilliant purple of their shining surface contrasts with the dark reed-beds which encircle them, and with the sombre hues of the desert sand. Here and there the way is marked by little heaps of stone ranged in a line, which once reached from the cells of Macarius to the monastery of Anba Bishôi. The track is called to this day the Path of the Angels: for legend tells that angels made the road to guide the hermits of Scete to church on holy days. At one point on the route, after Dair Anba Bishôi and Dair-as-Sûriâni, which stand within bowshot of each other, have risen above the horizon in front, the white walls of Macarius are still visible in the far distance behind: while on either side the broad valley spreads reposing in monumental silence.

---

[1] دير انبا بشوى.

We had heard that Anba Bishôi contained the best well of water of all the four monasteries, and we resolved therefore to make it our head-quarters for the remainder of our visit,—a decision which we had no cause to repent. We found our arrival was not expected : the iron-plated postern was closed, and we had to ring some time at the bell, which is hung on the convent wall and sounded by a cord swinging loose below. At last our Beduins and our beasts were admitted within the dair, and our tents pitched

A. J. B.

Fig. 20.—Dair Anba Bishôi from the north-west.

in the main courtyard, which is an oblong, bounded on three sides by cells, and on the fourth by a church dedicated to the patron saint of the convent. There are two other courtyards besides, in one of which is a large well about fifteen feet in diameter, worked with the usual Egyptian sakkiah or waterwheel and a string of pitchers. Water pumped up by this rude machinery, which doubtless dates from the days of the Pharaohs, is made to irrigate the monastery garden, which is almost a rood in extent, and grows some palms, olives, garlic, capsicum, and other vegetables, to the great pride of the monks.

The name Bishôi is no doubt an Arabic corruption

of the Coptic Isa, which corresponded probably to
Isaiah. The Coptic article ⲡ was prefixed in common speech, making the name Pisa, under which
name Anba Bishôi wrote an ascetic treatise, the
original MS. of which Curzon claims to have pro-
cured[1]. The Coptic form ⲡⲁⲏⲥⲉ is found in another
MS. of the fourth century[2]. There seems no more
to be said on the matter: for a demand for information on a point of philology or history has about as
much chance of a profitable answer from the monks
as a demand for the philosopher's stone. They
cherish the body of their founder, but his spirit is
indeed departed.

The principal church here, which bears the name
of Anba Bishôi, is an extremely fine building, the
main features of which are of the basilican order,
though the whole fabric is too Coptic in its mixture
of styles to be classed with any very definite form
of architecture. There are three entrances, one of
which on the north side is through a porch covered
in with a very fine dome of brick; another lies in
the corresponding position on the south side; while
the third is by a large central doorway in the west
end of the church. The body of the building consists of nave, with north and south aisle, and returned
western aisle or narthex. The roof of the nave is
a lofty pointed-arched vaulting: the aisles are also
vaulted, and are separated from the nave by massive
piers, which carry lofty pointed arches. These arches
are now mostly blocked up to strengthen the nave

---

[1] Monasteries of the Levant, p. 91.

[2] Fragmentum Evangelii S. Johannis Graeco-Copto-Thebaicum;
ed. A. Georgius. Rome, 1789. Praef. p. xcii.

walls, which the thrust of the vaulting seems to have
endangered: for a similar reason doubtless two additional piers have been thrown out laterally in the
middle of the nave, with the result of almost sunder-
ing it into two divisions. That this is not part of
the original design is proved by the fact that the
pier so thrown out on the north side is built across
the ancient stone ambon, entirely blocking the steps
by which it was mounted: and in replacement of the
ambon a wooden pulpit has been erected further
eastward. In the floor of the nave is set a small
marble basin, used at the ceremony of feet-washing.
The outer walls of the aisles once contained small
windows, now blocked: but traces of the starlike
design in stucco-work, which enclosed panes of
coloured glass, still remain visible.

The choir is entirely walled off from the nave,
with the exception of a very lofty arched opening,
the lower part of which closes with folding doors.
This is unquestionably part of the original arrangement of the church, and is very curious. It corresponds with the arrangement in one or two western
monastic churches, where women were admitted to
the service, and were thus effectually separated from
the men; but probably no woman has ever visited
these monasteries since their foundation. The choir
doors are set with panels of fine carving in relief,
enclosed in ivory borders: similar doors, though not
so lofty, shut off the aisles also from the choir: but
there are no steps between, the choir and the nave
being on the same level.

Like the nave, the choir is vaulted: but instead
of the vaulting of the nave and aisles being continued over the choir, it stops short; and the choir

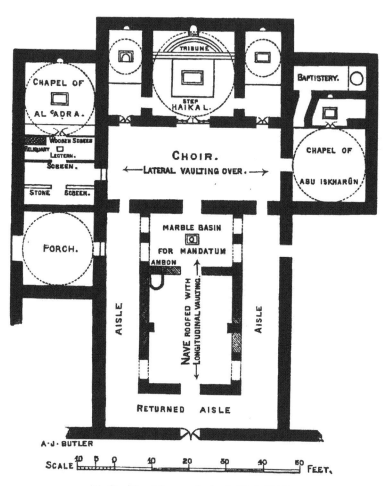

CHAPEL OF
AL ꞓADRA.

TRIBUNE

STEP
HAIKAL.

BAPTISTERY.

WOODEN SCREEN
RELIQUARY
LECTERN.
SCREEN.

STONE SCREEN.

CHOIR.
← LATERAL VAULTING OVER. →

CHAPEL OF
ABU ISKHARÛN.

PORCH.

MARBLE BASIN
FOR MANDATUM
AMBON

NAVE ROOFED WITH
LONGITUDINAL VAULTING.

AISLE

AISLE

RETURNED AISLE

A·J·BUTLER

SCALE 10 5 0 10 20 30 40 50 FEET.

Fig. 21.— Plan of the monastic church of Anba Bishôi.

has a separate vaulting at right angles to that of the nave. A decayed fresco of St. George on the south wall; the usual ostrich-eggs and a fine bronze corona hanging before the haikal-screen; and some small coloured windows of Arab stucco-work in the north and south gables of the roof—these are the only points of interest in the choir. But there are two satellite churches or chapels which open out from the choir, and deserve notice. That at the north side is dedicated to Al 'Adra, and contains the bones of Anba Bishôi in a reliquary: it is vaulted east and west, and has only a single altar. The other on the south side is larger, and is covered in with a most magnificent dome: the altar, which is dedicated to Abu Iskharûn, has for its slab a shallow marble tray of oblong form. A narrow passage north of the altar leads to the baptistery, which lies adjoining the chapel on the east: it contains a plain round font of the usual type, with a drain at the bottom to carry off the water.

Both these satellite chapels lie outside the main building, and are doubtless later erections; for the large church has its own three independent altars. The haikal is raised one step above the choir: the altar is further raised one step upon a platform, three sides of which stand clear, while the fourth runs into the eastern wall, which of course is straight not apsidal. Yet there is a tribune here of fine proportions. It consists of six steps, of which the lower three are straight, the upper three curved. The throne is gone entirely: but the broken masonry shows a cavity underneath it, which may have been intended for relics. All the steps are faced with vertical strips of coloured marble: the spandrels of

the niche above the throne still bear rich traces of
the finest opus Alexandrinum : and above is a large
panel filled with mosaic of marble on a larger scale, a
design of crosses in blue enclosed in a white border,
and containing what looked very like traces of gilt
vitreous enamel.   But I know no other instance of
this Venetian or Byzantine mosaic in Egypt, and the
impression is probably an illusion.   The niche itself
was once ornamented with a mural painting, which
has now quite vanished : but the ceiling of the dome
still retains its central cross, and many bright vestiges
of the graceful band of arabesques painted round it.
The peculiar structure of the haikal doors has already
been mentioned [1].   I have only here to add that in
addition to the ritual interest of their structure, they
are adorned with panels of the beautiful carving in
high relief noticed at the church of St. Macarius :
and above them rises a lofty arch of triumph.

There is a passage of communication between the
haikal and the two side-chapels.   Of these that on
the north is very small : the altar is raised on a step
and overshadowed by a tiny dome, but not by an
altar canopy.   The south side-chapel is likewise
domed, and rather larger.

All three altars at Anba Bishôi have their tops
formed of marble slabs, that in the north chapel
being of oblong form with a horse-shoe depression,
that in the haikal and other chapel being simple
oblongs with a raised border at the sides.   There
is no drain pierced through any of these altar-tops
here or elsewhere, as one would expect if they were
designed with a view to the rite of washing the altar.

---

[1] P. 31.

A bell-tower stands near the porch adjoining the courtyard, but it contains only a single small bell. One may follow the outer walls of the church round on the eastern and the southern side : indeed, altogether, it stands in greater isolation than any of the other churches ; yet there is no attempt whatever at outside adornment or even finish. Unhewn stones are used for the walls, which are left in the roughest state externally, with all sorts of chance buttresses, offsets, and inequalities. Even here, where there would seem to be no reason for denying that ornamentation to the outside which was lavished within the building, the Coptic architects, either from the force of habit or from some curious canon of taste, have entirely failed to produce a beautiful exterior.

The ḳaṣr contains little of interest except a series of lofty vaulted chambers, which, judging from the fragments of Coptic and Arabic volumes scattered about the floor, once served as the convent library. It has long since been ransacked : not a fragment of any work remains here, or, I venture to say, in any of the monasteries of the Natrun valley. On the top of the tower is a single chapel, dedicated to St. Michael, as was customary in the case of a sacred building raised on any lofty eminence, alike in eastern and western Christendom. The chapel is but rudely furnished. The pictures on the iconostasis dating from the last century, shew the twelve apostles vested in dalmatic, girdle, omophorion, and cope : but there is nothing else which calls for notice.

The ḳummuṣ or abbot of Anba Bishôi claimed for his monastery an antiquity of fifteen hundred years from its first foundation, but told me that the buildings had been largely repaired about a century ago. This was doubtless the time when the arches between the nave and aisles were blocked, and the cross-wall built in the nave of the principal church. Regarding the date of this edifice it is extremely difficult to speak with decision : for while the haikal points on the whole to the sixth or seventh century, other details, such as the enrichment of the loftier domes, the coloured glass and stucco-work, and possibly the structure of the nave, seem to belong rather to the tenth or eleventh century. The truth probably is that different features of the church are assignable to different epochs.

Dair-as-Sûriâni [1].

No one whose imagination has been kindled by the romantic story of Curzon's visit to the monks of the Natrun valley, could resist a feeling of keen excitement as he neared the walls of Dair-as-Sûriâni, where Curzon discovered that horde of ancient literary treasure which alone would make his name famous. The excitement is not lessened if the traveller carries, as the present writer carried, about his waist a heavy belt of gold, wherewith he hopes to retrieve some fragment of treasure still remaining : and even if the sense of adventure were wanting, one could not resist a novel feeling of fascination in surveying the singular beauty of the convent. For as the eye

-----

[1] دير السوريانى as dictated by one of the monks.

follows it, half-climbing the gentle slope of a desert hill, half-resting on the broad flat summit, its lines are extremely graceful; and while over the lower walls a little forest of palm-trees is seen waving its clustered foliage as in protest against the barren sands without, the great white tower and the walls above stand sculptured in azure clearness against the desert horizon.

A. J. B.

Fig. 22.—View from the tower of Dair-as-Sûriâni, showing the interior of that convent, and the neighbouring convent of Anba Bishôi.

The monastery seems to derive its name from a colony of Syrian hermits, who either founded it or occupied it very early. Traces of Syriac literature remain there even to this day, and many priceless Syriac MSS. were carried off by Curzon and Tattam. But there are no Syrian inmates now, nor are there either books or monks of Abyssinian origin, such as Curzon discovered.

The monks as usual received us with great kindness, and were eager to show us over the monastery. They pointed out to us the ancient and venerable tamarind—a rare but not unknown tree in Egypt—which is said to have grown from a walking-stick thrust in the ground by St. Ephrem : and they told us the legend, just as their predecessors have told it to travellers for generations before them [1]. They gave us tiny quantities of indifferent coffee, and peeled for us dry dates with soapless fingers : they talked with us about our journey and about their own life, they led us into the churches and over the tower ; showed us their books, their corn and their oil : and, like their brethren at the other monasteries, they refused to take our money.

There are two principal churches within the dair, both dedicated to the Virgin : but as the term Al 'Adra has already been applied distinctively to the larger and finer building, the smaller will here be called for clearness' sake Sitt Mariam—an alternative allowed by local usage. The church of Sitt Mariam then is aisleless and naveless, rather Byzantine in structure and nearly square in plan, and very dark. The entrance lies on the south-west. Over the doorway a block of white marble is inlet, sculptured with a very beautiful cross in low relief : and on the pier dividing the haikal from the south chapel within, there is another block of black marble, on which a cross is carved with splendid arabesques, and enclosed in a circular moulding. These I think are probably dedication crosses. The main divisions

---

[1] See for example Huntingdon's Epistles, xxxix. Huntingdon visited Egypt in 1695.

of the church are lateral, and include merely narthex, choir and sanctuaries : unless what I have called the narthex can be held to include a nave, in virtue of the low stone screen which runs north and south, making a sort of partition.   But the screen is only 4 ft. high, and the part behind it is so very shallow that it is more accurate to regard the whole as narthex : moreover the whole church, except the sanctuaries, is roofed with barrel-vaulting, in two spans with lateral axes : of these one span covers the choir, the other covers the remainder of the church westward of the choir, and renders it an architectural unit.   A solid wall pierced with two doorways separates choir from narthex, and helps to carry the vaulting.

In the choir one may notice a bronze corona of some merit, a reliquary, and an ancient pulpit, of which the decayed remains show traces of ivory figures of saints, which were once inlaid, one in each panel.   The haikal is rectangular, and has a conventional tribune of three straight steps, a deep eastern niche, and an aumbry at each side.   The altar is raised above the haikal floor by one step, which comes at a distance of 4 ft. from the screen : and at the four corners stand slender columns upholding a baldakyn.

Altogether different in style and structure, and far grander in design, is the magnificent church of Al 'Adra.   Whereas Sitt Mariam is only about 40 ft. by 40, Al 'Adra has about the same breadth with a length of 90 ft. : and whereas Sitt Mariam may possibly be called Byzantine, Al 'Adra belongs distinctly to the basilican order of architecture.   In its general arrangement it bears a strong likeness to the church of Anba Bishôi, but from internal evidence seems rather the model than the copy. By the kindness of the monks I was enabled to make a plan, which however defective is accurate as far as it goes, and will serve to give a good idea of the building. It will be seen that the main entrance is on the north side by a porch, although there is a small low western door somewhat singularly thrust aside from the centre of the western wall. But the church here is entangled in monastic chambers of one sort or another; and it is clear that the western doorway was not designed for a solemn processional entrance. The fabric consists of nave and two aisles with western returned aisle, choir, and sanctuaries: but the choir is shut off from nave and aisles by a thick and massive wall, which divides the church into two separate portions. This separation is made even more effectual by a pair of lofty folding doors (H), which close across the archway leading to the choir. The floor of the whole church is of one uniform level with the exception of the haikal, which is raised two steps above the rest: all three altars are also raised on a platform, one step above the level of the chapels in which they severally stand.

The nave is roofed with a very handsome and lofty vaulting, which runs from west to east and is slightly pointed. It is carried on piers divided by high pointed arches. The two westward piers are extremely heavy, the rest are lighter: and all seem to have massive columns more or less engaged. A large rib (L) further strengthens the vaulting: and a low stone screen (I) runs right across both nave and aisles, divided by open passages. Unfortunately the whole interior of the nave is so plastered with

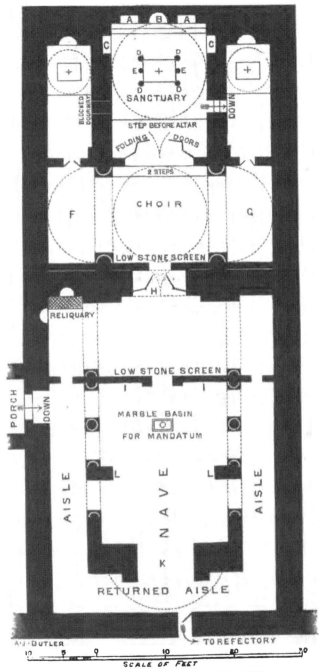

Fig. 23.—Plan of the Church of Al 'Aḍra, Dair-as-Sûriâni.

whitewash, that it is impossible to say whether any part of the fabric is of later construction than the rest.

Nearly in the middle of the nave floor lies a basin for the Maundy feet-washing. It consists of an oblong slab of marble, with a raised fillet round the edges, and a small circular hollow in the centre, about 9 in. across. One may notice also two bronze coronæ suspended in the nave: each consists merely of a flat plate of bronze, about 12 in. in diameter, pierced with holes to receive cups of oil. At the east end of the north aisle is a large wooden reliquary containing some holy bones, and close by it two aumbries.

At Anba Bishôi the choir, it will be remembered, is roofed with a vaulting at right angles to the nave vaulting: but here a different plan is followed. The choir roofing consists of a fine central dome, which covers the whole space before the haikal, and two semidomes, one at either end northward and southward. Each of these semidomes is adorned with very rich fresco paintings, which are still in fair preservation: northward the scene is the Death of the Virgin (F), and southward two subjects are depicted together, the Annunciation and the Nativity (G). In the latter our Lord wears the nimb crucifer. There is a large dome over the haikal altar; one of smaller size over each of the side-altars; and in the centre of the western returned aisle another semidome, frescoed with a scene representing the Ascension (K). In looking at the plan it is difficult to resist the impression that, in spite of the rectangular character of the church, the architect consciously studied a cruciform arrangement with his domes and semidomes. Regarding the merit of the mural paintings I may say at once that they are clear and strong in design, true in drawing, rich and mellow in tone, and, in a word, worthy of the church which they adorn and of comparison with any like work in Europe.

Curiously enough there is another stone screen against the western wall of the choir, where it is hard to say what purpose it can have served; for the monks could hardly lean upon it, as they do in ordinary cases. The doors between the choir and nave are evidently of extreme antiquity: they are inlaid with ivory figures of saints, each on a separate panel, but only the top panels are so decorated. Round the posts and lintel of the doorway runs a Syriac inscription, in raised letters, of a rude bold character, which fixes their date as not later than the seventh century of our era.

Between the haikal and the choir there intervenes a lofty chancel-arch, the lower part of which is closed by a pair of high folding-doors, each in three leaves. The leaves fold backward into the sanctuary, opening a full view of the altar: and these doors, like those of the choir, have their top panels inlaid in ivory with holy figures, which serve as icons, while all the lower panels are ornamented with geometrical designs in ivory inlay. The detail of these designs is very much simpler and more archaic-looking than the ivory designs at Abu-'s-Sifain: and is otherwise distinguished from them by the entire absence of the conventional acanthus, which is conspicuous no less in work of the ninth century and later among the churches and mosques of Egypt, than in carvings and illuminations of Anglo-Saxon, Irish, and other

Y 2

western artists. Here too a Syriac inscription runs round the jambs and lintel, but the lettering is rather later, although still of a kind not found subsequently to the eighth century. This church, then, claims the extraordinary interest of possessing two wooden screens, of which neither can be later than 700 or 800 A. D., and one must be considerably more ancient ; an interest which is partly shared no doubt with the neighbouring churches of Anba Bishôi and Al 'Adra Dair al Baramûs, but is otherwise unrivalled in all that remains of Christian architecture throughout the world.

There is no crewet-holder fastened on the haikal-screen here, although it is usually found in the desert churches, as in those of Cairo. The lintel of the door may be rightly called a rood-beam, for it carries in the centre a plain bronze cross. All three altars are raised one step above their several sanctuaries, but the platform is not detached at the sides. The central altar stands higher than the side altar, by reason of the steps before the haikal-screen, and behind it there is a tier of straight steps against the eastern wall, forming a sort of tribune. Four slender shafts at the four corners of the high altar (D) support a baldakyn : and at each side, north and south, there stands a solid marble candelabrum, 4 ft. 6 in. in height, touching the altar (E). The dome which roofs the haikal is high in pitch, and for some distance upwards has vertical sides before the spring begins : both in the cylindrical part and in the dome windows are pierced, filled in with stucco tracery and panes of coloured glass.

The interior of the haikal is most richly ornamented with designs in plaster of very elaborate and skilful

workmanship. The ornamentation begins at a height
of about 7 ft. from the ground, and consists of a belt,
4 ft. broad, which runs round the three walls. A
beautiful border of a very original design runs along
the lower edge of the belt : the remainder is divided
by vertical bands into panels, which are enriched
with the same design on a larger scale, alternating
with other designs no less sumptuous. The whole
of the work is finely moulded in plaster, and is cast
in high relief. In the eastern wall the niche (B) and
an aumbry on either side of it (A) are surrounded
by work in the same style, but even more beautiful.
At each side of the niche stands a pillar half-engaged
and covered with close flutes, which cross diagonally :
beside the pillars, and round about the arched heading
of the niche, runs a large and bold design of very
graceful arabesques ; and above the niche there is
a panel filled with crosses. Within the niche there
hangs a fine cross of bronze. The aumbries also
are roofed with circular arches followed round by
elaborate mouldings, and the spandrels are filled
with fine enrichments : moreover the aumbries in
the north and south wall, as well as the round arch
of the doorway into each of the side-chapels, are
lavishly ornamented in the same manner. It
will be noticed that the north doorway has been
blocked.

There is no Epiphany tank in this church, and
none at either of the churches of Anba Bishôi. One,
however, is found in the church of Abu Maḳâr, at the
monastery of that name, and one also in the restored
church at Al Baramûs.

The refectory at Dair-as-Sûriâni contains nothing
of special interest, except some rather rude and much ·

decayed frescoes : but it is worth remarking that
while all these desert monasteries contain a common
room for meals, like the frater of our English monasteries, there seems no instance of a common room
for sleeping, corresponding to the dormitory or
dorter. Each monk sleeps in his own cell, and
there seems no evidence of any other rule having
prevailed.

It is well worth while to ascend the tower : not
for the chapel of St. Michael at the top, where there
is nothing to repay a visit except a fine bronze lamp
like that engraved from Abu Kîr wa Yuḥanna at
Old Cairo : nor yet for the library, where all one's
hopes of hidden treasure swiftly vanish away : but
for the view, which opens in silent magnificence.
Nearly all the interior of the dair, with its churches,
cells, and garden of palms is visible : close by rise
the ancient walls of Anba Bishôi : farther to the
north, in the distance, the lakes flash like mirrors in
the sunshine : and all around the vast horizon is
bounded by desolate sands, more lifeless, more impassable, and more sublime than the ocean.

Dair Al Baramûs.

From our camp in the monastery of Anba Bishôi
to Dair al Baramûs was a ride of about three hours,
over loose sand and shale and ridges of limestone
rock, which in some places rose in little hills, and
had evidently been quarried to furnish stone
for the monastic buildings of the neighbourhood.

Our guide and herald, deputed by the patriarch, had gone on some way before us: and when on mounting the last ridge we sighted the monastery, dark figures were faintly visible upon the distant parapets.   As we neared, the monks descended, and stood grouped in clear relief outside, under the white walls of their fortress.   When we were within two hundred yards of the gate, the monks advanced towards us with waving banners.   They kissed our hands as we dismounted : then formed a procession in front of us, and advanced chaunting psalms and

Fig. 24.—Dair al Baramûs [1].

beating cymbals and triangles, while the great bell of the convent clashed out a tumultuous welcome. At the narrow doorway the banners were lowered, and we bent our heads; but the bell still boomed, and the chaunt continued, as we marched across the courtyard to the church of Al Baramûs.   There a service of song was held in rejoicing for our safe arrival; and when it was ended the abbot read an address of welcome such as is customary to read on,

---

[1] The above woodcut is borrowed from Sonnini with trifling corrections.

the arrival of any distinguished personage [1]. From the church we were led up to the guest-chamber, where we partook of the frugal fare offered by our kindly hosts : and we spent the day in talking to the monks, and in examining the various buildings.

---

[1] The address is worth giving ; it runs as follows :—

'Rejoice with me to-day, O my fathers, my brethren, because of these blessed people of Christ who have come to this wilderness, to visit this monastery and these lordly monuments, being favoured with all grace and divine blessing. Be glad with me to-day, O Christian people, chief of the clergy, revered deacons and honoured priests, and you, O blessed children, who come to-day into this wilderness, to these holy places which are bright with the light of saints. Sing tuneful hymns and psalms of David, saying, "Thy habitations, O Lord of Hosts, are bright, my soul longeth for thy courts," because herein the righteous fathers, saints without guile, abode.

'This is the convent of Al Baramûs, in which abode Maximus, Dûmatiûs, Anba Musa, and the priest Ad Darûs, and it bears the name of Mary the Virgin. This is the dwelling of brave soldiers, the place of heroes, who, being sons of kings and sultans, of their own will chose rather to be poor and needy, refusing the pomp and vanity of the world. They were lovers of Christ our God, and walked in his footsteps, bearing his cross.

'He who visits these mansions with firm faith, fervent desire, true repentance, and good works, shall have all his sins forgiven. Then, O my reverend fathers and my beloved brethren, come, that we may pray for these our dear and honourable brethren, who are come upon this visit and have reached these habitations. Let us pray that Jesus Christ, who was with his servants in every time and every place, saving them through all evil and sorrow, may now be with his servants who have come upon this visit, and may deliver them from all sins and iniquities. May he grant them the best of gifts and full reward, recompensing them for all they have endured through toil and peril and the weariness of the journey as they travelled hither ; give them abundance of blessing, of joy, and of grace ; grant them length of days, prosperity, and highest honour ; bring them back to their homes in safety, in health of soul and body, and after a long life transport them to the bright-

The church in which our solemn welcome was held is dedicated to Al Baramûs, a name of which the origin is uncertain; but the first syllable is supposed to be the Coptic article, and the remainder to represent some name like 'Ρωμαῖος. Unfortunately a restoration not quite finished had stripped the church of every single feature of interest, and apparently changed even the old lines of the building. An Epiphany tank has been constructed by raising the level of the ground in the narthex, a feat of which the monks are decidedly boastful: and every sign of antiquity has been swept away, except the haikal-screen, which is of no great moment.

There is, however, a fine ancient church still remaining, though not undamaged by the whitewash, in which this monastery rejoices. It is dedicated to Al 'Adra, and consists roughly of nave and aisles, with the usual three eastern sanctuaries. The nave is roofed with a pointed-arched vaulting, which is strengthened by three stone ribs: but the structure here is so far peculiar, not to say unique, that the ribs instead of running down the nave-walls to the ground stop short, and are received on corbels at the spring of the vaulting. Each corbel, moreover, is marked by a fine cross within a roundel, modelled

---

ness of Paradise and the life of bliss, through the intercession of our Lady the Virgin and of all our holy fathers. Amen.'

I may here note that the saints called Maximus and Dûmatiûs (مكسيمس او دوماتيوس) were sons of a Greek emperor Leo, who went into the desert of Scete, according to a fourteenth century MS. in the Bibliothèque Nationale. (Bib. Or. 258, fol. 16°.)

This address seems a very ancient institution : see Rufinus, ap. Rosweyde, p. 354: 'ubi autem ingressi sumus monasterium, *oratione, ut moris est, data* pedes nostros propriis manibus lavat,' sc. Apollonius.

in plaster and raised in low relief. Besides these six crosses, which unquestionably mark places signed with the holy oil at the consecration of the church, there are four other dedication crosses in the choir on the western face of the piers between the haikal and the aisle-chapels. These crosses in the choir are each enclosed in a circular border, no less than 20 in. in diameter: they are of the form called patonce, with the end of every branch cleft into three leaves, or rather a central pointed leaf between two half leaves. Both crosses and borders are filled with arabesques or other graceful tracery: the whole design is in plaster.

Here, as at Anba Bishôi, the haikal-screen consists of a pair of lofty folding-doors, each in two leaves; and here also, instead of opening back and showing the whole interior of the sanctuary, the four leaves have been permanently fixed, and the two inner leaves have been sawn through in such a manner that while the upper part of each remains immoveable, the lower swings open on hinges. The result of course is a fixed opaque iconostasis, with a low doorway in the centre, agreeing with the fashion which seems to have arisen in the eighth or ninth century. The carvings upon this screen stand out in very bold relief, and, though purely conventional, are singularly beautiful.

As usual, all three chapels are rectangular; but the haikal contains a niche so large as almost to be worthy the name of an apse. The floor of the niche is, however, raised so far above the floor of the haikal as to remove all doubt of the architect's intention. In the north-west corner of this sanctuary one may notice, embedded in the wall, a

piscina of earthenware; the monks told me that
the priest washes his hands here before the mass,
but after the mass at the altar.   The three altars
are undivided except by screens—a very unusual
arrangement in the desert churches; but each
is overshadowed by a lofty dome.

On the whole one may call the church rather
basilican than Byzantine, rather Coptic than basilican.   The nave is divided from the aisles at present by massive piers; but these in some cases
obviously, and conjecturally in all cases, enclose
marble columns of fine proportions.   In one or
two places capitals are dimly visible; and a very
splendid early Corinthian capital projects clearly
from the wall in one corner westward of the south
aisle.

Among the fittings of the church one may notice
that the basin for the Maundy feet-washing occupies its customary place in the nave floor; there are
two bronze coronæ hanging before the haikal, with
the usual ostrich-eggs; and in the haikal a larger
corona, 5 ft. high, built in three diminishing tiers.
But not a fragment now remains of the magnificent
Arab lamps of enamelled glass, several of which
Curzon saw in the church at the time of his visit;[1]
nor does one single specimen survive in any of the
churches of the desert.

Attached to the church of Al 'Adra are two
satellite churches or chapels, dedicated to Mâri
Girgis and Al Amîr Tadrus respectively.   The
former of these lies to the westward of Al 'Adra,
and is entered by a door opening out of the north

---

[1] Monasteries of the Levant, pp. 95–6.

aisle. Though now used only as a granary, it has
still a small haikal : the body of the chapel is nearly
square, and is covered with a dome. Curiously
enough the *western* wall contains three decided
niches, arched recesses which cannot have been designed for aumbries, but would seem to indicate
the possibility of there having been a western altar ;
of this, however, there are no other traces whatever
remaining, and the niches may have been meant
merely for lamps. The haikal is very small, only
about 8 ft. square, and nearly the whole area is
taken up by the altar, about which there is just
room to move. Over the altar is built a low dome
with graceful ornamentation ; the eastern niche bears
signs of an ancient mural painting ; the north and
the south wall each have a shallow flat recess, with
arched heading. But the most noticeable thing of all
about this chapel of Mâri Girgis is that the altar-
top projects beyond the sides about 3 in., with the
under edge bevelling inwards. This method of construction, so common as to be almost universal in
the early altars of our western churches, is so rare
in the churches of Egypt that I know of no other
example.

Al Amîr Tadrus very much resembles Mâri Girgis
in size and structure, but contains nothing of interest ;
it opens out of the middle of the north aisle, which
it adjoins. We may pass on to the refectory, which
lies south-west of Al 'Adra, and which is worth a
visit merely for the rude antiquity of its furniture.
The room is a long, dark, vaulted chamber, lighted
only by two unglazed holes in the roof ; the walls
are, or once were, adorned with a profusion of simple
and clumsy frescoes ; the table is formed by a solid

bench of stone running down the middle of the room, with lower stone benches ranged along either side : and near the entrance there stands a curious ancient book-rest of stone in the shape of a thick-limbed letter Y, with short branches, and a large cross sculptured on the stem.   I cannot think that this refectory is later than the fifth or sixth century.

One more chapel remains, that of the Archangel Michael, which is in the ḳaṣr or tower : a small plain uninteresting building.   Here, however, lies a pile of loose leaves of MS., which cover nearly half the floor of the chapel to a depth of about 2 ft. : and here I thought at last was a real chance of undiscovered treasure. So I spent some hours in digging among the pile, in choking and blinding dust ; armful after armful was taken up, searched, sifted, and rejected.   Here and there a tiny fragment of early Syriac, Coptic, or even Greek on vellum ; half a leaf of a Coptic and Ethiopic lexicon ; several shreds of Coptic and Arabic lexicons ; countless pages of mediæval Coptic or Copto-Arabic liturgies : this was the only result of the most diligent search, and the quest ended in final disappointment.   The monks were very good-natured, allowing me to take away my little pieces of worthless paper as memorials of my visit, but declining with courteous firmness to give or sell the whole collection of rubbish ; for they required the leaves, they told me, to bind their new books, and all the paper in Cairo would not answer their purpose so well.

We had much talk with the kindly old abbot, who was in special distress because the lay council at Cairo were threatening to sequester the revenues of the monastery, and administer the estates as a sort

of ecclesiastical commission. The abbot had a great
idea of our influence with the English and Egyptian
governments, and surrounded his appeal to us for
counsel with some state and solemnity; but our
answer conveyed cold comfort. The poor old man
was wearing a leathern girdle on our behalf, a more
serious matter than it sounds; for it meant that
he was doubling all his offices, or, in other words,
making six hundred daily prostrations instead of
three hundred, and praying fourteen times a day
instead of seven. He was, however, greatly pleased
to find that one of my clerical companions was also
wearing a leathern girdle; and we spared him the
shock of discovering that it was only a revolver-belt.
Generally the monastery appeared more clean and
cared for than the others. Huntington found here
twenty-five monks two centuries ago, and the number is about the same to-day. One among them is
remarkable for being able to read Hebrew and
Syriac; for generally they have neither art nor
knowledge, beyond reading and writing Arabic and
sometimes Coptic. Certainly a great change for
the better has come over Al Baramûs, since Sonnini's visit one hundred years ago, if indeed one
can accept his obviously prejudiced story[1]. He

---

[1] Voyage dans la Haute et Basse Egypte. Paris, 1798; vol. ii.
pp. 179–207. Sonnini's account of his farewell to the monks of
Al Baramûs is so amusing, and the work so little known in England, that I may be pardoned for transcribing a few pages :—

'L'un des Bédouins avoit tué sur les bords d'un des lacs de
Natron un phénicoptère, qu'il me présenta. Quoique ce fut un
assez mauvais gibier, il devenoit un mets délicat pour gens qui
vivoient depuis plusieurs jours d'une rude abstinence. Mes com-
pagnons s'empressèrent de le faire rôtir : mais au moment où nous
nous disposions à en faire un excellent repas, les moines se jetèrent

tells, for instance, that the reliquary is full of donkey and camel bones, gathered at random in the desert; that the chalice and paten used at celebration are of ordinary table glass; that the services are exceedingly disorderly; and that the

---

dessus avec une voracité comparable à celle de chackals, animaux carnassiers et immondes, déchirant lâchement une proie facile et dégoûtante qu'ils n'ont pas eu le courage de ravir, et dans un clin d'œil notre oiseau disparut sous les ongles et les dents de ces chackals enfroqués.

'En nous disposant de quitter d'aussi vilains hôtes, je me proposois de leur faire quelque cadeau, pour le séjour désagréable que nous avions fait parmi eux. Je reconnus bientôt que j'avois affaire à des hommes plus dangereux que les Bédouins, francs et généreux dans leur amitié et qui conservent dans l'exercice même de leurs brigandages une sorte de loyauté. Le Supérieur me dit qu'il convenoit que je donnasse d'abord pour le monastère, ensuite pour l'embellissement de l'église, puis pour les pauvres, et enfin pour lui-même. J'écoutois patiemment cette longue énumeration de besoins, et curieux à savoir jusqu'à quel point on en éleveroit la valeur, je demandai quelle seroit la somme suffisante pour y subvenir. Après quelques instants de supputation, le moine me répondit que le couvent ayant besoin d'être blanchi en entier, il pensoit que cinq à six cent sequins rempliroient tous ces objets. Bagatelle, sans doute, pour une pension de cinq jours au pain de lentilles et aux lentilles à l'eau. Je fis à mon tour ma proposition. Ma bourse sortoit des mains des Arabes, qui me l'avoient presque toute épuisée ; il m'en restoit six sequins, que j'offris au Supérieur. Nous étions un peu loin de compte : aussi le moine entra dans une fureur difficile à peindre ; il se répandit en invectives, et jura les saints de son église que je ne tarderois pas à repentir de ce qu'il appeloit mon ingratitude. Le misérable osa invoquer la justice du ciel sur laquelle il fondoit des espérances sacriléges, et qui, disoit-il, ne manqueroit pas de lui amener bientôt des Arabes auxquels il indiqueroit ma route, et qu'il chargeroit de sa vengeance. A ce trait mon sang-froid m'abandonna et j'allois assommer le coquin sur la place, si les Bédouins qui étoient venus me chercher ne l'avoient enlevé et soustrait à mes coups.

'Je sortis enfin d'un séjour infernal et j'étois prêt à monter sur

monks are unspeakably churlish, dirty, ignorant, and vicious. This highly flavoured description doubtless owes much of its acidity to the fact that Sonnini was robbed by the Beduins and narrowly escaped murder, and that he quarrelled with the monks. Altogether his journey seems to have been extremely unpleasant, and his misfortunes soured his remembrance. He got as far as Dair-as-Sûriâni, which he says was better built, 'et les religieux m'ont paru moins sales et moins stupidement féroces' (!), and thence made his way back from the desert,

---

l'âne qui m'étoit destiné quand le vieux moine me fit prier de lui donner les six sequins que je lui avois offerts. Le scheick Arabe s'étoit chargé de la commission, et à sa considération .je les remis. Nous vîmes alors le scélérat faire, pour notre heureux voyage, une prière au ciel, dont quelques minutes avant il invoquoit contre nous toute la vengeance.

'Cet homme n'existe plus probablement: il étoit déjà vieux et décharné, et sa vilaine figure s'accordoit parfaitement avec la laideur de son âme: son nom étoit *Mikaël*. Mais . . . il est très important de faire connoitre à nos concitoyens qui sont en Egypte, le caractère de perfidie de ces prétendus religieux, car, à quelques nuances près, ils se ressemblent tous. Quels que soient les dehors qu'ils affectent, l'on peut être certain que leur haine contre les Européens est plus profonde et plus atroce que celle des Mahométans, et que leurs maisons dans le désert seront le point d'appui des excursions des Bédouins, leur magasins d'approvisionnement, et le lieu des délibérations propres à assurer le succès de leurs brigandages.'

Contrast this account with that of Rufinus, whose visit was in the year 372 A. D. After telling how the monks ran out to meet him with bread and water, escorted him in procession with chaunting to the church and washed his feet, he remarks: 'nusquam sic vidimus florere charitatem, nusquam sic vidimus opus fervere misericordiae et studium hospitalitatis impleri. Scripturarum vero divinarum meditationes et intellectus atque scientiae divinae nusquam tanta vidimus exercitia, ut singulos paene eorum credas oratores in divina esse sapientia.'

angrily disdaining a visit to Abu Makâr. One may question whether the Frenchman's temper was not somewhat overweening; but, however that may be, although the ignorance of the monks is generally deplorable, they are good kind-hearted people, and welcome strangers with the utmost power of their simple hospitality. And so far from being avaricious, they declined the coins we proffered with a quiet but decisive dignity.

Not far from the monastery of Al Baramûs, in a westerly direction, there lies the great valley or channel which the Arabs to this day call ' Al Bahr bilâ Mâ,' or the Waterless River. No doubt it represents an ancient branch of the Nile once flowing westward of the Libyan hills, and reaching the sea near Lake Mareotis; but whether it parted from the main stream near Dongola, according to the tradition current in the Sudân, or from some other point further north, has not been decided. A few years ago, when the western branch of the Nile burst its banks near Bani Salâmah, the stream, instead of passing down along the Delta, rushed through a gap in the range of hills, and forced its way along the Waterless River; and this fact proves that even so far north there is still a considerable difference of level between the present river and the ancient channel. In prehistoric times, ere the Nile left its old bed, the whole intervening desert was doubtless rich cultivated land; and traces of its richness may still be found in the gigantic trunks which lie scattered about the sands at the 'petrified forest' beyond Al Baramûs. The monks have a characteristic legend for the scene; for they relate that the Waterless River was dried up at the prayers

of St. Macarius, in order to punish the pirates, whose
depredations vexed the early Christian anchorites;
and they point to the logs cumbering the ground
as the wrecks of the pirate fleet, which was turned
to stone[1].

From Al Baramûs we made our way back to our
camp at Anba Bishôi, whence we were to start directly on our homeward route across the desert.
Early on the morning of our departure the monks
requested us to attend a service in the church. They
met us in the porch, their procession headed by a
large cross, which was wreathed in branches of olive
and palm and decked with burning tapers: and they
went before us singing and beating their cymbals,
while the convent bell pealed, until we passed through
the large church, and came to the chapel of Al 'Adra.
We found the dim building illumined with scores of
tapers, which were planted on the lattice screen of
the choir and above the haikal door, and scattered
all over the reliquary containing the bones of Anba
Bishôi, or rather his body, which is said to rest within
it incorruptible. The cross was set upright in the
doorway of the haikal, and censers full of burning
incense were swung till the air became heavy with
the fumes, while the monks united in chaunts and
prayers and earnest intercessions for our safety.

This little service was the last scene in our visit,

---

[1] See Huntington, l.c., who however records little else of interest.
He describes Anba Bishôi as 'non adeo rimis fatíscens ut cetera.'
Another traveller of not much later date, Le Sieur Granger, who
visited Egypt in 1730, is equally disappointing: giving little more
information than that neither at Abu Makâr nor As-Sûriâni would
the monks allow him to enter the library. See Relation du Voyage
fait en Égypte, p. 179.

but not the least impressive. Among those who came to bid us farewell were some brethren from Dair-as-Sûriâni, and one poor monk from Al Bara-mûs, whose presence was somewhat pathetic. He was the proud possessor of one of three venerable watches owned by the monastery, but silent from time immemorial : and, unknown to the abbot, he had entrusted his treasure to me, begging me to take it to the patriarch, and pray his holiness to have it mended. When the abbot discovered what had happened, he was very angry, and made the poor Lôga start on foot across the desert at three o'clock in the morning to catch us before we left Anba Bishôi. There was no help for it : so I unpacked the watch and gave it back to the monk, who received it with touching sorrow, and who doubtless often mourns in secret over his disappointment and his broken toy.

When our camels were all loaded and our beasts got out of the low postern of the dair, we exchanged our last farewells and compliments without the walls, where the abbot gave us a parting prayer and blessing. Thence we rode down towards the lakes, distant about an hour's journey, and found their surface covered with hundreds of flamingoes and other waterfowl of brilliant plumage flashing in the sun. As we looked, the flamingoes all rose together in a scarlet cloud, and swept away over the water. We passed among the great reed-beds, where the Beduins cut the reeds which they make into mats ; round the south end of the lakes ; then upwards, ridge over ridge, till at the summit we paused, turned our horses' heads, and looked back over the beautiful desert valley. We were now eastward of Dair Macarius, which did not lie quite on our homeward route, though it was still the nearest in view: and all four monasteries were visible together, Al Baramûs just within the far azure of the horizon. This was the view we had missed on our arrival owing to the nightfall. It is a sight beyond description, but never to be forgotten. As we turned away, and the ridge behind us finally closed the scene, shutting out the vast and shining desolation of the valley of the monks, we felt as if we had been living with fifteen centuries of history cancelled, moving in the ancient monastic world of Egypt, undreaming of things to come: but now the sense of reality rushed back upon us, and we found ourselves alone in the desert.

CHAPTER VIII.

The Churches of Upper Egypt.

The Monasteries of St. Antony and St. Paul in the Eastern Desert. —The Convent of the Pulley.—The White and the Red Monastery. —Church at Armant.—The Churches of Naķâdah.—Church at Antinoë.—Miscellaneous.

P to this point the descriptions of churches and places of interest in Egypt have been drawn entirely from my own observation and experience: but there now comes a large branch of the subject which is still almost absolutely unexplored, and to which I can unhappily contribute nothing, except a collection of scanty notes derived from other travellers. The hurried yet formal progress of the khedive, which I accompanied through Upper Egypt to the First Cataract, did not give me a chance of a single visit to a Coptic church: nor can I well hope ever again to ascend the valley of the Nile. But it will be something to indicate some portion of the work which has yet to be done, especially in these troubled times, when the danger is lest a surge of Muslim fanaticism should sweep away all the still unchronicled remains of Christian antiquity, ere a 'learned rover' can be found to record them.

The number of monks and monasteries in Upper Egypt, from the fourth century onwards, seems to have been prodigious. Rufinus relates that in the region about Arsinoë he found ten thousand monks : at Oxyrynchus the bishop estimated his monks at ten thousand, and his nuns at twenty thousand, while the city itself contained no less than twelve churches. Pagan temples and buildings had been turned to monastic uses : the hermitages outnumbered the dwelling houses[1]: in fact the land 'so swarmed with monks, that their chaunts and hymns by day and by night made the whole country one church of God.' If one can believe these and the like stories, Egypt at this time was one vast convent; and the wonder is that the nation was not extinguished by universal celibacy. But, with all due allowance for oriental weakness in arithmetic, it is certain that every town of importance along the valley of the Nile had its churches and friars, while many parts both of the country and the desert were occupied by vast monastic settlements.

Among the earliest and most interesting of these, though unfortunately also the most inaccessible, must be counted the monasteries of St. Anthony and St. Paul in the eastern desert by the Red Sea. St. Anthony is generally called the first monk, but St. Ammon, or Piammon, as he is often called in Coptic, was contemporary, if not earlier. It is Piammon of whom the legend is told that he saw an angel standing at the altar, and recording the names of such among the monks as received the eucharist worthily,

---

[1] See Rosweyde, pp. 350, 363, especially the passage 'aedes publicae et templa superstitionis antiquae habitationes nunc erant monachorum, et per totam civitatem plura monasteria quam domus videbantur.'

omitting the others : and when he died, St. Anthony is said to have seen his soul ascending to heaven. How soon monasteries, in our sense of the term, were built upon the sites hallowed by St. Anthony's devotions in the desert, cannot be easily determined ; but it may be conjectured that the first foundation was not long after the death of the saint. At present Dair Mâri Antonios is the largest of all the dairs of Egypt: a fact which in itself perhaps militates against its claim to the remotest antiquity.

As the monasteries of the Natrun valley have their little bases of supply in the Delta, so those of the eastern desert depend for provisions on some smaller dairs upon the Nile, one situated near Bani Sulf, and another opposite the village of Maidûm called after St. Anthony[1]. The church of St. Anthony has already been briefly mentioned[2]. I may add, on Mr. Chester's authority, that the domes here and in the adjoining Abu-'s-Sifain are supported by columns ; and that the church contains an ancient chalice, and several porcelain ostrich eggs painted with crosses and figures of the cherubim. These porcelain eggs are now very rare, but one or two with Muslim designs may still be seen in the mosque of Kait Bey, without the walls of Cairo.

Tradition relates that St. Anthony lived here, but the throng of wayfarers for ever passing up and down

---

[1] My information about the eastern desert monasteries is derived from Mr. G. Chester's 'Notes on the Coptic Dayrs' (Arch. Journ. vol. xxix), and from Vansleb's 'Nouvelle Relation d'un Voyage fait en Égypte,' Paris, 1698. To the latter author also I am indebted for much material concerning the other churches mentioned in this chapter.

[2] P. 7.

the Nile drove him to seek the seclusion of the
desert mountains: and Pococke heard from the
monks at the time of his visit that, owing to the special
sanctity of the spot, crocodiles were afraid to pass it,
and hence were never found in Lower Egypt.   The
journey from Bûsh to the Red Sea monasteries
occupies about three days.   According to Vansleb
there are two routes; of which the northern follows
the Nile for some distance, then turns to the right,
and passing a deep well in the natural rock filled with
water, leads in three easy stages to the convents.
The other, by which he himself travelled to avoid
encounters with hostile Beduins, trends south-east for
a day and a half, then due east, and requires four
stages.   The monastery of St. Anthony lies on the
slope of Mount Kolzim, at the foot of a gigantic
precipice, and looks over the gulf of Suez to the
distant mountains of Sinai.   It is oblong in shape,
girt by a lofty wall, and encloses about six acres of
ground.   Unlike the Natrun monasteries, it has no
doorway at all, but man and beast are hoisted up by
pulleys on the wall.   At the time of Vansleb's visit
the place was still in ruins, not having yet recovered
from the period of wreckage and desolation which
followed the murder of the monks, some four hundred years ago, by the Muslim slaves whom they
iniquitously had purchased.   But since that time
there has been a good deal of restoration.   The
gardens are described as being very beautiful;
watered by a mountain stream, which gushes, clear
as crystal, from the rock; and abounding in palms
and olives and the richest vegetation.   Two hundred
years ago the monks had vines, from which they
made a sort of white wine, used at the mass and set

before any guest of distinction. Whether the vine is now cultivated or not, I cannot say.

There are three churches within the monastery, besides the quite new church of Al 'Aḍra. That of Anba Markus is dedicated to a brother of that name, an inmate of the convent in ancient times, who died there in the odour of sanctity, and whose body is preserved in the church. The building is roofed with twelve domes. Similar in structure, but smaller, is the church of the apostles Peter and Paul, which Vansleb erroneously says is remarkable for possessing the only bell in Egypt. Mr. Chester saw there two ancient enamelled glass lamps, but nothing else of interest is mentioned. Neither of these churches is anterior to the period of abandonment: but the third and most important, dedicated to St. Anthony, is extremely ancient; indeed the monks aver that St. Anthony was its builder. Even Vansleb is convinced of its great antiquity, and remarks that it is the only thing which escaped the violence of the Arabs. Apparently[1] it consists of narthex, nave, choir, and haikal; the nave is divided from narthex and choir by two stone screens: and the whole church is covered by domes, except the choir, which is vaulted. The altar stands at a considerable elevation above the floor of the nave. All over the walls of the church are remains of very rude and early frescoes, which even in Vansleb's time were blackened with smoke; which arose, not, as he thinks, from ages of incense, but from the camp fires of the Beduin. Yet a figure of Christ in glory encompassed

---

[1] Mr. Chester's account is not as clear as could be wished.

by angels, and other figures in the eastern niche, are still discernible: and it is probable that with careful cleaning nearly the whole might be recovered.

The square tower, resembling those in the western desert, contains a chapel dedicated to St. Michael, a library of books which deserve examination, a fine processional cross of silver, a silver-mounted shade held over the silver gospel on the occasion of the annual procession to the cave of St. Anthony, and 'a fine bronze lamp of at least as great antiquity as the foundation of the convent itself.'

St. Anthony's cave lies outside the monastery, higher up the mountain: it is a natural cavern in the sheer face of the cliff with a ledge in front, and seems one of a number of caves inhabited by the early anchorites.

Two days' journey south of this monastery there lies another, dedicated to Mâri Bolos or St. Paul—not the apostle, but the friend of St. Anthony and fellow-anchorite. Here too the story runs that slaves were purchased, and joined in the conspiracy which annihilated the monks of the eastern desert. But this far convent has scarcely ever been visited by a European traveller: and its beauties and its treasures must be left to their ancient silence.

Before however quitting this part of the subject, it will not be out of place here to give some particulars of the rule of life observed at Mâri Antonios, at the time of Vansleb's visit, and doubtless unchanged at the present day. The monks renounce marriage, kindred, and possessions: they vow to live in the desert, to dress in woollen habits with a leathern girdle, to eat no meat and drink no wine, to use abstinence and fasting, to pray and to work. All but the abbot and the sick must sleep on a mat on the ground, never removing their dress or their girdle. They must say the canonical hours, and every evening must make one hundred and fifty prostrations, falling flat on the earth with outspread arms, and making the sign of the cross each time as they arise. These prostrations are called metanoë or penance. Seven additional prostrations are required at church, one before each of the hours.

The monastic dress consists of seven vestments: (1) a shirt of white wool next the skin : (2) a tunic of coarse brown wool, which does not open in front : (3) a black serge overall with wide sleeves: (4) a small close-fitting hood of black serge: (5) a girdle of leather: (6) a large mantle of black stuff with white lining, seldom used except on journeys : and lastly (7) the 'asklm[1],' or 'angelic habit.' Those who wear the angelic habit are as few and far between as the very angels ; for the wearer is bound to make three hundred daily prostrations, and to undergo a special system of almost impossible fasting and mortification. All carry a staff in the shape of a tau-cross, on which they lean while walking or praying ; and their head-dress consists of a ṭarbûsh wound round with a white and blue turban.

On fast days they eat but once a day, at three o'clock in the afternoon ; they have two meals on Saturday and on Sunday. Fish is not forbidden, but very rarely seen among them, although the Red Sea is within an easy distance. At Eastertide they are

---

[1] The word seems derived from the Greek σχῆμα; but the Arabic is الاسكيم and the Coptic ⲡⲓⲙⲙⲟⲣⲥ̄ⲛⲁϩ : ⲙⲁⲣⲥ̄ⲛⲁⲣ is said by Peyron to mean a 'monastic girdle.'

allowed eggs and milk, which are sent from the Nile convents. Of the twenty inmates at the time of Vansleb's visit only two were priests, the rest lay brethren; and all were blind or deaf or lame, or broken by age and by the terrible rigour of their monastic rule [1].

Dair al Bakarah, or the Convent of the Pulley.

We must now return to the valley of the Nile, where the churches are legion, but for the most part quite unknown. Some few, however, have been visited from time to time by travellers, from whose writings information may be gleaned enough to tantalize. Among the convents which have attracted most attention is Dair al Bakarah [2], or the Convent of the Pulley, which crowns the summit of a lofty mountain rising sheer from the river. Gabal-aṭ-Ṭair, as the mountain is called, lies on the right bank of the stream, about halfway between Girgah and Miniah. The entrance to the convent is by a deep natural shaft, cleft through the solid rock from the summit to the base, where a cave opens on to the river [3]: and the ascent is generally made by a pulley, whence the name of the monastery. The dair is a

---

[1] Vansleb had the same unpleasantness with the monks at his departure that Sonnini had when leaving Al Baramûs; and, like Sonnini, he encountered serious perils. See pp. 313-331.

[2] البكري.

[3] See Curzon's Monasteries, p. 111 seq.

square enclosure, about 200 ft. each way, built originally of hewn stone of Roman workmanship, but
showing considerable traces of Arab repairs.

The church is partly cut out of the solid rock, and
may be called subterranean. Curzon gives a plan of
it—unfortunately without scale—which I have borrowed with a slight alteration, showing the southern
recess under the staircase. The body of the church
seems to lie in the open, only the choir and haikal

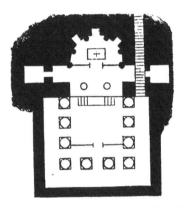

Fig. 25.—Rock-cut Church at the Convent of the Pulley.

being actually hewn in the rock. Upon the columns
dividing nave from aisles and returned aisle there
rests a heavy wooden architrave. The choir is raised
about three feet above the nave, and is approached
by a double flight of steps—a most unusual arrangement. Obviously the wooden screens of the choir and
of the haikal are mediæval or modern; doubtless the
original haikal-screen consisted of folding-doors like
those still in use at Dair-as-Sûriâni. Deeply recessed
niches, showing as such on plan, are characteristic of
fourth century churches in Upper Egypt. The
chambers opening out of the choir north and south,

though not described as containing altars now, were no doubt originally chapels; so that the church possessed the normal number of altars. The dedication of the church, and indeed of the whole monastery, is to Al 'Aḍra or the Virgin, and the monastic legend ascribes its foundation to the Empress Helena.

There is no reason to doubt the truth of the tradition: and there is a curious point about the church hitherto unnoticed. I mean its resemblance to the rock-cut temple of ancient Egyptian work at the not far distant town of Girgah. There is the same descent by a flight of steps in each case[1] : the vestibule of the temple is marked off from the aisles and returned aisle in precisely the same manner, and by the same number of columns, as in the church : there is an ascent of steps corresponding to those before the choir : and, omitting merely the central hall of the temple, one finds a space like the choir at Al 'Aḍra with rock-hewn chambers opening north and south, and three recesses eastward, which do not greatly differ from the Coptic haikal with its three niches. The comparison is further borne out in a remarkable manner by the fact that only part of the temple is subterranean, and the part which stands in the open is the pillared vestibule, answering to the pillared nave of the Christian edifice.

It is of course not surprising that Coptic architects should have been influenced by the magnificent buildings of the ancient Egyptians : the wonder is rather that this influence should not have been more decided. For while it is easy to understand a studied avoidance of pagan models, one would still expect to

---

[1] See plan in Baedeker's Lower Egypt, p. 168.

find more generally some sort of likeness, some details at least reproduced by unconscious imitation.

***

The White Monastery.

Quite the most remarkable instance of resemblance between Coptic and ancient Egyptian architecture is found in Dair al Abiaḍ, or the White Monastery, so called from the white ashlar of which it is built. It lies at the foot of the Libyan hills as far south as Sûhâg, with some miles of desert intervening between it and the present bed of the Nile. It is a large, quadrangular fortress-like building, having its outer walls finished off upwards with a fine cornice, after the manner of the old Egyptian temples. This cornice is of white marble. The walls are relieved by two rows of small windows like loop-holes, one half way up, the other near the top: there are twenty-seven[1] windows in each row on the north and south side, and nine in each row on the east. At present, however, all the windows are blocked up. Each stone of the ashlar is 3 ft. to 4 ft. long and 1 ft. broad. There were six gates, not of white limestone but of red granite; now, however, only a single entrance on the south has been left open, called the mule gate, from a legend which tells of a pagan princess who came riding on a mule to desecrate the church, when the earth opened and swallowed her up. According to an authentic tradition, the White Monastery was founded by the Empress Helena. The external dimensions of the dair are variously given, but seem

---

[1] Curzon gives the number as twenty.

to be about 240 ft. by 133[1]. Its dedication is to
Anba Shanûdah[2]. A splendid basilican church once
occupied the whole interior, with the exception of a
corridor along the southern side, in which were
crowded together the cells and other domestic buildings of the monks in two stories. The church had

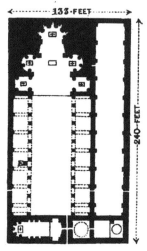

Fig. 26.—Plan of the White Monastery.

a true narthex with central western entrance : a central passage divided the narthex into two portions
north and south, both of which were entirely walled

---

[1] Vansleb makes the measurement 280 ft. by 111 ; but this is
merely a rough calculation. Curzon gives 200 ft. by 90 ; but
Denon and Sir G. Wilkinson both give 250 ft. by 125.

[2] Pococke writes it 'Embeshnuda'; Sir G. Wilkinson, 'Anba
Shnoodeh or St. Sennode' (!), deriving the latter name apparently
from Vansleb. Even Curzon is at fault about the name, calling
Sanutius a Muslim saint ! Doubtless this mistake arises from the
fact that the Copts, with prudent ingenuity, did manufacture a
Shaikh Abu Shanûd for the benefit of their superstitious oppressors,
and so secured protection and reverence for the Christian shrine.
Shanûdah, or ϣⲉⲛⲟⲩϯ, as he was called in Coptic, lived in the
time of St. Cyril, and was famed for his theological writings.

off the church.　In the northern half of the narthex are traces of the most magnificent decoration, which roused the enthusiasm of Curzon, whose
description is quite worth quoting.　It runs as
follows :—

　' The principal entrance was formerly at the west
end, where there is a small vestibule, immediately
within the door of which, on the left hand, is a small
chapel, perhaps the baptistery, about 25 ft. long, and
still in tolerable preservation.　It is a splendid
specimen of the richest Roman architecture of the
later empire, and is truly an imperial little room.
The arched ceiling is of stone ; and there are three
beautifully ornamented niches on each side.　The
upper end is semicircular, and has been entirely
covered with a profusion of sculpture in panels, cor-
nices, and every kind of architectural enrichment.
When it was entire, and covered with gilding, painting, or mosaic, it must have been most gorgeous.
The altar in such a chapel as this was probably
of gold, set full of gems ; or if it was the baptistery,
as I suppose, it most likely contained a bath of the
most precious jasper, or of some of the more rare
kinds of marble[1].'

From the arrangement of the chamber with its
apse and circlet of columns, one would rather imagine
that it served as a chapel than as a baptistery ; and
this conjecture is made certain by the evidence of
Denon, who, in his adventurous travels during the
campaign of Bonaparte in Egypt, paid a visit to the
Red and White Monasteries, upon the day following

---

[1] Monasteries of the Levant, p. 131.

that on which they had been fired by the Mamelukes.
It is from Denon[1] that I have borrowed the plan in
the text, making such modifications or additions as
are warranted by his own or by independent information: and it must be remembered that his description is thirty-nine years anterior to that of
Curzon. Denon very distinctly speaks of an altar
as standing within the apse of the narthex—though
it was adorned with neither gold nor gems in his
day: and not only does he place the baptistery in
the southernmost division of the narthex in the plan,
but in the text he expressly describes it as containing
a 'superbe citerne,' a magnificent font or basin for
total immersion. This basin seems to have been
sunk in a platform of masonry, which was ascended
by a short flight of stairs. Here then it was that in
the days of the foundation of the church neophytes
and proselytes were baptized, and immediately afterwards received their first communion in the opposite
chapel: but it will be noticed that the baptistery has
its outer vestibule.

Regarding the adornment of the chapel, Denon
does not contribute much to our knowledge: but he
mentions that the columns round the wall were
joined by a circular architrave, with frieze and cornice above, and that the whole entablature was
surmounted by a conch. Precisely the same architectural features are found in each of the three
eastern apses, which vary curiously from the usual

---

[1] See Voyages dans la Basse et la Haute Égypte en 1798–9, par
V. Denon. London, 1807. The narrative is in vol. i. p. 157 seq.;
the elevation and plan are given in the volume of plates, pl. x; the
description of the plate is in vol. ii.

disposition of the three eastern chapels in having a sort of trefoil arrangement. The conch of the haikal, as well as the conches of the other two apses, still showed their original frescoes as late as half a century ago : in the central conch was a large figure of the Redeemer, while the paintings in the side-chapels represented various saints. All three apses had the curve broken by numerous recesses or niches, which were very richly ornamented ; and if the plaster which now covers them were removed, probably more frescoes or other ancient decoration of great interest would be discovered underneath.

The body of the church consists of nave and two aisles, each aisle being divided from the nave by a row of fourteen columns, carrying a classical architrave. Most of the capitals are of late Corinthian order, and Pococke remarks that many of them have crosses carved among the foliage : but neither the capitals nor the shafts seem to be uniform, as they were taken from pagan buildings, and not designed for the structure in which they are placed, as was the case in the adjoining Red Monastery. Vansleb expresses great admiration for the capitals of the two granite columns beside the door of the haikal. He adds that on one of the shafts was a Greek inscription, recording the name of Heliodorus : while all over the walls and the floor of the building, as well as on the great staircase leading to the dormitories, one might notice stones covered with hieroglyphics, which were generally set topsy-turvy. At the time of his visit all the columns were standing, although the nave was already roofless.

If one may believe that the plan represents the

original arrangement of the church, it contains another feature no less exceptional than the trefoil arrangement of the apses, namely the position of the aisle-chapels. These seem in the present instance to be an addition to the regular complement of three chapels, so that the church contains a total of five eastern chapels: and if the two apsidal chapels at the side are remarkable in not standing more nearly abreast of the haikal, these two rectangular aisle-chapels are still more eccentric In the very same particular, standing as they do in the body of the nave. They have too this further irregularity, that neither chapel has any western doorway, but one opens southward, the other northward. From the general structure of the basilica, it certainly looks as if these aisle-chapels were not originally walled off from the aisles, and in fact did not exist: or if they existed originally, it was as part of the choir, and not as separate chapels. Yet, in face of Denon's explicit testimony, one cannot press a mere conjecture.

The ambon for the epistle, which stood in the middle of the north aisle, rested on four heavy columns, and was ascended by a short stone staircase. It is described as consisting of two enormous blocks of granite, but further details of its construction are unfortunately wanting. The spot marked in the centre of the choir seems to denote the ambon for the gospel: it is lettered in Denon's plan, but the explanation has been altogether omitted. It is however decidedly not an altar: and the ambon in the north aisle is specially described as being 'for the epistle.' Only the choir and the haikal now remain intact, and are still used for services. All

that could perish by fire perished in the flames which
Denon saw smouldering.

About two miles from Dair al Abiad lies another
monastery, almost exactly similar in plan, and called
Dair al Aḥmar, or the Red Monastery, from the red
brick of which the outer walls are built.   It lies in a
small village sheltered by palms, instead of standing
isolated in the open desert : it is rather smaller than
the White Monastery, but has an additional building
covering the well, which seems to have lain outside
the original enclosure.   Its patron .saint is Anba
Bishôi[1].   From the plan given by Pococke[2] the
church seems to contain an Epiphany tank in the
centre of the narthex, and a basin for the Mandatum
near the western entrance of the nave.   The northern
half of the narthex is apsidal, the apse of course
being internal, and columns are set against the apse
wall.   Apparently Dair al Aḥmar is in better preservation than its neighbour : for Pococke gives a
section of the nave which shows a continuous wooden
architrave resting on the columns, with rather highly
stilted relieving arches above, one between every
pair of pillars.   The columns used for both these
Christian churches were probably taken from the
ancient Egyptian towns of Aphroditopolis or Athribis
in the vicinity : but Vansleb remarks, that, while
those at the White Monastery are of different shapes
and sizes, here at the Red Monastery all the columns
are of uniform design and of one thickness : here too
the details of the enrichment are finer, and the

---

[1] Pococke calls it ' Der Embabishai,' vol. i. p. 79.

[2] Vol. i. pl. lxxi. p. 246 : but I am afraid Pococke's plans are
not very trustworthy.

capitals of the two pillars by the haikal-door Vansleb declares to be the most beautiful he has ever seen.

The orientation of these churches is not exact, but the axis points between N.E. and N.E. by E. in both cases.

The buildings themselves are doubtless of the fourth century, and must be ranked among the most splendid remains of that epoch. It is curious that Pococke, in mentioning them, should not class with them the church at Armant, the ancient Hermonthis, near Thebes, which is built on almost precisely the same model, and which Pococke insists upon regarding as a pagan temple converted to Christian uses[1]. This church is of rectangular form, about 150 ft. by 100: it consists of narthex, nave, aisles, haikal, and eastern chapels. The narthex and nave have both a central western entrance: the narthex is divided off eastward by a solid wall from the aisles: but in the centre opposite the haikal the wall curves out and forms a large apse projecting westward into the narthex. It is therefore the external western wall of the church, and the curve of this interior apse which are divided by central doorways; but it is quite obvious that this western apse was designed merely for symmetry, and can never have contained an altar. The narthex itself shows a curious arrangement, consisting of five chambers: of these, two on the north and two on the south side are rectangular, and were used probably for baptistery, places of penance, or sacristies, while the central chamber is of course irregular in shape, and served merely for a passage. Although now in ruins this church must

---

[1] Pococke gives a plan, vol. i. pl. xliv. p. 110.

have been extremely fine : for it has the advantage over the Red and White Monasteries in being a double-aisled basilica, i. e. in having two parallel aisles both north and south of the nave, and four parallel rows of columns with eleven in each row. Although the haikal wall is apsidal, the curve is broken by five deep irregular recesses, and the apse is wholly internal. The side-chapels are rectangular.

The Churches of Naḳâdah.

About twelve miles north of Thebes, on the left bank of the Nile, stands a very interesting group of monasteries, just mentioned by name in Vansleb [1] and Murray, but otherwise unknown in literature. The first of these, which stands detached, is evidently a Byzantine building, but differs in several particulars

---

[1] Vansleb mentions (1) 'Deir il Salib,' or the Convent of the Cross, (2) 'Deir il Megma,' (3) 'Deir Mari Poctor,' and adds that the two latter are uninhabited. Murray names four : (1) 'Dayr es-Seleeb,' (2) 'el Melâk,' (3) 'Mari Boktee,' (4) 'Mar Girgis.' If Murray is right as against Vansleb in (2), the names should be as follows : (1) Dair-as-Sullîb, (2) Dair al Malâk Mikhaîl, (3) Dair Mâri Buḳtor, (4) Dair Mâri Girgis ; i. e. the monastery of the Cross, the Archangel Michael, St. Victor, and St. George. For the plans in the text I am indebted to Sir Arthur Gordon, who however has been prevented by his absence in Ceylon from communicating in time for this work the information needful to explain them. I have not even been able to ascertain the dedication of the churches : but the plans are so good and so interesting that I do not hesitate to publish them : and from what Murray says one cannot be wrong in identifying the second plan as that of Dair al Malâk Mikhaîl.

from those hitherto noticed. For there seems to be
a narrow atrium at the western end, with a single
entrance into the church : the narthex and the nave
are of equal length, and each is covered with a single
large dome, but at the angles of the nave dome are
placed four semidomes. Moreover, although the
aisles, which once extended from the choir to the
western wall, are now walled off at the narthex, and
are merely coextensive with the nave, still each of
the remaining aisles north and south retains the

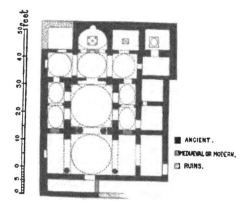

CHURCH AT NAKÂDAH.

Fig. 27.--(Communicated by Sir Arthur Gordon.)

original arrangement by which it was divided into
two portions, with an archway between, each portion
crowned with an elliptical dome. The choir also is
subdivided into three parts, each with a dome of its
own. Eastwards the church has a plain apsidal
haikal with two square side-chapels, and an arch of
triumph : but it is worth notice that the front of the
haikal seems to have been open originally, or closed

only with a folding screen, precisely in the same manner as the haikals of the churches in the western desert. At present the centre of the haikal archway is blocked by a short wall of modern masonry, which leaves two side-doors, one against each pier—an arrangement perhaps copied from one of the churches at Dair al Malâk : but each of the other chapels was built with a single central entrance. The baptistery lies at the south-east corner of the sacred building, through which alone it is accessible.

Dair al Malâk, as will be obvious from the plan, contains in itself a group of contiguous churches, of which the most important in the centre is dedicated to St. Michael. This church is one of the most remarkable Christian structures in Egypt, possessing as it does some unique peculiarities. There are four churches, of which three stand side by side in such a manner that they have a single continuous western wall. Two of the four have an apsidal haikal with rectangular side-chapels, while the other two are entirely rectangular : but the two apses differ from all other apses in Egyptian churches by projecting on plan beyond the eastern wall, and by showing an outward curvature. They form a solitary exception to the rule that the Coptic apse is merely internal, and so far belong rather to Syrian architecture than to Coptic. The principal church shows two other features which do not occur elsewhere in the Christian buildings of Egypt, namely an external atrium surrounded with a cloister, and a central tower with a clerestory. Here again we may, I think, trace the work of an architect more familiar with Syrian than with Coptic models. Possibly the same remark may apply to the structure of the

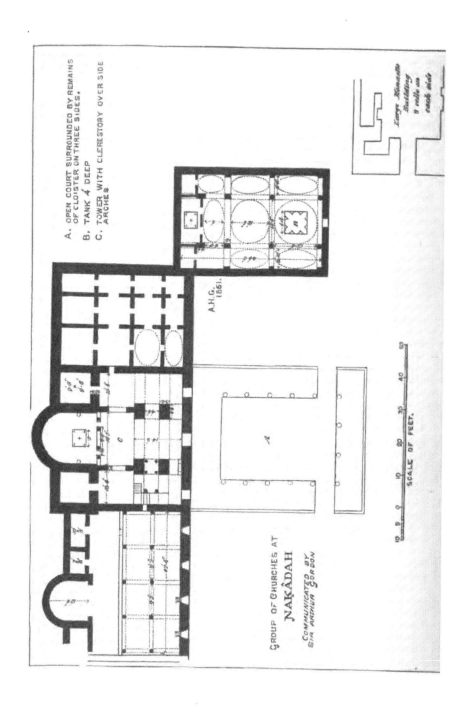

A. OPEN COURT SURROUNDED BY REMAINS
   OF CLOISTER ON THREE SIDES.

B. TANK 4 DEEP.

C. TOWER WITH CLERESTORY OVER SIDE
   ARCHES.

A.H.G.
1861.

GROUP OF CHURCHES AT

NAKÂDAH

COMMUNICATED BY
SIR ARTHUR GORDON

SCALE OF FEET.

Large Monastic
Building
3 miles on
each side

iconostasis, which has two side-doors and no central entrance, though this arrangement is not quite un-paralleled in the churches of Upper Egypt, and may be a later alteration.   It will be noticed that the church has a triple western entrance from the cloisters [1].

The northernmost of the group of churches has also some points which deserve remarking ; for it seems to have contained four or more altars instead of three, unless indeed one of the rectangular spaces was rather a baptistery—an unlikely supposition. Again, the structure of the body of the church is most peculiar, there being no sort of division into nave and aisles, but merely a series of columns set in quadrilaterals, and joined either by beams or arches.   Lastly, the church seems to have had no western doorway, but several western windows, with a considerable splay inwards.

Of the remaining two churches, one seems re-markable for the subdivision of both nave and aisles by walls or stone screens, each into three compart-ments : it is curious too that the north aisle is con-siderably wider than the nave, and the nave than the south aisle.   But the whole building, apparently, is in a ruinous condition, the altars having been demolished, and all the domes but two having fallen.   In contrast to this irregular structure the last of the four churches is beautifully symmetrical, but entirely different from any of the three former.

---

[1] The steps in the north aisle seem to indicate the ambon, but I have not been able to refer to Sir A. Gordon for information. The arrangement of the doorway by the steps appears in any case awkward.

The nave is of unusual width in proportion to the aisles, but the whole design is extremely graceful and quite Coptic in character; except that here also, as in the main church of St. Michael, the haikal-screen is formed by a solid wall of masonry pierced by a doorway at each side, but having none in the centre. Towards the western end of the nave a very fine Epiphany tank is sunk in the floor. Two columns and a pier divide the nave from each aisle, one pair of columns standing against the western wall, the other pair being detached. From the latter, and from the isolated piers, arches spring in all four directions, and carry domes above, which must be as light and elegant in structure as they are beautiful in design and arrangement. For of the nine, or perhaps twelve, original domes eight are now remaining : of these only two are circular on plan, the remaining six being elliptical. The elongation of these ellipses is very bold and striking : indeed the whole roofing of this church, as indicated in the plan, is an architectural triumph.

The Convent of St. John, near Antinoë.

Two degrees further north than Naḳâdah, on the right bank of the Nile, lie the ruins of the ancient Antinoë, and near them the town of Madînah, where, in an ancient quarry, may be found the subterranean church of St. John, which is said to have been built by the Empress Helena, the mother of Constantine.

Were there no mote of evidence besides to determine the truth of this tradition, the plan of the haikal
would decide it beyond question.   The persistence
with which certain churches are ascribed to Helena,
by a people utterly ignorant of history or architecture,

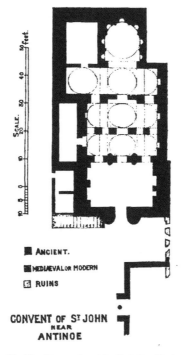

ANCIENT.

MEDIÆVAL or MODERN

RUINS

CONVENT OF SᵗJOHN
NEAR
ANTINOE

Fig. 29.—(Communicated by Sir Arthur Gordon.)

is in itself remarkable : and it is still more remarkable
to find that these churches are always marked by a
particular form of haikal.   Witness the Red and
White Monasteries, the church at Armant, and many
others.   Indeed so regular is the coincidence, that a
deep apsidal haikal with recesses all round it, and

columns close against the wall, may be almost infallibly dated from the age of Helena. In these churches there is no communication between the haikal and aisle-chapels, the front of the haikal is open, and the apse is of course internal.

But the church of St. John differs from those at the Red and White Monasteries, in being of the Byzantine rather than the basilican order, or in containing that admixture of the two orders, which, even at this early epoch, seems often to have been characteristic of Coptic architecture. For while the general plan of the building seems at first sight rather basilican, the narrow aisles, with lateral divisions, the heavy piers at either end and in the middle of the nave, the arches joining them, and the many domes and semidomes of the roofing, are decidedly Byzantine features. The narthex at St. John's is unusually large, and has a fine western entrance approached by a modern flight of steps from above. This church is very rich in mural paintings, the walls being covered with New Testament subjects and figures of saints, which have their legends in Coptic. The same is true of the adjoining chapel.

A great number of vast caverns hewn in the mountains of this neighbourhood still bear witness to the zeal of the early anchorites who frequented them: the inscriptions, crosses, and figures carved upon the walls have never been examined. About a mile further is another Christian settlement, called the Dair of the Palm-Tree.

MISCELLANEOUS.

THE other churches of Upper Egypt are, alas, mere names and shadows of a name; and their number is so great that I cannot pretend to give them all, even in a dry and barren catalogue of names[1]. Vansleb speaks of a rock-cut church of the Virgin on a mountain near Siût; and near it are the ruins of a monastery dedicated to St. Severus, where once there were three hundred and sixty monks all engaged in alchemy, searching for the philosopher's stone,—'belle occupation pour des gens qui ont renoncé au monde et aux richesses'[2], as the traveller drily remarks. Ten leagues from Dandarah, westward of the Nile, he saw an ancient convent dedicated to Anba Balamûn, and another near it called after Mâri Mîna. At Balliânah was a very fine underground church of the Virgin; and two convents at Bahgûrah. Near Asnah is a monastery dedicated to the Holy Martyrs, and built by the empress Helena[3]. Vansleb mentions also another subterranean church beneath the church of St. Gabriel, in the monastery of 'Casciabe,' in the Faiûm[4]. The upper church is said to have been built by a retired magician named Ur, the son of a still more famous sorcerer, one Ibrasclt, who

---

[1] It scarcely needs remarking that Neale's list of Coptic monasteries (Eastern Church, Gen. Introd. vol. i. p. 119), which he calls 'correct,' and which gives twenty-six as the number for all Egypt, is ridiculously incomplete, and in itself a tissue of errors: for example, it omits the desert monasteries altogether; mentions six only at Cairo, including one which does not exist; and gives such names as 'The Two Swords,' 'Beysheuy,' and 'Bersaun.'

[2] Voyage, p. 380.   [3] Ib. p. 406.   [4] Ib. p. 275.

married a king's daughter. Ur, abandoning his arts, became bishop of the Faiûm and erected the church, of which the Virgin Mary laid the foundations, and St. Michael designed the choir and the other details.

There are said to be several other ancient churches in the Faiûm, such as those at the convent of Kalmûn[1]: but their description has yet to be written. It only remains to indicate a few other sites of Christian buildings in Egypt and to close this sadly imperfect chapter. At Bibbah, about seventy miles south of Cairo, is a monastery to which the Copts have attached the name of an imaginary Muslim saint, Al Bibbâwi, as their talisman. The quarries of Suâdi, opposite Miniah, contain some remains of early Christian times. Isbaidah, below Antinoë, is remarkable for some ancient grottoes, in one of which a church has been cut with an eastern apse. A few miles further south the famous catacombs of Tal al Amarna show frescoes, niches, and other traces of Christian occupation. Dair al Kussair, on the same bank of the river a little higher up, is said to date from the time of Constantine. The Libyan mountains near Siût are full of caves and tombs, once the dwelling-places of Christian hermits. There is a Coptic church at Tahtah, above Sûhâg. Akhmîm was rich in ancient churches, and the Convent of the Martyrs, mentioned by Al Makrîzi, probably still exists. The same writer records a monastery of Mûsah, south of Siût, and a church at Darankah dedicated to the

---

[1] Al Makrîzi says this is the only place where the famous Persea grows. See Rev. S. C. Malan's Notes on the Coptic Calendar, p. 61.

Three Children. Leo Africanus mentions the Convent of Mâri Girgis, at Girgah, as the largest and richest monastery in Egypt. Near Abydus is a very ancient and curious monastery, within the ring-wall of what seems to be an old Egyptian fortress or sacred enclosure; it contains the church of Anba Musâs[1] and some satellite chapels, which together are roofed by no less than twenty-three domes. The sanctuaries are all rectangular, and the architecture generally Byzantine. The remains of another dair, called the 'Greek Court,' close to Anba Musâs, appear to be of the same antiquity.

In the Great Oasis of the western desert, which lies a long way south-west of Abydus, the necropolis by the temple of Al Khargah contains a Christian church and many inscriptions in both Coptic and Arabic, which have never been copied. Here, too, among the most frequent devices on the walls of the tombs, may be seen the tau-cross, the ancient Egyptian emblem of life, which the early Copts seem to have adopted before the Greek form of the cross prevailed. Other Coptic and Arabic inscriptions are found in the Oasis, among the ruins of Ad-dair.

Returning to the Nile valley one may remark, in passing, a Coptic settlement at Hû, on the western bank. A little further south was the island of Tabenna, where St. Pachomius retired with fourteen hundred of his brethren and built monasteries; but the shifting course of the river has long since

---

[1] Murray's Egypt, vol. ii. p. 437. The spelling of the Arabic names in Murray is unfortunately very haphazard, and the descriptions of Coptic churches, where intelligible, are not as a rule accurate.

annexed the island to the mainland. Ad-dair below
Dandarah, as the name declares, is of Christian
origin. Ḳibt, the ancient Coptos on the eastern
bank, the town from which it is at least plausible
that the Copts are called, is still a mine of Christian
antiquities, although it never recovered from the
wreck of the Diocletian persecution. At Madinat
Habû, near Thebes, a Christian chapel was built
in one of the courts of the great temple; and the
name Dair al Baḥari, or the Northern Monastery,
is an abiding witness to the site of other religious
buildings in the vicinity.

Two ancient monasteries still survive near Asnah,
one dedicated to St. Matthew, the other to SS. Ma-
naos and Sanutius. The latter church, which is said
to have been founded by the empress Helena, contains some very ancient mural paintings of figures
with legends in Coptic, besides sepulchral inscriptions, among which occurs a stone graven with the
labarum[1],—a symbol which does not occur elsewhere in Egypt within the writer's knowledge.
From this point down to the First Cataract even
the names of the churches are unrecorded, though
so large a tract cannot be devoid of Christian antiquities; for the traces of the religion of the cross
are found to the remotest south of Egypt. Part
of the great temple of Isis, on the island of Philae,
was turned into a Christian church, and dedicated to
St. Stephen, in the sixth century, as the sculptured
tokens on the walls still testify. Tâfah, close upon
the tropic of Cancer, contains a temple, which was in
like manner converted to Christian uses; upon the

---

[1] Murray's Egypt, vol. ii. p. 506, is my authority for this statement.

walls is graven a calendar, dating from the fourth or fifth century. The temple at Amâdah, near Korosko, is another instance of a pagan fane adapted to Christian worship; and the region about Abu Simbal is rich in monuments, which prove that even there the religion of Christ was carried by the Copts, who fled for shelter from the fury of Diocletian.

So must end the confused and broken tale. Enough has been said, however, to show what work must yet be done in order to give the world anything like a complete account of the Christian antiquities of Egypt. Remains so vast in extent, so venerable in years, so unique in character, so rich in known and unknown possibilities of interest, are surely as well worthy of research and exploration as the colossal monuments of pagan Egypt. Yet day by day they are perishing, unknown to western travellers, and little regarded by the Copts themselves; and nothing, absolutely nothing, has been done or is doing to rescue them from oblivion, or to save them from destruction[1].

---

[1] There is an Arabic MS. of the highest interest in the Bibliothèque Nationale (No. 307 in the new catalogue), the title of which is 'History of the Monasteries of Egypt.' This precious document is unique, and I have been unable to obtain a loan of it, or even to consult it, in time for publication.

INDEX TO THE FIRST VOLUME.